...SHI
RAR
1972
RVE

W9-DHT-402

THE QUEST FOR
REGIONAL COOPERATION

CALIFORNIA STUDIES IN URBANIZATION
AND ENVIRONMENTAL DESIGN

THE COMMUNITY BUILDERS
by Edward P. Eichler and Marshall Kaplan

CHANDIGARH: A STUDY OF THE CITY AND ITS MONUMENTS
by Norma Evenson

THE QUEST FOR REGIONAL COOPERATION: A STUDY OF THE
NEW YORK METROPOLITAN REGIONAL COUNCIL
by Joan B. Aron

The Quest for Regional Cooperation

A Study of the New York
Metropolitan Regional Council

———————

JOAN B. ARON

University of California Press

Berkeley and Los Angeles 1969

University of California Press
Berkeley and Los Angeles, California
University of California Press, Ltd.
London, England
Copyright © 1969, by
The Regents of the University of California
Library of Congress Catalog Card Number: 69–16738
Printed in the United States of America

HT
394
N5
A7

T, 6 Ap 72

PREFACE

Councils of governments, more popularly known as "COG's," are rapidly gaining acceptance in the American governmental framework as useful devices for handling some of the difficult problems facing metropolitan areas. Virtually unknown as instruments of government fifteen years ago, the number of councils in the United States has now grown to over one hundred, with more being organized almost daily.

This study deals with the failure of the initial effort to create a viable council of governments in the New York metropolitan region. First organized in 1956 by a relatively small group of far-sighted local officials in the tri-state region embracing New York City, the Metropolitan Regional Council reached a peak of regional activity in the early 1960s but was almost defunct by 1966. It has been revived recently with federal help and is just now beginning to reassess its role in the complicated political environment in which it exists.

I hope that the Metropolitan Regional Council in New York will derive benefit from this critical analysis of its past history and will be able to avoid some of the difficulties which beset it in its first ten years. It is my further hope that a study of the obstacles facing a council of governments in the New York metropolitan area will be of some use to councils of governments elsewhere. Perhaps they are experiencing similar uncertainties and growing pains in the course of their cooperative endeavors. While the New York area may be unique with respect to its composition, problems, and complexities, some of the self-destructive potentialities of a council are likely to be universal.

Work on this study was begun during an internship in the

HC

office of Maxwell Lehman, First Deputy City Administrator of New York City from 1961–1965, who likewise served as Executive Secretary of the Metropolitan Regional Council. A further period of employment as a Council staff member, with access to all correspondence, records, and documents, was a great help in expanding my understanding of the Council's behavior, past and present. During this time, Arthur Prager, Assistant Executive Secretary of the Metropolitan Regional Council, was particularly helpful to me, and I owe him special thanks for his cooperation, encouragement, and good will.

I am deeply grateful also for the advice and guidance furnished by Professors Ralph A. Straetz and Charlton F. Chute of the New York University faculty. The additional material and insights provided by William N. Cassella, Jr., Assistant Director of the National Municipal League, were enormously helpful. I owe special debts to Professor Victor Jones of the University of California at Berkeley, John P. Keith, Executive Vice President of the Regional Plan Association, and Professor Robert G. Smith of Drew University, all of whom read this manuscript at an early stage and whose comments were invariably instructive. Finally, I wish to acknowledge the encouragement of my husband, without whose patience and understanding (and direct help in caring for our five children) this book would never have been written.

CONTENTS

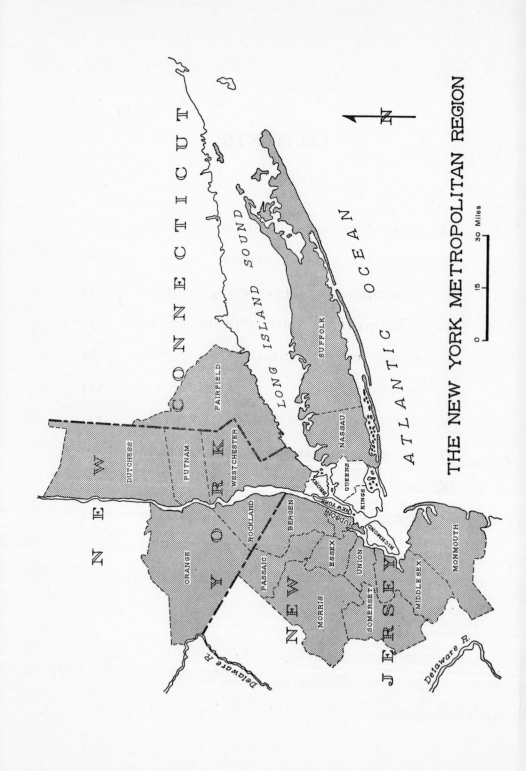

THE NEW YORK METROPOLITAN REGION

I

INTRODUCTION:

THE REGIONAL COUNCIL APPROACH

Since the turn of the century, the United States has experienced a dramatic growth of large urban areas. In the decade ending in 1960, 84 percent of our total population growth took place in the 212 areas of our country then recognized as metropolitan. Approximately 113 million people, or roughly two-thirds of our entire population, now live in "standard metropolitan statistical areas,"[1] and by 1968 these areas had increased in number to 233. This pattern of population growth is expected to continue. By 1980, it is anticipated that 190 million persons, or three-quarters of the projected population of 260 million, will be residing in urban areas.

Metropolitan growth and change have created special tensions within communities, new patterns of life, and governmental problems of unprecedented dimensions which have taxed existing facilities to the limit. The numerous individual government units which characterize the metropolitan areas can no longer perform independently the many functions their citizens consider

[1] A "standard metropolitan statistical area" is defined by the U.S. Bureau of the Budget as "a county or group of contiguous counties which contains at least one city of 50,000 inhabitants or more. . . . In addition to the county . . . , contiguous counties are included in an SMSA, if, according to certain criteria, they are essentially metropolitan in character and are socially and economically integrated with the central city" (U.S. Bureau of the Census, "Population of Standard Metropolitan Statistical Areas: 1960 and 1950," 1960 Census of Population, Supplementary Reports, PC (S1)–1, April 10, 1961, p. 4).

necessary in such fundamental fields as mass transportation, water supply, sewage disposal, water and air pollution, and recreation, where services spill over local boundary lines. Nor can the autonomous jurisdictions handle adequately the pressing social and economic needs of the poor and nonwhite groups in metropolitan areas. Problems associated with duplication and overlapping of governmental efforts, uneven public services, diffused responsibilities, inequitable distribution of financial resources, and lack of area-wide planning have received a great deal of attention from writers on urban affairs.[2] Less noteworthy have been the political adaptations of our local governments to meet the challenges of demographic and economic change. Metropolitan areas have been likened to international organizations insofar as competition and jealousies among their component parts are concerned.[3]

Efforts to Deal with Fragmentation

Numerous plans have been devised over the years to reorganize the boundaries of local political jurisdictions in an effort to establish some sort of rational order in urban areas. Proposals have ranged from informal cooperative agreements between local governments to suggestions for a basic reordering of local governmental units into a general governmental jurisdiction coextensive with the metropolitan area. This latter approach has received persistent

[2] E.g., John C. Bollens (ed.), *Exploring the Metropolitan Community* (Berkeley and Los Angeles: University of California Press, 1961), p. 92; Roscoe C. Martin, *Metropolis in Transition: Local Government Adaptation to Changing Urban Needs* (Washington: Housing and Home Finance Agency, 1963), p. 142; Advisory Commission on Intergovernmental Relations (hereafter cited as Advisory Commission), *Governmental Structure, Organization and Planning in Metropolitan Areas: Suggested Action by Local, State and National Governments* (Washington: U.S. Government Printing Office, 1961), particularly "Problems of Governmental Structure and Services," pp. 12–17; Beatrice Dinerman, *Organization and Structure of Local Government in the United States* (Los Angeles: Bureau of Governmental Research, 1961), p. 43; Morris Janowitz (ed.), *Community Political Systems*, I, International Yearbook of Political Behavior Research (Glencoe, Illinois: The Free Press of Glencoe, 1961), particularly Chap. IV by Amos H. Hawley and Basil G. Zimmer, "Resistance to Unification in a Metropolitan Community."

[3] Victor Jones, "The Organization of a Metropolitan Region," *University of Pennsylvania Law Review*, CV (February 1957), 538.

support in the literature.[4] However, a large group of urban observers has become increasingly critical of the prescriptions that
call for creation of area-wide government and does not necessarily
regard metropolitan reorganization as a panacea for urban needs.
These writers point out that the establishment of a new structural
framework would have little effect on the quality of life in metropolitan areas and might even generate new problems, such as
bureaucratic unresponsiveness.[5]

As a matter of record, most of the efforts to develop a constituency and a government as large as a metropolitan area have not
been successful. In the period 1950–1961, only a small number
of proposals for significant change in local governmental structure which were submitted to popular referendum in eighteen
of the nation's standard metropolitan statistical areas were passed.
In all of these proposals the issues centered about common problems relating to inadequacies of existing local governmental opera-

---

[4] Some of the early proponents of governments with sufficient authority
to remedy the inadequacies of local governmental units in metropolitan
areas were Chester C. Maxey, "The Political Integration of Metropolitan
Communities," *National Municipal Review*, XI (August 1922), 229–253;
Thomas Harrison Reed, *Municipal Government in the United States*
(New York: The Century Co., 1926), particularly Chap. XVIII, "The
Government of Metropolitan Areas"; Paul Studenski, *The Government of
Metropolitan Areas* (New York: National Municipal League, 1930), p.
389; and Victor Jones, *Metropolitan Government* (Chicago: University of
Chicago Press, 1942), p. 52. For more recent proposals, see Luther Halsey
Gulick, "Metropolitan Organization," *The Annals of the American
Academy of Political and Social Science*, CCCXIV (November 1957),
57–65, and *The Metropolitan Problem and American Ideas* (New York:
Alfred A. Knopf, 1962); John C. Bollens, *The States and the Metropolitan
Problem: A Report to the Governors' Conference* (Chicago: Council of
State Governments, 1956), p. 22; Advisory Commission, *Government in
Metropolitan Areas: Commentaries on a Report* (Washington: U.S. Gov-
ernment Printing Office, 1962), particularly the comments of Thomas H.
Reed (p. 2), Jefferson B. Fordham (p. 18), and Guthrie S. Birkhead
(p. 95).

[5] E.g., Edward C. Banfield and Morton Grodzins, *Government and
Housing in Metropolitan Areas* (New York: McGraw-Hill, 1958), par-
ticularly pp. 30–56; Vincent Ostrom, Charles M. Tiebout, and Robert
Warren, "The Organization of Government in Metropolitan Areas: A
Theoretical Inquiry," *American Political Science Review*, LV (Decem-
ber 1961), 831–842; Charles R. Adrian, "Metropology: Folklore and
Field Research," *Public Administration Review*, XXI (Summer, 1961),
152–154; Robert Warren, "Political Reform and Metropolitan Reform,"
Public Administration Review, XXIV (September 1964), 185.

tion and the need for urban services in outlying areas. Review of the difficulties inherent in gaining popular support for proposals of governmental reorganization compelled the Advisory Commission on Intergovernmental Relations to conclude in 1963 that "political realities . . . preclude shattering the [system] in order that it might be remolded in conformity with an updated model."[6]

Local governments have, therefore, resorted to a variety of alternative devices in order to meet the extraordinary demands caused by urban pressures. These take various forms: isolated instances of city-county consolidation, as in Nashville–Davidson County, Tennessee; formation of the urban county, as in Dade County, Florida; and the "federation" approach, as in Toronto, Canada. More common are partial or expedient measures. These include enlarged governmental strength for the county, as in Westchester and Nassau counties, New York; the establishment of a single-purpose agency to administer one or more designated functions in a metropolitan area, such as the Port of New York Authority; intergovernmental agreements, where one unit of government contracts for performance of certain functions with another governmental unit, as is done in the Los Angeles area; and varying types of voluntary and informal cooperative arrangements between two or more governmental units.[7]

The Cooperative Effort

With the abandonment of proposals to secure metropolitan government, the voluntary cooperative approach became more

[6] Advisory Commission, *Performance of Urban Functions: Local and Areawide* (Washington: U.S. Government Printing Office, 1963), p. 9. Refer to the Advisory Commission's analysis of *Factors Affecting Voter Reactions to Governmental Reorganization in Metropolitan Areas* (Washington: U.S. Government Printing Office, 1962) for complete accounts of the successful and defeated proposals.

[7] For more detailed treatment refer to Advisory Commission, *Alternative Approaches to Governmental Reorganization in Metropolitan Areas* (Washington: U.S. Government Printing Office, 1962), particularly p. 19; Victor Jones, *University of Pennsylvania Law Review*, CV (February 1957), 542; Martin, *Metropolis in Transition*, pp. 3–10; and W. Brooke Graves, *American Intergovernmental Relations: Their Origins, Historical Development and Current Status* (New York: Charles Scribner's Sons, 1964), particularly Chap. XXI, "Interlocal Relations."

attractive to officials in different parts of the country in the 1950s. This alternative attempted to provide coordinated effort in dealing with problems facing metropolitan areas without destroying the individual identity of the cooperating local governments. The voluntary council, or "conference," as it was often called, was generally composed of the chief elected officials of local units of government within a metropolitan area. These persons came together "to seek a better understanding among the governments and officials in the area, to develop a consensus regarding metropolitan needs, and to promote coordinated action. . . ."[8]

A council is a voluntary organization with no governmental or operating powers and no powers to compel attendance or participation. In contrast to some type of "structural" adaptation, where direct action is undertaken through the creation of a new unit of government (as in the case of a special district), the council foresees negotiation of agreement for common action within the framework of existing local governments. For this reason, the council has been termed a "pragmatic" approach which capitalizes on existing values and eliminates the need for creation of a metropolitan government in its attempt to bring order into metropolitan areas. Other attributes of the council are generally considered to be its easy initiation, political palatability, grass-roots contact, broad geographical base of representation, flexible boundaries, locally controlled policy, limited partisan contact, and lack of legal compulsion.[9]

Until 1965, the principal councils in the country and their respective core cities were the Supervisors Inter-County Commit-

[8] Samuel Humes, "Organization for Metropolitan Cooperation," *Public Management*, XLIV (May 1962), 106.

[9] For early information on the usefulness of the conference approach, refer to Martin, *Metropolis in Transition*, pp. 2 ff.; Advisory Commission, *Governmental Structure*, pp. 24–25, and *Alternative Approaches*, pp. 37–38; Victor Jones, "Associations of Local Governments: Pattern for Metropolitan Cooperation," address to the 67th National Conference on Government, Miami Beach, Florida, November 30, 1961; "Summary of Discussion, Workshop on 'Voluntary Multi-Purpose Regional Organizations,'" mimeographed (Washington: American Municipal Association, 1961); "AMA–NACO Workshop on 'Voluntary City-County Regional Cooperation,'" mimeographed (Washington: National League of Cities, 1965); and Roscoe C. Martin et al., *Decisions in Syracuse: Metropolitan Action Studies, No. 1* (Bloomington: Indiana University Press, 1961), p. 230.

tee (Detroit, Michigan); Metropolitan Regional Council (New York, New York); Puget Sound Governmental Conference (Seattle, Washington); Metropolitan Washington Council of Governments (Washington, D.C.); Mid-Willamette Valley Council of Governments (Salem, Oregon); Regional Conference of Elected Officials (Philadelphia, Pennsylvania); Association of Bay Area Governments (San Francisco, California); Metropolitan Atlanta Council of Local Governments (Atlanta, Georgia); and Southern California Association of Governments (Los Angeles, California). These are all relatively young organizations. Most are less than ten years old.

Two recent federal laws, the Housing and Urban Development Act of 1965 and the Demonstration Cities and Metropolitan Development Act of 1966, have stimulated a greater number of local governments to undertake regional planning on a cooperative basis and to form regional councils for this purpose. This development has been further encouraged by the establishment in 1967 of a national clearing house and service program for councils under the joint auspices of the National League of Cities and the National Association of Counties—with initial funding provided by the federal Department of Housing and Urban Development—to evaluate the work already performed by councils of governments and to encourage the establishment of such bodies in additional metropolitan areas.[10] By March 1968, when the research for this study was completed, there were more than ninety councils in existence, and another twenty were in the process of formation. About 75 percent of these had been created since January 1966.[11]

Councils of government have been established in different regions by a variety of means. They may be created by virtue of specific state enabling legislation, joint exercise of powers agreements, interstate compacts, intergovernmental agreements, and

[10] The American Municipal Association and the National Association of Counties first embarked on a joint program to encourage the development of new regional councils in 1962. Their efforts became more significant with the passage of the two federal laws which have been mentioned briefly here. The impact of federal legislation on the development of councils of governments will be discussed in detail in Chapter V, pp. 106–108.

[11] Recent information on the number of councils of governments comes from Richard Hartman, "Expand Service to Regional Councils," *National Civic Review*, LVII (March 1968), 159.

corporate charters; some may be simply informal organizations without legal status. The councils vary widely in the number and type of governmental units eligible to participate in council affairs. Each council is composed of elected officials of local governmental units, but membership is not uniformly limited to local governments. Thus the Washington, D.C., council includes representatives of the United States Congress and the general assemblies of Maryland and Virginia, as well as officials of the governing bodies of the District of Columbia and the counties and independent cities of the region. The Salem, Oregon, council includes representatives of the school district and the state, as well as representatives of the city of Salem and the two counties involved. And the new Southeast Michigan Council of Governments authorizes direct participation by representatives of the school districts as well as by other local governmental representatives.

The councils generally provide for participation of counties and cities in their affairs, but most do not encourage membership by smaller governmental units. Special-purpose districts are usually excluded, but in some councils these may be included as nonvoting members. Each council defines its own geographical service area, and this can be altered to include additional units as desired.

All of the councils have a general deliberative body which meets once or twice each year and serves as a policy-making and review mechanism. Smaller executive committees or boards are formed from the representatives serving on the general body. The councils operate with small staffs for the most part and derive financial support, in addition to federal funds they receive for specific purposes, from contributions by member units, with the amount of the contributions usually being determined on the basis of population.[12]

Cooperation in the New York Metropolitan Region

The New York metropolitan area, the largest, most complicated, and most populous metropolitan area in the United States,

[12] Much of the material presented here is based on a comprehensive report prepared by Royce Hanson, *Metropolitan Councils of Govern-*

has more reason than most to establish a council of governments. The "region" itself was identified as a conceptual and statistical entity more than a half century ago, but its most commonly accepted definition stems from research studies prepared for use in the *Regional Plan of New York and its Environs*, the first volume of which was published in 1929 by the Regional Plan Association, a civic research and planning association. The region then defined by the Regional Plan Association (hereafter known as RPA) was composed of twenty-two counties: nine in northeastern New Jersey, twelve in New York State, including the five counties of New York City, and one in Connecticut. It extended in a radius of roughly 50 miles from mid-Manhattan and included 6,907 square miles in land area, of which New York City occupied 315.[13] (See map facing p. 1 for the New York metropolitan region as it was then defined.)

The New York metropolitan area is unique in many respects, particularly in the complexity of its intergovernmental arrangements. In 1959, all types of governments in the region totalled

---

ments: An Information Report (Washington: Advisory Commission on Intergovernmental Relations, 1966). The reader is also referred to Citizens Research Council of Michigan, "Research Brief on Membership, Representation and Voting Procedures of Councils of Governments," memeographed (Detroit, 1966); and to *A Summary of Proceedings: First National Conference of Governments* (Metropolitan Washington Council of Governments, 1967).

[13] Early attempts at definition of the New York region were made by the U.S. Bureau of the Census in 1911; by Maxey, *National Municipal Review*, XI (August 1922), 237; and by Thomas H. Reed, "The Region, A New Governmental Unit," *National Municipal Review*, XIV (July 1925), 417–423. Refer also to the Staff of the Regional Plan, *The Graphic Regional Plan: Atlas and Description*, Vol. I of *Regional Plan of New York and Its Environs* (New York: Committee on the Regional Plan, 1929).

The RPA regional area should be distinguished from the New York "standard metropolitan statistical area," which is limited by the United States Census Bureau to nine counties with a 1960 population of 10,700,000, and from the New York–Northeastern New Jersey Consolidated Area, which is defined by the Bureau of the Budget for statistical purposes as seventeen counties with a 1960 population of 14,700,000. The Tri-State Transportation Commission, a tri-state planning body, embraces a region of 7,989 square miles and includes twenty-two counties in New York and New Jersey and six planning regions in Connecticut. The Tri-State "region" had a 1960 population of 17,104,000.

1,417, a figure which includes counties, cities, towns, villages, boroughs, townships, school districts, and various forms of special-purpose districts in such fields as fire, housing, sewerage, health, parks, water, drainage, and waste disposal. By 1961, Robert Wood counted as many as 1,467 distinct political units in the area which he described as "one of the great unnatural wonders of the world."[14]

This labyrinth is made more intricate still by the presence of three sovereign states with different governmental philosophies and arrangements, which often work at cross-purposes with each other, and by a large number of federal programs with substantial local impact. Since local jurisdictions exhibit great variety in formal powers, political arrangements, structures, and boundaries, a large number of autonomous decision-making centers attempt to cope with the problems associated with urban growth: traffic congestion, declining railroad facilities, polluted air and water, inadequate recreational facilities, substandard housing, and social and economic segregation. Public corporations and metropolitan authorities have been created to handle the most critical public services. These vary politically, financially, and geographically from the local governments and further impede a coordinated approach to area-wide problems.

The region's governments have severe financial problems as well. Wood provides a vivid description of the impact of environmental forces in the New York metropolitan region which results in wide discrepancies between the needs of different communities and their taxing potentials, or in the "segregation of resources from needs." For the most part he finds that those communities with the highest population density and which are

---

[14] Robert C. Wood, *1400 Governments: The Political Economy of the New York Metropolitan Region* (Cambridge: Harvard University Press, 1961), p. 1. For further analyses of the political fragmentation of the New York region, see Michael N. Danielson, *Federal-Metropolitan Politics and the Commuter Crisis* (New York and London: Columbia University Press, 1965), particularly pp. 2 ff.; Jameson W. Doig, *Metropolitan Transportation Politics and the New York Region* (New York and London: Columbia University Press, 1966), particularly pp. 42–43 and 232–250; and Benjamin Chinitz, "New York: A Metropolitan Region," *Scientific American*, CCXIII (September 1965), 134.

under the most severe pressures to spend, show a marked tendency to be unable to meet these pressures. To cope with increased demands, the localities manipulate assessments for the levying of property taxes, rezone, increase taxes or levy new ones, raise debt limits, or create special-purpose districts. There is no uniformity in land-use control among the region's governments, and little attention is paid to the pattern of development of the region as a whole.[15]

As the nation's largest metropolis in terms of population, economic wealth, education, and cultural resources, New York City occupies the dominant position among the region's local governments. While the region has two other very large cities, Newark and Jersey City, about one-third of the region's jobs are located in downtown Manhattan and approximately one-half of the region's residents live in one of New York City's five counties. The city also has a high concentration of low-income, unskilled groups: in 1960, one-fifth of its residents were Negro and one-sixth were Puerto Rican.

As in most metropolitan areas in the country, the older cities of the region have ceased to grow in population. In 1960, the region's population totalled 16,139,000, an increase of roughly two million people over the 1950 census. Since New York City's population declined by a hundred thousand in the decade between 1950 and 1960, all of the region's growth took place in the suburban counties. By 1965, the region's population had increased to 17 million, and a continued trend of growth on the one hand and decentralization of business, industry, and residential development on the other is projected for the future.[16]

Enumeration of some of the difficulties facing the New York metropolitan region makes it abundantly clear that no unit of government can solve them alone. The need for a coordinating mechanism seemed equally clear more than a decade ago, and many individuals and groups, including Dr. Luther H. Gulick

[15] Wood, *1400 Governments*, p. 50. See also Raymond Vernon, *Metropolis 1985* (Cambridge: Harvard University Press, 1960), p. 181.

[16] Edgar M. Hoover and Raymond Vernon, *Anatomy of a Metropolis* (Cambridge: Harvard University Press, 1959), particularly Chap. IX, "The Jobs, the People and the Future." For a more recent study, see RPA, *The Region's Growth: A Report of the Second Regional Plan* (1967).

(then City Administrator of New York City), the Citizens Budget Commission (a private New York City civic organization), and RPA called for official recognition of regional needs.[17] Responding to the cooperative challenge, Mayor Robert H. Wagner of New York City took the unprecedented step of inviting the chief elected executives of local communities in New York, New Jersey, and Connecticut to meet at City Hall, New York, on June 18, 1956, to discuss the possibility of joint action for problems transcending local boundary lines.

A Brief History of the Metropolitan Regional Council

Mayor Wagner opened the first meeting of what was to become the New York Metropolitan Regional Council by defining the New York metropolitan area in terms of the geographic boundaries used by RPA; he went on to enumerate some of the regional authorities and commissions then in existence and asked: "Are present governmental mechanisms adequate to deal with the problems of the metropolitan community?" Wagner answered the question himself by pointing out that mutual cooperation would enable local officials to understand regional needs, identify mutual problems, work out solutions by voluntary local action, and create a force to protect the region's prosperity. Cooperation would also help them to "get to know each other better, breaking down the walls that may have existed . . . , and replacing them by mutual trust as we work toward mutual objectives."

There was general agreement about the existence of disturbing problems, particularly with respect to transportation, teen-age drinking, and housing. The only executive present who expressed satisfaction with existing governmental "machinery" (in the form

[17] Luther H. Gulick, "The Next Twenty-Five Years in Government in the New York Metropolitan Region," address to the 25th Anniversary Meeting of RPA, October 6, 1954; Harold Riegelman, counsel to the Citizens Budget Commission, address proposing a metropolitan council of municipalities, January 12, 1955; RPA *News*, No. 48 (1955) and No. 49 (1956). See also Robert H. Wagner, "Problems of the Metropolitan Area," address to the American Municipal Association, Miami, Florida, November 28, 1955.

of the coordinating efforts of City Construction Coordinator Robert Moses) and distrust of any " 'junior United Nations' of metropolitan officials being formulated under some impressive name" was Holly A. Patterson, County Executive of Nassau County. Despite his skepticism, agreement was sufficiently widespread for James D. Hopkins, then Westchester County Executive, to draw up a joint policy statement and proposal for continued action by the group. The statement noted:

> The region is bound together by the integrated economy and well-being of each community as related to the prosperity of the region as a whole. . . . The communities of the region face many common problems extending along jurisdictional boundary lines which cannot be met entirely by local jurisdictions acting separately. These problems include traffic and transportation, recreation, water supply, air and water pollution, sewerage disposal, and planning for future population growth and economic expansion.[18]

The Hopkins statement called for a request to Mayor Wagner to act as pro tem chairman of the new Metropolitan Regional Conference, to appoint a steering committee to study and make recommendations concerning the form of regional organization, and to delineate the regional problems to be given first priority. The steering committee met in July 1956 and decided to include as members of the Conference all communities which had attended the original meeting and all other counties and cities in the New York metropolitan region. The Conference accepted New York City's offer of the use of the City Administrator's office as secretariat and proposed that technical assistance be furnished by participating communities. Two working committees were created to deal with the problems of transportation and teenage drinking, with additional committees to be added when needed.

The first membership meeting was held at Rutgers University in December 1956, and Mayor Wagner hailed the beginning of "what may well turn out to be the most significant new development in local government in our time." The Conference reit-

---

[18] The material presented here comes from a transcript of Conference on Metropolitan Regional Development, City Hall, New York, June 18, 1956.

erated its support of the four basic principles which had been accepted by the steering committee as follows: (1) "The organization shall be voluntary in character both in composition and in binding policy determination." (2) "Membership shall consist of the top elected public officials." (3) "The organization shall respect the principle of home rule and the integrity of the communities." (4) "The organization shall be non-political in motivation and action."

The Conference also adopted the plans proposed for membership, organization, and committee work. It was decided that only the elected chief executive of each community would be eligible for membership, but each elected official might bring with him any staff members he wished to participate in discussions, make studies, and deliver reports. The vote at Conference meetings would be cast only by the elected official representing his community in view of the "recognition that responsibility for decision ultimately rests with the elected official who is directly answerable to the people."[19] The chairman and other officers were to be selected by vote of the entire membership. Each community was to have one vote and all proposals would be carried by majority action.

On May 27, 1957, the Conference had its next full meeting and voted to establish a permanent organization. The steering committee was replaced by an executive board consisting of the chairman and eight chief executives of member governments elected by the Conference, three from New York, three from New Jersey, and two from Connecticut. The general membership gradually increased in number thereafter to a total of thirty-seven member communities: nine New Jersey counties, eleven New Jersey cities and towns, six Connecticut towns, six New York counties, and five New York cities.[20]

[19] Maxwell Lehman, "The Metropolitan Region Gets Together," address to the Women's City Club of New York, December 2, 1958.
[20] For the Council's purposes, the region consisted of twenty-one counties: Bergen, Union, Hudson, Essex, Middlesex, Somerset, Morris, Passaic, and Monmouth in New Jersey; Nassau, Suffolk, Westchester, Rockland, Orange, and Putnam in New York; the five counties included in the City of New York; and Fairfield County in Connecticut. However, the New York City counties and Fairfield were not eligible for member-

By 1958, Conference committees were functioning smoothly in their respective fields of traffic and transportation, water pollution, air pollution, water supply, housing and redevelopment, and recreation and land use. Studies then underway included an evaluation of the future park and recreational needs of the region (in conjunction with RPA), an inventory of housing needs, a master map of water pollution, a study of regional commuter lines, and a formulation of an air-pollution warning system. At its semi-annual meeting, the members voted to change the organization's name from the Metropolitan Regional Conference, which "sounded like a debating group rather than the action organization that it is," to the Metropolitan Regional Council (hereafter referred to as MRC), a name "more precisely delineating the work and objectives of the organization." Simultaneously, the title of Maxwell Lehman, Deputy Administrator of New York City, who had been acting as "Secretary," was changed to "Executive Secretary." Mayor Wagner was sufficiently encouraged by the group's progress to point out that "metropolitan cooperation is working, [and] that this Conference already has acted as an intermediate layer of administrative assistance for its member-governments on governmental problems jointly shared." An additional committee was created to study the future direction of the Council, with instructions to report back in the near future.

---

ship in the Council. New York City had one vote and Fairfield was represented by the mayors or first selectmen of six cities and towns. The counties enumerated here are identical to those included in the RPA definition of the region with the exception of Dutchess County, New York. The criteria used in drawing the boundaries of the Metropolitan Regional Council's region were "rather loose" according to the assistant executive secretary. It was felt that all counties fifty miles from Manhattan were tightly bound to the economy of the region and included many people who commuted to and from work in the city each day. It seemed to the Council that Dutchess was not involved in this way with New York City. However, Dutchess County was not barred from membership and was always invited to send observers to meetings.

In addition to the New Jersey and New York counties enumerated above, Council members included Bayonne, Elizabeth, Hoboken, Jersey City, Linden, Morristown, Newark, Passaic, Paterson, Plainfield, and Rahway, New Jersey; Darien, Greenwich, New Canaan, Norwalk, Stamford, and Westport, Connecticut; and Mount Vernon, New Rochelle, White Plains, Yonkers, and New York, New York.

On June 10, 1958, Mayor Wagner again addressed Council members and listed certain "intangibles" that had emerged as a result of the organization's operations during its first two years of life. Since these represented the expectations of many of the officials who were among the original participants, and since they were restated by them frequently over the next six years, they are set forth here briefly as follows:

1. We are a going concern, and a vigorous one.
2. By looking at the region as a whole, we begin to work away from the fragmented manner in which many of our common problems have been approached. . . .
3. By establishing a mode of swift, simple, direct communication among the elected officials of the area, we have been able to identify more clearly what our mutual problems are.
4. We have found that informal contact has enabled us on many occasions to assist each other on specific governmental needs.
5. We have established a clearing-house for the exchange of information and cross-fertilization of ideas.
6. We have undertaken to work out solutions to some of our major governmental problems by voluntary local action.
7. We have been able to present our views and our needs as a region to the three states of which we are a part, and to the federal government.

One year later, Mayor Wagner foresaw continued growth for MRC as a recommending agency to the state and federal governments on regional matters, as a central information agency, as a liaison between the region's local governments, as a coordinator of the activities of the existing interstate agencies, and as an actor in a "participating or supervisory capacity in new bi-state or tri-state agencies to be created."[21]

As trailblazers in the first cooperative attempt among local governments in the New York metropolitan region, Mayor Wagner and his colleagues on the executive board seemed pleased with their progress in the years between 1956 and 1961. In 1960 Mayor Wagner quipped that "there are some political theorists who claim that local government is not equipped to handle this growth

[21] MRC meeting, June 16, 1959. The balance of the information given in the foregoing pages comes from minutes of the executive board meeting, January 8, 1958, and from addresses by Robert H. Wagner to MRC members on February 5, 1958, and June 10, 1958.

and predict the eventual establishment of super-governments throughout the country or increased federal control. . . . The spirit of regional cooperation engendered by the MRC is the best antidote that I know to prevent erosion in the exercise of local control."[22] Later the same year, at least two of these political theorists noted that MRC has had such a "vigorous start and warm response that its influence appears likely to increase gradually but steadily in the years ahead."[23] During the following year, however, another point of view emerged. Robert Wood found that the Council had made very slow progress in developing into the kind of goal-setting, program-developing agency it wished to be. He noted little change in customary behavior patterns among local political officials who, he said, "continue to cling to their favorite slogan 'cooperation' as the panacea for the very real conflict which exists."[24]

The chairman's customary speech to the full membership meeting in June 1962 indicated for the first time that the future might not be as bright as originally anticipated. Mayor Wagner took public note of the "myths" currently surrounding the Council and tried in particular to dispel popular notions that MRC was a kind of supergovernment, with an expensive bureaucracy, through which New York City was seeking to "take over" its neighbor communities. By 1962, a strong, vocal minority had developed in opposition to the Council's attempt to gain legal recognition, and this effort was reluctantly abandoned the following year. In May 1964, in an editorial headed "The 1500 Little Kingdoms," the *New York Times* noted that MRC, "launched eight years ago with high hopes that it would pioneer new inter-community relationships, has fallen on evil days."[25] While most of the top officials who participated in Council activities were convinced of its value, they were unsuccessful in the attempt to persuade their local legislative bodies to ratify an agreement pledging regular financial contribution to the Council.

The Council has never recovered from its downward course.

[22] Address to MRC members, February 23, 1960.
[23] Wallace S. Sayre and Herbert Kaufman, *Governing New York City: Politics in the Metropolis* (New York: Russell Sage Foundation, 1960), p. 596.
[24] Wood, *1400 Governments*, p. 194.
[25] *New York Times*, May 15, 1964, p. 42.

At a membership meeting held at City Hall, New York, in the spring of 1964, reorganization of the Council as an organization of elected officials, rather than communities, was the main topic of discussion. An agenda outline for a meeting in September 1964 of the Technical Advisory Committee of MRC, which consisted of knowledgeable metropolitan consultants who were interested in the Council, included many of the same items relating to membership provisions, budgetary needs, and future activities which had appeared in the minutes of steering committee reports eight years previous. No agreements were reached at that meeting, and no firm leadership was exercised for many months thereafter. By 1965, the Council's activities were practically non-existent, and the prognosis for the future was dim. In 1966, an attempt was made to revive MRC under the chairmanship of John V. Lindsay, the newly elected Mayor of New York City. Casting a covetous eye at the federal aid being dispensed to regional councils in other metropolitan areas, MRC members voted to incorporate as a nonprofit body and to attempt to secure federal funds under the provisions of the Housing and Urban Development Act of 1965. The Council received approval of its grant request in the spring of 1968, and it is once more attempting to gain a foothold for itself as a viable regional organization in the New York metropolitan region.

At this particular point in MRC's life, it seems appropriate to pause and examine the reasons for the Council's inability to achieve its own objectives during its first ten years of operation. In view of the growing national tendency of local governments to form councils of governments within their respective metropolitan areas, the failure of the initial effort in the nation's largest and most important metropolitan region takes on added significance. Whether councils can develop into the regional planning and coordinating mechanisms their federal benefactor envisions depends upon many factors including the character of the region, the jurisdictions and the personalities involved, support from other levels of government, public orientation, the strength of competing regional forces, and, of course, the strategies pursued by the councils themselves. All of these factors will receive consideration herein.

The following chapters will attempt to make clear some of

the formidable obstacles which hampered MRC's early effort in the New York metropolitan region, and which rendered it impotent after the first five years of its life. The account does not intend to suggest that the successful creation of a cooperative and coordinating mechanism, per se, would have enabled the region's local governments to deal with the many social and economic pressures confronting their communities. But it does assume that some type of regional agency of political responsibility, with active local representation and participation, can exert considerable influence upon the future development of the region. For this reason, the account highlights the pitfalls to be avoided if MRC is to survive, and if it is going to help local governments respond to urgent metropolitan needs. Similar hurdles are likely to be found elsewhere, and other councils, in formative stages of development, might well give them heed.

II

VOLUNTARISM AND ITS LIMITATIONS

Varying Perceptions of "Regional" Problems

The assertion has been made previously that voluntary councils are useful devices for helping local communities solve common problems which they are unable to resolve by individual action. However, this statement should not obscure the finding that agreement has not always been forthcoming, or self-evident, on the nature of the appropriate metropolitan problem requiring common action, or on the form of action needed. To those familiar with the current literature in urban affairs, this is hardly surprising. Early works in the field tended to look upon fragmentation of governmental units in metropolitan areas as *the* metropolitan problem requiring attention.[1] Current observers regard questions of governmental structure as but one of the many problems with which metropolitan areas have to cope and recommend for further investigation a comprehensive view of "all the major dimensions of life in urbanized areas."[2]

[1] E.g., Reed, *Municipal Government in the United States*, p. 337; Bollens, *The States and the Metropolitan Problem*, p. 17. See also Chap. I, n. 4.

[2] Stanley Scott, "Research on Governmental Reorganization in Metropolitan Areas," *Two Notes on Metropolitan Research*, Second Annual Faculty Seminar on Metropolitan Research, August 28–September 7, 1960 (Maxwell Graduate School of Citizenship and Public Affairs, Syracuse University, 1961), p. 18. See also Scott, "The Metropolitan Scene: Some Recent Views," *Public Administration Review*, XXVI (December 1966), 334–343; Charles Press, "Research on the Metropolis: Foundation for Conservation," *Public Administration Review*, XXII (Spring, 1962), 91; Martin et al., *Decisions in Syracuse*, p. 320; Guthrie S. Birkhead (ed.), *Metropoli-*

For the purpose at hand—at this initial stage of consideration—it seems sufficient to point out that a great number of diverse governmental functions are necessary to assure the social, economic, cultural, and physical development of the communities making up a metropolitan complex. A "metropolitan problem" then may be simply stated as the inability of local governments to perform independently the many functions which are area-wide in nature. The multiplicity of governmental units is not the problem in and of itself; rather, the problem is the inadequacy of local governmental capacity to provide certain common services which the people wish and need.[3]

But what are the services "common" to the counties and municipalities which comprise a large metropolitan area such as New York? Further difficulties arise in defining appropriate geographical boundaries within which to perform different types of public functions. The logical sector for planning for commuter transportation may be very different from that suitable for recreation, water, sewage disposal, and other essentials. Vincent Ostrom, Charles M. Tiebout, and Robert Warren suggest that even a new large governmental entity would not ensure the appropriate organization for *all* types of public services required for the diverse political jurisdictions constituting a metropolitan area.[4] In confirmation, Oliver P. Williams and his colleagues draw a graphic picture of some of the different, highly specialized, and relatively autonomous communities surrounding the central city of Phila-

---

tan Issues: Social, Governmental, Fiscal, Background Papers for the Third Annual Faculty Seminar on Metropolitan Research, August 20–30, 1961 (Maxwell Graduate School of Citizenship and Public Affairs, Syracuse University, 1962), p. 11.

[3] For further discussion, refer to Roscoe C. Martin, *The Cities and the Federal System* (New York: Atherton Press, 1965), p. 181, *Metropolis in Transition*, p. 129, and "Action in Metropolis: I," *National Civic Review*, LII (June 1963), 304–305; Scott Greer, "Social Change and the Metropolitan Problem," *Metropolitan Issues*, ed. Birkhead, p. 13; and Charlton F. Chute, "The Honolulu Metropolitan Area," *Public Administration Review*, *XVIII* (Winter, 1958), 8–9.

[4] *American Political Science Review*, LV (December 1961), 835–837. Also refer to Advisory Commission, *Performance of Urban Functions*, for further discussion of the political and economic criteria to be considered in organizing to provide different types of services in metropolitan areas.

delphia, each of which requires special types of services and financial resources to sustain the system of governments as presently constituted.[5]

The New York metropolitan area is even more highly specialized and diverse. While the "regional" focus furnished by RPA is a help in conceptual definition of the area, local communities, limited by jurisdictional considerations and subjected to peculiar local pressures, vary widely in their perceptions of "essential" regional services. For this reason, the MRC staff discovered that the problem of air pollution was of great concern to some parts of the region but relatively unimportant to others. When the Council considered "common" needs of a limited geographical area, such as the northeastern sector of New Jersey, it was still confronted by a wide variety of responses: Jersey City wanted more housing for its aged population; Plainfield was troubled by trash and garbage disposal; Bergen County preferred to handle its problems locally; Newark needed more housing for middle-income people; Elizabeth requested help in air-pollution control; and Rahway needed protection from mosquitoes flying in from Staten Island, from water flowing in from Linden, and from the people who crowded her recreational facilities on weekends.[6] Fortunately for MRC, all of these communities agreed on overwhelming traffic and transportation problems, a field in which the Council had been active for several years.

The attempt to influence individual governments to consider regional issues from the point of view of a larger metropolitan constituency was a constant challenge—and source of frustration —to MRC. Many communities, which were less adversely affected than others by certain inadequate regional services, proved unwilling to share in the administrative or financial responsibilities for study or research unless they perceived some direct benefit to themselves. The Council's difficulties in securing the participation of the region's governments are well illustrated in its effort to assemble on one comprehensive "regional water map" all

[5] Oliver P. Williams et al., *Suburban Differences and Metropolitan Policies: A Philadelphia Story* (Philadelphia: University of Pennsylvania Press, 1965), pp. 299–305.

[6] Memoranda on interview data, MRC, August 2, 1960.

information regarding existing and proposed programs of water-pollution control. First attempted in 1958 under the impetus of Nassau County, the project received a good deal of time and attention from a few interested communities before its eventual abandonment in 1962 due to a lack of material aid and assistance from MRC's members.[7]

The Search for Consensus

In addition to varying perceptions of "needed" metropolitan projects, both the representative structure and the voluntary character of a regional council hinder it in formulating new policies for regional development. The local communities which comprise the general membership would like to preserve their distinctive perspectives and policies in as pristine a state as possible. Lacking a central governing body (with sanctions to enforce decisions), the council finds it difficult to act as the central forum for negotiation and compromise. Since many of the member officials and governments have never communicated effectively before—except in the adjustment of border conflicts between neighboring communities—it may take a long time for mutual confidence to develop and for accommodation to be reached. Unanimity of action is not a prerequisite, but some kind of substantial or reasonable consensus must emerge for positive action to follow.[8]

This requirement of "near unanimity" is a large drawback to council effectiveness. It may lead to unnecessarily prolonged study or avoidance of sensitive or controversial issues by council members. The teen-age drinking problem in the New York metropolitan area is a case in point.

[7] This effort will be discussed in detail in Chap. VIII, pp. 176–178.

[8] For detailed accounts of adjustment of conflict situations among neighboring communities, refer to Williams et al., *Suburban Differences*, pp. 19, 29–30, and 299–305; and Paul Studenski, "Metropolitan Areas, 1960," *National Civic Review*, XLIX (October 1960), 470. Further discussion of consensus requirements can be found in Hanson, *Metropolitan Councils of Governments*, pp. 5 and 33; Martin et al., *Decisions in Syracuse*, p. 109; Charlton F. Chute, "Problems Common to Metropolitan Areas," address to the Third Annual Spring Planning Assembly, Akron, Ohio, April 10, 1958; and Jones, "Associations of Local Governments," address to Conference on Government, 1961.

As early as June 1956, the mayor of Elizabeth, New Jersey, suggested that this problem receive study by the Council in the hope that the New York State legal minimum drinking age might be raised from eighteen to twenty-one years of age to conform with New Jersey and Connecticut state laws. MRC established a committee to consider the problem, requested it to assemble the necessary information, and subsequently resolved that a study of "teen-age problems including the proper age . . . for the drinking of alcoholic beverages" be undertaken by the three state legislatures. The committee was disbanded in January 1958 on the basis that it had gone as far as it could with its assignment.

In August 1960, immediate reactivation of the teen-age drinking study was recommended to the MRC executive secretary as a means of retaining support of the New Jersey members. The recommendation went unheeded until February 1962, when Jersey City requested publicly and vociferously at a general membership meeting that the Council undertake a study of automobile accidents caused by teen-age drinkers in the New York metropolitan area. Six months later, a panel discussion was held by MRC on the advisability of raising the New York State minimum drinking age to twenty-one. While no transcript of the proceedings is available, newspaper accounts indicate that the discussion threatened to "split" Council members. Sal J. Prezioso, then executive officer to Westchester County Executive Edwin G. Michaelian, questioned the Council's right to delve into the question while a New York legislative committee was studying it. He pointed out that many municipalities and counties were having a difficult time convincing the voters of the benefits of joining MRC and felt that "the quickest way to kill . . . [MRC] would be for the panel to make a strong recommendation of any kind at this time."[9] A resolution was adopted urging the New York State legislature to pass "equalizing legislation," and the subject was promptly forgotten, both by MRC and the state legislature.

At the very time that MRC needed support from all of its members to sustain itself as a functioning organization, New Jer-

[9] Robert P. Kalter, "Drink Age Dispute Threatens to Split Tri-State Council," *Newark Star Ledger*, June 20, 1962. See also "New York Drinking Age Spurs Hot Controversy in Tri-State Council," *New York World Telegram and Sun*, June 20, 1962, p. 25.

sey officials became increasingly bitter over the Council's failure to press the New York legislature to raise the minimum drinking age. The *Newark Evening News* found a "discouraging contrast between New York's pious talk about regional cooperation and its uncooperative ruthlessness when that serves its interest."[10] In view of the strong resistance by New York members to any change in existing legislation, the attempt by New Jersey members to raise the drinking age was probably a lost cause from the beginning. On the other hand, the Council was under intense pressure to make the effort or lose face very early in its history. The simplest way out was to appoint a committee which would collect data and then emerge with a recommendation for further study.

The inability to secure majority agreement with respect to a large number of controversial issues served as a constant stumbling block to the Council's operations. When a subject became too "sensitive" for discussion or action, it was likely to be set aside for further study or suffer dilution of content. In some cases, these "solutions" merely assured continuing stalemate.[11] In others (as in the teen-age drinking problem), they led to a resolution that could not be carried out within the existing governmental framework without additional pressure from potent political forces. On still other occasions, when the Council succeeded in effecting a compromise among conflicting points of view, it often was unable, on a voluntary basis, to sustain the effort needed to carry forth the project to a successful completion.

Lack of Funds and Staff

Financing by voluntary contribution is one of the largest drawbacks to voluntary cooperation. Without legal authority, MRC

<hr>

[10] "Nobody Loves It," *Newark Evening News*, March 23, 1963.

[11] For another example of MRC's inability to undertake positive action (in the form of a recommendation to the federal government) because of the sensitive nature of the material, see Chap. VIII, pp. 183–184. Royce Hanson's study of the Metropolitan Washington Council of Governments indicates that it too avoided certain subjects, such as uniform taxicab rates, because of their controversial nature (*The Politics of Metropolitan Cooperation: Metropolitan Washington Council of Governments* [Washington, D.C.: Washington Center for Metropolitan Studies, 1964], p. 48).

had no guarantee that it could assess member governments, and it was unable to raise the necessary funds to perform its work or to staff its organization properly. The chairman of the Metropolitan Washington Council of Governments once pointed out: "Everyone's for cooperation until it costs money,"[12] and MRC's experience indicated a membership fearful of high costs and taxes which yield little or no tangible return.

It was suggested at an early MRC meeting that Council members attempt to secure appropriations from the legislative bodies of their particular governmental subdivisions at the rate of $.01 per resident to pay for an executive secretary, a staff, and an office for MRC. The Council was then seeking legal recognition by the three state governments, and it was felt that this time-consuming task would be greatly facilitated if MRC had competent staff personnel. The Vice-Chairman of MRC, Westchester County Executive Michaelian, who was presiding in Mayor Wagner's absence, silenced the heated discussion which followed this suggestion by directing attention to the lack of a quorum at the meeting. The motion could not be acted upon at that time and was not suggested again in this form in the future.[13]

The federal impact upon the financing of councils of governments will be discussed in detail in Chapter V. For the present, it should be noted that the lack of a reliable source of funds is not as severe a problem for a voluntary council now as it was for MRC ten years ago. In 1965, the federal government offered councils financial aid to establish themselves and provided them the opportunity to participate directly in the planning of pro-

[12] Anne A. Wilkins, address to "AMA–NACO Workshop on 'Voluntary Regional Cooperation Councils,'" mimeographed (American Municipal Association, 1963). For confirmation by a MRC member, see memorandum from Arthur Prager, Assistant Executive Secretary, MRC, to Lehman concerning "MRC Visit to Essex County," September 6, 1962. It is reported here that James L. McKenna, Director of the Board of Freeholders in Essex County, New Jersey, told Prager that the freeholders were not opposed to the MRC idea "in principle" but felt that "there was no benefit to be gained in proportion to the money spent."

[13] The suggestion was made by Louis Greenbaum, Chairman of the Mayor's Advisory Committee of Stamford, Connecticut, to the MRC membership, June 16, 1959. See Chap. VII, pp. 154–157, for further discussion of MRC finances.

grams with regional implications.[14] This means that councils of governments are now obligated to raise less money for their activities by voluntary subscription. However, a council must be established as a legal entity in order to qualify for federal grants, a requirement with which MRC was not able to comply during the first ten years of its life.

Inability to Implement Recommendations

In addition to difficulties in securing a steady source of funds, a voluntary council also lacks an adequate administrative process for assuring reasonably effective implementation of decisions that are reached. While the action required varies with the nature of the particular problem, voluntary organizations generally depend on cooperative action among themselves, or on action by another governmental level, for implementation. Any local group can refuse to be bound by decisions if it does not agree with majority considerations. Without substantial unanimity of opinion among its members, a council's recommendations for action by other governments carry little weight. To many observers, this inability to implement recommendations offers little prospect of providing immediate action in dealing with the critical problems facing metropolitan areas.[15]

In the New York metropolitan area, MRC had no power to compel action. It could only meet to discuss and make recommendations that were not binding upon any of the member communities. Because the Council consisted only of chief elected officials and did not include representatives of local legislative bodies (except from those governmental units lacking an elected chief executive), it was not even certain that a given local community would sustain commitments undertaken by its chief executive officer. Even if a community were a formal member of the Council (under the interlocal agreement of 1962 or the new articles of incorporation drawn up in 1966), it could not be

[14] Section 701(g) of the Housing Act of 1954, as amended through August 10, 1965.
[15] E.g., Advisory Commission, *Alternative Approaches*, p. 38; York Wilbern, "The Changing Ecology of Urban Local Government," *Metropolitan Issues*, ed. Birkhead, p. 58; Martin, *Metropolis in Transition*, p. 49.

compelled to retain membership. A member would terminate its membership simply by failing to make its annual contribution.

Had MRC gained the legal status it sought for so many years, it would have been no more than a public advisory body. Yet it regarded this recognition as the most urgent of objectives, to open the way to "unlimited . . . [opportunities] in the field of regional problem-solving."[16] While this was probably an over-optimistic appraisal of the Council's potential in 1962, legal status would certainly have eased its financial and staffing problems, and would have enabled it to make agreements and/or contracts with other agencies to perform additional activities. MRC's quest for legal status developed into the Council's major activity from 1959 to 1966 and affected all aspects of its operation during these years. It is useful to explore this attempt in detail, since MRC's prolonged effort to gain the approval of the state legislatures initially —and of the voters of the region ultimately—exemplifies many of the obstacles facing a council of governments.

Agreement to Seek Statutory Recognition

Late in 1957, Maxwell Lehman, Executive Secretary of MRC, requested opinions from a number of community leaders as to whether the Council should continue operations on a purely voluntary basis or begin consideration of an expanded role in regional matters. While the answers to this request are not available, Lehman must have found them sufficiently encouraging to advise Columbia University students a short time later that: "Whatever new governmental machinery is set up as an intermediary layer between the local communities and the three states, the Metropolitan Council will be the permanent base upon which the machinery will rest."[17] At the June 1958 membership meeting, a committee was appointed to determine the direction the Council should follow in the coming years. Karl Metzger, Director of the Board of Freeholders of Middlesex County, New Jersey, was named Chairman of this "Committee on the Future of the MRC,"

[16] Letter from Prager to James Schrader, American Society of Planning Officials, Chicago, Illinois, October 18, 1962.

[17] Maxwell Lehman, address to Columbia University planning students, April 8, 1958.

which included as members: Ray Manahan, Mayor of Morristown, New Jersey; Griffith E. Harris, First Selectman of Greenwich, Connecticut; A. Holly Patterson, County Executive of Nassau County, New York; and Edwin G. Michaelian, County Executive of Westchester County, New York.

In order to carry out its charge, the committee scheduled four public hearings at different locations throughout the region and invited elected officials, civic leaders, and consultants to offer recommendations as to MRC's future: Should the Council (1) continue as a voluntary organization, (2) attempt to seek statutory recognition, or (3) develop into some form of regional government? Fifty organizations and individuals were heard. The majority of the witnesses favored an attempt to seek statutory recognition, so that the Council might eventually "be able to come to grips with the governmental problems which beset the region."[18]

On the basis of the opinions expressed at the public hearings, the committee proposed to the membership at the February 1959 semiannual meeting that:

> (1) MRC receive legal recognition as a federation of municipal and county governmental officials from the three states, authorizing consultation, research, and studies, but no operating powers; (2) the states of Connecticut and New Jersey enact legislation patterned on Article 14G of the General Municipal Law of New York State which permitted a variety of specific cooperative projects to be undertaken by adjoining communities, even across state lines; (3) a full-time secretariat be set up; (4) the Council should be supported by all of its members, perhaps at the rate of $.01 per resident; and (5) membership in MRC should be by resolution of the legislative body of the community seeking membership, followed by affirmative action by the executive board of the Council.

No vote was taken on the committee report in order to permit the members time to study it until the next meeting, six months later.

Despite Nassau County's objections to proposals (1) and (2) dealing with legal recognition, the executive secretary felt sufficiently confident of ultimate acceptance to prepare a "Draft

[18] Report of the Committee on the Future of the MRC, February 19, 1959. See Chap. IV, pp. 53–63, for a detailed discussion of the recommendations offered at the public hearings.

of an Act to Establish a Tri-State Metropolitan Regional Council" for discussion at the June 1959 meeting. The members were more hesitant in their approach. While most seemed to approve of the committee's proposals, they nonetheless directed the executive secretary to forward ballots to all of the members asking them to vote for or against the recommendations as given. Results of the balloting indicate that twenty-six members voted affirmatively on all counts, three voted partial approval, six did not respond, and one (Bergen County, New Jersey) voted "no" on all counts.[19]

On February 23, 1960, a roll-call vote of the general membership was taken on the committee's three recommendations of legal status, financial support, and the creation of a full-time secretariat. The results show twenty-nine approvals of all three items. Negative votes were cast by Bergen County on all counts, by Essex County on legal status, and by Hackensack on financial support. Four communities abstained: Morristown, New Jersey, and New Rochelle, Nassau County, and Suffolk County, New York. On the basis of the affirmative vote of the majority, the members approved a resolution to seek formal legal status for MRC, and authorized the committee to prepare the necessary legislation, an annual budget, and a plan for organization of the secretariat.[20]

Preparation of the MRC Bill

A second draft of legislation establishing a "Tri-State Council"

[19] A memorandum from Leslie Slote, then Senior Management Consultant, City Administrator's office, to Maxwell Lehman, October 17, 1960, indicates that affirmative votes on all counts were cast by Hudson, Middlesex, Monmouth, Morris, Somerset, and Union counties, New Jersey; Elizabeth, Hoboken, Jersey City, Newark, Passaic, Paterson, Plainfield, and Rahway, New Jersey; Darien, Greenwich, Norwalk, Stamford, and Westport, Connecticut; Orange, Putnam, Rockland, and Westchester counties, New York; and by New York, White Plains, and Yonkers, New York. Negative votes were cast by Bergen County, New Jersey (on all counts), Essex County, New Jersey ("no" on legal status), Hackensack, New Jersey ("no" on financial support), and New Canaan, Connecticut ("no" on Article 14G). Abstentions were cast by Passaic County, Linden, and Morristown, New Jersey, and by Nassau County, Suffolk County, and New Rochelle, New York. Consult the map facing page 1 for the location of place names.

[20] It is interesting (and ironic) to note that Bergen County, the one

was prepared and sent to the Committee on the Future and to the executive board before submission to the membership at the regular June 1960 meeting. This was found acceptable with the exception of a section which proposed a "board of managers" for the Council consisting of one member from each state to serve for one year. Karl Metzger was sharply critical of this suggestion and certain that "the entire membership would be horrified at the thought of a triumvirate. Certainly it would give Bergen and Nassau Counties a lovely opportunity to shout that their fears were justified."[21] After correction of the offending words, the membership approved the reciprocal state legislation and authorized the Committee on the Future to prepare to introduce it into the three state legislatures. The committee was also authorized to urge enactment in Connecticut and New Jersey of legislation patterned after Article 14G of New York State Law. In making his customary report to the membership at the June 30, 1960, meeting, the executive secretary noted that "the whole matter had [already] been discussed and debated for a period of more than eighteen months."

This proved to be just the beginning of the complex and cumbersome procedures required to draft legislation that would be equally acceptable to the legislative bodies of the three states. As an added complication, the Council was ambivalent about how to proceed vis-à-vis the state legislatures and was faced with conflicting suggestions. On the one hand, there were those who encouraged the Council to continue in its efforts to secure new

---

community which cast a completely negative vote on both occasions, on the basis that the establishment of MRC as a legal entity would remove governmental power farther from the local voters, had experienced a 44 percent increase in population growth between 1950 and 1960, and was expected by RPA to undergo a similar increase in population between 1960 and 1975, with the northern part of the county doubling in the number of residents. As a result of this growth, Bergen was expected to have overwhelming internal problems which the local level of government would be incapable of solving by itself. (Industry and employment were also expected to expand faster in Bergen than in any other county in the region.) These projections come from an address by Joseph M. Lieper, Director of Transportation Planning, New York City Planning Commission, to the Transit Committee of Bergen County, March 18, 1960.

[21] Letter from Metzger to Lehman, April 28, 1960.

state legislation specifically designed for it, on the grounds that passage of an "interstate compact" would lend increased status and "dramatic impact" to the new organization. This point of view was buttressed by advice from the Corporation Counsel of New York City, who wrote: "In view of the relatively simple organizational structure . . . [and] the severe restriction to advisory and informational powers . . . the bill raises no serious problems of a strictly legal nature and these features should overcome objections of the state legislature."[22]

But "these features" did not quiet all voices of protest. State Senator Elisha T. Barrett, Chairman of the New York Joint Legislative Committee on Interstate Cooperation, strongly recommended that MRC proceed with the "obvious step" of abandoning its effort to secure new legislation and concentrate on the passage by New Jersey and Connecticut of legislation patterned after existing Article 14G of the New York State Law with respect to interlocal agreements. Enacted in 1957, this section of the law enabled local governmental units in New York State to cooperate with governmental units of other states "on a basis of mutual advantage." The law permitted the establishment of an interlocal advisory board (by interlocal agreement) to recommend programs and policies for cooperative or uniform action in a variety of functional fields, including municipal planning. It also permitted the contracting public agency to furnish such office supplies and personnel as might be needed to carry on the work of the advisory board and share in the expenses involved. Barrett felt that this legislation furnished a "legal method to achieve" the Council's three goals of legal recognition, a full-time secretariat, and financial support by members. While the bill failed to give specific authorization to the joint employment of

---

[22] Memorandum on "Legal Aspects of the Proposed Metropolitan Regional Council" by Charles H. Tenney, then Corporation Counsel of New York City (undated). See also the minutes of an informal meeting of Leslie Slote of MRC and consultants C. McKim Norton, Bernard Richland, John Keith, William Cassella, Jr., Edward Kresky, and John Bebout, March 15, 1960. While these men agreed that legal status should be secured via new legislation, it was also suggested that Article 14G should be kept as a safeguard for the future in the event that the attempt to secure such legislation failed.

personnel by localities on an interstate basis, this shortcoming could be circumvented "in a circuitous fashion."[23]

Barrett noted that Connecticut was already favorably disposed toward regional cooperation and recommended that the executive secretary use the weight of the important New Jersey communities participating in MRC to secure such legislation in that state. He offered the services of the staff of the Joint Legislative Committee to aid the Council in formulating legislation authorizing agreements across state lines.

Barrett's position was unequivocal. As he later explained in a letter to State Senator Walter J. Mahoney, he found MRC's new legislation undesirable and unnecessary. The proposed MRC statute was too vague, and it did not provide adequate control by the state over financial matters and personnel practices. In Barrett's opinion, sufficient state law already existed to permit interlocal cooperative agreements, and this could be amended to provide for MRC's specific needs.[24]

The Council appears to have paid little attention to this advice from a powerful, strategically placed, state legislator. The files of the City Administrator's office bulge with material concerning the specific provisions of the new bill but fail to include background information for use by state legislators, which might serve to justify the new legislation or integrate it with existing state law. There is likewise no indication that the Council attempted to line up backers for the new bill. At this point, the bill's greatest support seems to have emanated from its authors—in New York City.

Between June 1960 and March 1961, MRC continued to clear provisions of the new bill with its members and with attorneys

[23] Letter from Barrett to Lehman, February 23, 1960, reprinted in the Annual Report of the Joint Legislative Committee on Interstate Cooperation, Legislative Document (1960) No. 6, Sec. V, "Interlocal Cooperation," pp. 191–193. The appropriate sections of Article 14G of the General Municipal Law discussed herein are subdivisions (a) and (b) of sections 462 and 463 respectively.

[24] Letter from Barrett to Mahoney, December 6, 1960 (in the files of William N. Cassella, Jr.). Barrett pointed out that Article 5G of the General Municipal Law, enacted in 1960, also provided for the carrying out of joint or cooperative municipal undertakings through interlocal agreements. He felt that this legislation, in addition to Article 14G, would be adequate for the Council's legal needs.

"acquainted with legislative practice."[25] Corrections and additions were made for the third and last time; these were "relatively minor changes" involving nomenclature, population requirements for membership, and fringe benefits to Council personnel.[26] "An Act to Establish a Tri-State MRC" was introduced into the New York Assembly (Print #5808, Introd. #4993) on March 25, 1961, the last day of the legislative session. It was referred to the Rules Committee and was never reported out.

Passage of Enabling Legislation

By late spring, 1961, the Council was ready to proceed along the lines mapped out by Senator Barrett and others a year before. Bills were introduced into the legislative bodies of New Jersey and Connecticut providing for the establishment of interlocal advisory boards, and a bill was introduced in New York to amend Article 14G of New York's General Municipal Law. This amendment was designed to permit more flexible arrangements in the making of interlocal agreements by giving cooperating communities authority to hire their own interlocal staffs and receive federal assistance. This legislation was vetoed by Governor Nelson A. Rockefeller on technical grounds: Article 14G did not specifically provide for the establishment of interlocal agencies and the proposed bill failed to specify the employing entity of interlocal employees.[27]

On June 14, 1961, Public Act 429, "An act concerning interlocal agreements between governmental units of this state and other states," was signed by Governor John N. Dempsey of Connecticut, providing for the establishment of interlocal advisory boards through an interlocal agreement. While the Connecticut

[25] Letter from Lehman to Metzger, January 6, 1961.

[26] The words "tri-state federation" were substituted for references to a tri-state "agency" and "council"; these changes were made to quiet the fear that the Council was trying to set itself up as a supergovernment. Membership was restricted to municipalities with a population of 50,000 or more (instead of the "45,000" figure which had appeared previously), and provisions for retirement and other benefits were made for present and prospective employees. Report of the Committee on the Future of the MRC, February 28, 1961.

[27] Veto message of Governor Rockefeller of S. Bill Print 1879, Introd. #1811, April 24, 1961.

law paralleled New York State's 14G, it was a bit broader than the latter in allowing civil service and pension benefits to interlocal employees and in authorizing federal grants to interlocal boards.[28] Both of these features were likewise contained in New Jersey legislation S. 226 (providing for the establishment of interlocal boards), which passed the State Senate in May 1961. Two other amendments were planned for the New York statute to provide for employee benefits and eligibility for federal grants.[29] For the first time, MRC felt confident that legal status was imminent.

Drafting of the Interlocal Agreement

Passage of the three state statutes would enable the Council to draw up an interlocal agreement and hire a full-time staff to carry on its work. Accordingly, the Committee on the Future referred to the membership in June 1961 a set of principles to serve as a guide in the preparation of the interlocal agreement. This "Scope of Activities" spelled out the kinds of activities MRC would pursue in the fields of "intergovernmental cooperation, research, technical assistance, and community relations." A Technical Advisory Committee was appointed to use this statement as a guide in drafting an interlocal agreement that would comply with the laws of the three states.[30]

[28] Considerable help was given in the passage of the Connecticut legislation by the Council of State Governments, which brought the MRC proposal to the attention of the Connecticut Commission on Intergovernmental Cooperation, a mixed body of Senate and House members and gubernatorial appointees. Intervention by the Council of State Governments helped to create a favorable atmosphere for consideration of the new proposal by the Connecticut legislature, and was an important factor in gaining final approval of it.

[29] New York State S. Bill Print 2046, 2495, Introd. #1974, January 29, 1962, an act to amend the general municipal law in relation to providing authorization for agreements concerning interlocal employees or officers to assist in the work of interlocal advisory boards, and S. Bill Print 2089, Introd. #2003, January 29, 1962, to amend the general municipal law and the commerce law, in relation to acceptance of federal aid by interlocal advisory boards, were introduced into the Senate in 1962 but were not reported out of committee.

[30] MRC's Technical Advisory Committee included the following persons: John Bebout (Chairman), Frederick L. Zimmerman, William N. Cassella, Jr., John Keith, George Deming, and W. Bernard Richland.

In February 1962, the fourth draft of the interlocal agreement was approved. Its provisions followed closely the principles and activities set forth in the earlier tri-state council act. In essence, the agreement provided for the creation of an interlocal advisory board known as the Metropolitan Regional Council, through which the member localities "by association, consultation, and study" might be helped in dealing with common problems. The Council was composed of contracting units of government, represented by their elected chief executive officers, and each unit had one vote. The work was advisory in nature and was to be performed by an executive director and a staff, with assistance from participating communities. Funds were to be provided by member governments, with the budget not to exceed contributions of more than $.01 per capita of the population of the contracting units of government. The agreement became effective when adopted by the City of New York and any four additional local governmental units, providing that at least two of the latter were from outside New York State.[31]

Each Council member from New York State and Connecticut was authorized to present the interlocal agreement to his respective governing body for action required by state law, and to report back before May 1, 1962. New Jersey members were excused from similar action until their state had enacted the appropriate legislation.

Temporary Setback in New Jersey

S. 226, an act authorizing counties and municipalities to enter into agreements with governmental units in other states, was still pending in New Jersey. Despite a report in the *New York Times* that Governor Robert B. Meyner's approval was "assured,"[32] the bill passed both houses of the legislature and then languished on

[31] MRC Committee on the Future Development of the Region, "Interlocal agreement among the undersigned contracting units of government, establishing the Metropolitan Regional Council, pursuant to Article 14–G of the General Municipal Law of the State of New York (1957), Public Act 429, 1961 session, General Assembly, State of Connecticut, now designated as sec. 7–339a through 7–339l, Connecticut General Statutes, 1961 supplement, and Chapter 46, Laws of the State of New Jersey (1962)."

[32] *New York Times*, July 23, 1961, p. 58.

the Governor's desk, unsigned. Last-minute appeals were made by Karl Metzger, Joel Jacobson, head of the New Jersey AFL-CIO, United States Senator Harrison Williams, Jr., and Amory Bradford, then Vice-President and General Manager of the *New York Times*, but Governor Meyner expressed fear that the bill would open the way to "haphazard, unnecessary, wasteful bureaucracy" and vetoed the legislation shortly before his term expired in January 1962. Meyner found further faults with the bill: it was "loosely drawn," represented "the antithesis of orderly coordinated planning," imposed no maximum salary limits, failed to provide authority for intrastate interlocal agreements, made insufficient provision for state supervision and review, and lacked a "compelling showing of need."[33]

It seems clear that MRC had not anticipated this hostile reaction from Governor Meyner. Misreading the political situation in Trenton, the Council had informed the press that it expected "complete tri-state legal authority" by August 1961,[34] and then failed to convince its last important holdout of the need for interlocal cooperation on regional problems. The Council did not repeat this omission. Governor Richard J. Hughes, who succeeded Meyner in office, was approached directly by Mayor Wagner and MRC members in New Jersey and proved to be a good deal more sympathetic to the cause of regional cooperation than his predecessor. A bill was introduced into the legislature soon after he took office, and the "Regional Advisory Council Act of 1962" was passed and signed by the Governor on May 18, 1962.

Further Legal Problems

At this time, MRC still had legal difficulties ahead. The first sign of trouble came in a letter from Mayor Wagner to Governor Hughes raising a question about a provision in the New Jersey bill designating the State Commissioner of Conservation and Economic Development as a nonvoting member of MRC. To

---

[33] Veto message of Governor Meyner of S. 226, January 9, 1962.
[34] *New York Times*, July 23, 1961, p. 58.

Wagner, this provision detracted from one of the principal purposes of MRC, "which is to promote . . . cooperation between local governments, giving to such local governments the sense of independence which encourages the ideal of home rule."[35] It also rendered the proposed law inconsistent with laws already enacted by the states of New York and Connecticut. This inconsistency was overcome by amending the interlocal agreement at the June 1962 membership meeting to provide for state review and examination of books and for the states to be represented on the Council as nonvoting members.

Opinions from the requisite legal officers in each of the three states were then sought to make sure that the amended agreement conformed with the recently passed state legislation. Only New Jersey found the interlocal agreement in compliance with the conditions and requirements set forth in the statute. The Connecticut Assistant Attorney General and the Attorney General objected to the agreement on technical and substantive grounds respectively, and the Comptroller in New York State did not feel that Article 14G of the General Municipal Law as amended permitted the Council to hire its own personnel. After a good deal of correspondence and discussion between New York City and Albany, it was agreed that express statutory authority for the hiring of personnel "should be implied," and the interlocal agreement was found to be in accord with the applicable provisions of the General Municipal Law of New York.[36]

Although the objections of Connecticut's Assistant Attorney General were easily overcome, the Council's problems with the Attorney General took a little longer to resolve. Once the Attorney General found the "substance" of the agreement satisfactory, he questioned the "policy" considerations underlying Connecticut's seemingly unequal representation by two representatives on the executive board as compared with three representatives from contracting units of government from each of the other two states. In explanation, the executive secretary pointed out that the interlocal agreement was made among thirty-seven

---

[35] Letter from Wagner to Hughes, May 14, 1962.
[36] Letter from Alfred W. Haight, First Deputy Comptroller, New York State Department of Audit and Control, to Lehman, October 18, 1962.

counties, cities, and towns in the region, and not among the states. The executive board had always operated with this pattern of representation, as had the steering committee before it, and this question had never been raised. Moreover, the New Jersey sector had twenty members, with a total population of 3,788,000, and the New York sector had eleven members, with a population of 11,086,000; Connecticut was represented by six units in the lower portion of Fairfield County with a total population of 267,000 persons. If "population" were to be considered, the six Connecticut towns and cities were well represented on the Council with one vote each, as compared to such communities as New York City and Bergen County, which were also entitled to one vote each on Council matters. By April 1963, the Attorney General was convinced that there was no discrimination against his state or the communities therein, and found the agreement to be in accord with state law.[37]

In this slow, tedious fashion—with legal and technical obstacles to overcome every step of the way—the interlocal agreement was reconciled with the enabling legislation of the three states. Had there been just one state to contend with, the difficulties would have been sufficiently great; with three states, the problems seemed endless. It was, of course, critical to gain approval of the interlocal agreement as a legal document. During this whole period of travail with state attorneys, the agreement was under consideration for ratification by member communities of the three states. If the interlocal agreement needed further revision, local legislative bodies would have to pass new ordinances and resolutions.

Ratification of the Interlocal Agreement

By March of 1963, ten communities had ratified the interlocal agreement: Middlesex County, Union County, Jersey City, Plain-

[37] Letter from Attorney General Albert L. Coles of Connecticut to Lehman, April 23, 1963. Previous letters from Assistant Attorney General Carl D. Eisenman had raised minor objections: that the full title of the Connecticut enabling legislation was not set forth in the interlocal agreement, and that the reference to "cities and towns" should be expanded to include the participation of "boroughs" as well. All of these objections were answered in full and corrected by MRC.

field, and Rahway, New Jersey; Westport, Connecticut; and Orange County, Rockland County, White Plains, and Yonkers, New York. Suffolk County had voted against affiliation in May 1962, and Nassau County Executive Eugene H. Nickerson, who controlled only a few votes on his Board of Supervisors, was reluctant to present the agreement for ratification because of the board's almost certain refusal.

One of the biggest setbacks in MRC's drive to attain greater permanence and legal standing occurred in March 1963, when Westchester County voted against membership for a variety of reasons including alleged fear of takeover by New York City, fear of supergovernment, and fear of loss of home rule.[38] By the time the membership convened a short time later, MRC was apprehensive about the "irrational" anti-MRC arguments that were receiving increased attention in areas where approval had already been given, as well as in places like Bergen County, where the agreement had not yet been considered.

Karl Metzger's report to the membership on the status of the interlocal agreement in March 1963 answered charges of "unconstitutionality" and "supergovernment" by pointing out that the MRC agreement was not an interstate compact, that the Council had no operating powers, that the agreement had been found legal and proper by the legal officers of three states, and that MRC was a council composed of local officials, and not a council "imposed on them." He appealed to the membership to consider the four following possibilities: (1) organization on a formal basis with the ten units which had ratified; (2) continuation on a voluntary basis and abandonment of the quest for legal status; (3) intensive education of the public to clear up misunderstandings; or (4) abandonment of voluntary cooperation altogether. In reply, the membership resolved:

> that MRC reaffirm its determination to move toward the goal of effective cooperation among the communities of the New York–New Jersey–Connecticut metropolitan region; and that the Committee on the Future be mandated to prepare new recommendations that will advance the organization toward this goal; that as

[38] For a detailed discussion of "The Westchester Story," see Chap. VI, pp. 126 ff.

action toward formal legal status continues, informal arrangements be maintained permitting participation of member communities in the Council's work.[39]

The Committee on the Future met shortly thereafter and agreed to continue MRC as a voluntary organization of public officials and carry on its work "if possible more vigorously than before." A special subcommittee was appointed to suggest revisions to the interlocal agreement so that it would be more acceptable to the legislators of the region's local governments. The members were instructed to hold off further submission of the agreement to their respective legislative bodies until the new document was prepared.

It was also decided that New York City should not formally ratify the agreement to create MRC as a formal legal body, on the basis that MRC without Suffolk, Nassau, and Westchester counties would be less effective than MRC as an association informally composed of all the counties and municipalities of the region. There was a good deal of discussion of this point at subsequent meetings. Some members felt that New York City should ratify immediately and thus allow MRC to gain legal standing, set up a permanent secretariat, and become eligible for federal grants. On the other hand, the MRC executive secretary felt that it would be best if unanimous approval by all members were to precede action by the City Council of New York in view of accusations by certain political groups that MRC was an attempt by New York City to "take over" the region.[40]

The subcommittee met in August 1963 to revise the interlocal agreement and suggested that the name "MRC" be changed to the "Council of Local Governments," that a different chairman assume office, and that the Council be reconstituted as an organization of elected officials, rather than communities. Imposition of modest dues was recommended, based on a starting budget not to exceed $50,000. The executive board did not convene to consider these suggestions until early in 1964. At that time, it was

[39] MRC membership resolution, March 19, 1963.

[40] The information presented here comes from minutes of a meeting of the Committee on the Future, April 11, 1963, and meetings of the special committee to amend the interlocal agreement, August 22, 1963, and September 10, 1964.

decided to retain the existing name and to adopt the motion "that MRC abandon its attempt to gain legal status as an organization of communities, but reorganize itself as an organization of elected officials, and that MRC set up a system of dues payment by members to make itself self-supporting." This change was submitted to the few members who appeared at a general meeting in April 1964 and was approved. Mayor Wagner offered to appoint a Budget and Charter Committee to draw up a new constitution and set up a dues schedule for the reorganized MRC.

Subsequently, the entire effort to reorganize MRC ground to a halt. The Technical Advisory Committee met on September 9, 1964 to discuss the items to be included in a new charter, such as budget, future programs, new sources of funds, and public relations activities, but no action followed. A draft of a new agreement drawn up by the county attorney of Nassau was never distributed to the membership.[41] Karl Metzger, who had been in the forefront of the effort to gain legal status, admitted to a "deep sense of dismay and frustration" after the Westchester defection,[42] and it was apparent that outside consultants, staff officials, and MRC members had lost interest in carrying on. Ratification of the interlocal agreement, which had been taken for granted during the entire effort to gain state legislative approval, was now an unpopular cause. The ten approvals by member communities were already obsolete, since any amended agreement would have to be reconsidered by local legislative bodies.

Epilogue: Incorporation as a Legal Entity

Almost two years later, the current effort was begun to revive the Council. The executive board convened in March 1966 and voted to establish MRC as an official entity so that it might

[41] The new agreement was titled "Constitution of the Council of Local Governments: An Organization of the Elected Municipal and County Chief Executives of the New York, New Jersey, Connecticut Metropolitan Area," July 21, 1964. This document appeared to follow the same lines of the original interlocal agreement except that it set up an advisory board of "local chief executives" rather than one of "local governmental units." The powers assigned were identical in both cases.

[42] Report to MRC membership, March 19, 1963.

qualify for federal funds available for comprehensive planning under the Housing and Urban Development Act of 1965 (Title II). At a membership meeting held in June 1966, MRC members elected Mayor John V. Lindsay of New York City as Chairman, voted to "incorporate," and authorized the new Executive Secretary, Mathias L. Spiegel, First Deputy City Administrator of New York City, to prepare drafts of articles of incorporation for general distribution. By October 1966, the incorporation papers had been approved by all of the former members and MRC met as an official body for the first time in its history.[43]

The certificate of incorporation of MRC states that the Council's purpose is: "to provide an agency for the cooperation of the elected chief executive officers of municipalities in the New York–New Jersey–Connecticut metropolitan region in the practical study of questions affecting the region, the holding of meetings for discussion of problems of current concern to the region, and the furnishing of information on matters of common interest to the members. . . ." The Council is given permission to receive and administer grants, finance research, execute agreements, accept appropriations from communities, and hire a full-time staff. The articles of incorporation forbid the Council to engage in such activities as political campaigning, lobbying for legislation, and issuance of propaganda. The voluntary nature of the Council is kept intact by Article IV which provides that: "No resolution or other act of the Corporation shall be binding on any municipality."

By the act of incorporation, MRC gained legal status, but it

---

[43] In going the "incorporation" route, MRC followed the example of the Metropolitan Washington Council of Governments, which became a tax-exempt, nonprofit institution in 1965. The Certificate of Incorporation of the Metropolitan Regional Council, Inc., Pursuant to the Membership Corporation Law of the State of New York, November 2, 1966, was signed by Mayor John V. Lindsay of New York City, county executives Eugene H. Nickerson of Nassau and Edwin G. Michaelian of Westchester, and Robert P. Slocum, Chairman of the Board of Supervisors, Rockland County, New York; by Mayor Hugh J. Addonizio of Newark, Mayor Thomas J. Whalen of Jersey City, and George L. Burton, Jr., director of Freeholders, Middlesex County, New Jersey; and by Mayor Thomas C. Mayers of Stamford and First Selectman Herbert E. Baldwin of Westport, Connecticut.

still lacked a formal organizational framework. This was provided in the "By-Laws of the MRC, Inc.," which were officially adopted on March 3, 1967. These restate the purpose of the Council to be "association, consultation and study," and give the Council power to render technical assistance, establish committees, accept grants, and open a permanent office. Membership is restricted, as before, to chief executive officers, with one vote for each member regardless of his community's size. The new board of directors consists of nine members: four from New York, three from New Jersey, and two from Connecticut. The by-laws provide for annual contribution of dues by Council members according to a population formula, but "no member shall be responsible for any contribution unless such sum is appropriated by his municipality according to law." In May 1967, MRC filed an application for a federal grant of approximately $210,000 to cover the cost of staff, office space, and program. MRC was to raise approximately $105,000 in matching contributions, or one-third of its total proposed budget. At the end of 1967, the MRC application was being processed by the regional office of the U.S. Department of Housing and Urban Development.

Despite avowals of vigorous pursuit of plans and programs, MRC moved at an increasingly slow pace after its initial drive for legal status was halted in the early 1960s. In view of the stumbling blocks it encountered in the form of legal technicalities, complicated procedures, and dissimilar state requirements, this reaction was not altogether unexpected. The tenacity and fortitude of those who worked unceasingly over a five-year period to secure legal standing for the Council merit admiration.

At the same time, it might be questioned whether more forthright handling of legal and political issues as they arose might not have moved the whole procedure along more expeditiously, and thus hindered the development of a full-blown opposition. In directing attention to the scarcity of cooperative arrangements in the New York metropolitan region, Wood points out that "protracted negotiations . . . and political and administrative finesse"[44] are required for a number of municipalities to tackle problems in

[44] Wood, *1400 Governments*, p. 118.

common. Without the money, staff, and full-time leadership that legal status would have provided, MRC lacked the machinery to sustain the monumental effort that was required.

The relative ease with which MRC was able to incorporate as a nonprofit corporation under long-existing state law stands in sharp contrast to its earlier efforts. However, the Council would probably have been unwilling to settle for this modest, undramatic entrance into the regional scene in former years. Specific recognition as a public advisory body—by means of state enabling legislation—was regarded as a necessary first step which would pave the way for the Council to assume a more active role in the formulation of regional policy. There was never consensus among MRC members as to what the specifics of this role should be but merely agreement that legal authority would be useful in whatever direction the Council might be headed.[45]

It will become increasingly clear, in subsequent chapters, that this lack of a well-defined sense of purpose hampered the Council considerably, both in its initial effort to gain approval of the states and in its later effort to gain ratification by the region's local communities. If MRC saw itself only as a study and advisory group, local officials questioned the need for an interlocal agreement—with vaguely defined powers—to which "By-Laws" would be added at some future date. A look at some of the traditional norms of local government may help to indicate why MRC encountered such fierce resistance from some of the autonomous communities surrounding New York City.

[45] In this connection, note should be taken of the emergence of the Tri-State Transportation Commission in the New York metropolitan region in 1965 as a legal entity for research and study but with no power to enforce public policy. Originally established by the governors of the three states as a tri-state planning "committee," the Commission has recently been assigned the considerable task of reviewing all local requests for federal funds in a large number of functional fields. For further discussion of Tri-State, see Chap. V, pp. 99 ff., and Chap. IX, pp. 207 ff.

III

TRADITIONAL APPROACH OF LOCAL GOVERNMENTS

Desire for Home Rule

Voluntary councils need all the support they can enlist from local communities if they are to function as effective representative bodies. This, however, is not easy to obtain. Thomas Jefferson provided a philosophical justification of local authority which is still part of our cultural mores. Vigorous, prominent, local governments were, to Jefferson, the best guarantee of liberty and protection against arbitrary government, and they would be efficient as well.

Suburban governments manifest a persistent tendency toward this inherited independence, although the justification for their long-standing convictions rests on increasingly shaky foundations. Recent studies find no supportive evidence for the widely held claim that small governmental units foster active political participation by their residents. Rather, they raise "serious doubts about the validity of the belief that small political units constitute the best means of keeping government in the control of the people."[1] Nevertheless, the desire for local autonomy and preser-

[1] Bollens (ed.), *Exploring the Metropolitan Community*, p. 87. See also Janowitz (ed.), *Community Political Systems*, I, particularly the findings of Hawley and Zimmer (p. 177) and Scott Greer (p. 199). Other observers have also stressed the undemocratic nature of grass-roots decisions: e.g., Rexford G. Tugwell and Edward C. Banfield, "Grass-Roots Democracy—Myth or Reality?," *Public Administration Review*, X (Winter, 1950), 54–55; Robert C. Wood, *Suburbia: Its People and Their Politics* (Boston: Houghton Mifflin, 1959), p. 289 and *passim*.

vation of local values is more pronounced now than in Jefferson's time. Separate competing governments continue to draw back from any joint action which might mean a loss of independence or threat to home rule.

No Breakdown in Sight

The impact of urban pressures has not yet been sufficiently severe to compel the suburbs to engage in joint action on major regional problems. Without substantial alterations in existing governmental arrangements, most of the local communities in the New York metropolitan region have been able to fend off a breakdown in the provision of essential public services. Informal coordinating devices, contractual arrangements, special districts, and metropolitan authorities have enabled local governments to maintain acceptable standards of existence. Increased state and federal assistance programs—as yet largely uncoordinated—have provided the means for existing governments to meet their most pressing financial burdens. The suburban governments are thus able to function with a minimum of coordination and preserve their independence, without too great a concern for urban needs.[2]

Nor is there a "crisis" in governmental services so far as the suburban public is concerned. While cooperative planning would appear to be more acceptable than "metropolitan government," regional cooperation runs into suburban opposition from elected officials, bureaucrats, civic associations, commercial groups, and homeowners, all of whom feel a deep stake in the preservation of the status quo. A cooperative plan becomes "supergovernment" to the suburbanite who is fond of his neighborhood, his way of life, and his isolated refuge. Since proposals generally must be approved by the electorate or their elected representatives, any proposal for changing important features of existing political arrangements has a limited chance of success.[3]

Furthermore, leadership from the central city is frequently

[2] Wood, *1400 Governments*, pp. 173–199; Bollens (ed.), *Exploring the Metropolitan Community*, pp. 71–80, 198, 314; Greer, in *Community Political Systems*, ed. Janowitz, I, 188–201, and *Governing the Metropolis* (New York: John Wiley and Sons, 1962), p. 129; and Williams et al., *Suburban Differences*, p. 294.

[3] For further discussion of some of the groups opposed to reorganization

unacceptable to suburban units of government, who fear the intrusion of problems from unwelcome elements of city life. This feeling of distrust is intensified by the substantial differences in "income level, ethnic identities, family composition, and living conditions," which are found among the local communities in the New York region.[4] The predominantly white, middle- or upper-class suburb wishes to preserve its political autonomy and distinctive view of the "public interest" free from involvement with the political leadership, racial tensions, and social costs of the central cities. It has been questioned, therefore, whether it is reasonable for the voluntary council to expect local officials to play a large part in restructuring their own roles.[5]

Other questions arise concerning the validity of the attempt to change the suburbanite's view of the "metropolitan problem." Robert Wood's studies of *Suburbia* and *1400 Governments* point up the close relationship which the suburbanite feels to his customary political patterns, and which he does not want to relinquish. One of the pressing problems still to be answered by students of urban affairs concerns the means of preserving the values inherent in local government within a pattern of govern-

---

proposals, refer to Advisory Commission, *Factors Affecting Voter Reactions*, p. 13; and to *Report of the Joint Legislative Committee on Metropolitan Areas Study to the Legislature of the State of New York*, March 20, 1959, Legislative Document (1959) No. 19, particularly p. 43.

[4] Vernon, *Anatomy of a Metropolis*, p. 15. See Charles R. Adrian, *Governing Urban America*, 2d ed. (New York: McGraw-Hill, 1961), p. 163; Greer, *Governing the Metropolis*, p. 52; and Edward C. Banfield and James Q. Wilson, *City Politics* (Cambridge: Harvard University Press, 1963), p. 46, for further discussion of differences between suburbanites and city dwellers. However, due caution must be exercised with regard to the classic stereotypes of the poor, underprivileged, nonwhite central city on the one hand, and the comfortable white suburb on the other. In investigating economic, social, and racial disparities between central cities and suburbs in the metropolitan areas of the United States, the Advisory Commission finds that "very few meaningful generalizations . . . can be applied to all metropolitan areas." Disparities are found mostly in the Northeastern section of the United States, and in general there are broad variances from region to region and from one metropolitan area to another. (*Metropolitan Social and Economic Disparities: Implications for Intergovernmental Relations in Central Cities and Suburbs* [Washington: U.S. Government Printing Office, 1965], p. 11.)

[5] Roscoe C. Martin, "Action in Metropolis: II," *National Civic Review*, LII (July 1963), 366.

mental arrangements that will permit broad policy-making in matters of more than local concern.[6]

MRC proponents felt that the Council provided an obvious answer to this question. Their rationale held that the local sub-urban communities and the regional organization would "complement" each other, and that the Council would "strengthen existing local units of government by making them more effective."[7] Once common problems could be identified, mutual understanding would develop, and suburban officials would join together with their urban counterparts in a cooperative venture. The voluntary nature of the effort would help to overcome the suspicions of those who feared the motivations of the new group.

"Parochialism with a Vengeance"[8]

This line of reasoning, appealing as it might have been to MRC and its boosters, was not always self-evident to some important suburban political officials. At the very first MRC meeting, for example, A. Holly Patterson, chief executive officer of Nassau County, expressed hesitation about joining a "Metropolitan Council of Municipalities," or a "Regional Commission for Metropolitan Planning," or a "Metropolitan Council for Government and Civic Agencies," or a "Metropolitan New York Planning Commission," or any other such "vanguard of utopia." If the chief elected officials of the New York metropolitan region were to form merely a "conference" to study common problems, Nassau would be willing to cooperate fully, but only on an "entirely voluntary" basis.[9]

---

[6] For some discussion of this point, refer to Greer, in *Community Political Systems*, ed. Janowitz, I, 205; Adrian, *Public Administration Review*, XXI (Summer, 1961), 157; Banfield and Grodzins, *Government and Housing in Metropolitan Areas*, pp. 44–56; Jefferson B. Fordham, "Introduction," *A Symposium on Metropolitan Regionalism, University of Pennsylvania Law Review*, CV (February 1957), 441.

[7] Samuel Humes, "A Comparison of Voluntary Metropolitan Regional Organizations," in "Workshop on 'Voluntary Multi-Purpose Regional Organizations,'" p. 6.

[8] *Newsday*, editorial, October 2, 1959.

[9] Transcript of Conference on Metropolitan Regional Development, City Hall, New York, June 18, 1956, p. 17.

Patterson was as good as his word. As the Chairman of MRC's Water Pollution Committee, he took the lead in developing a program of water-pollution analysis and planning, and budgeted funds to permit Nassau to support the development of a water-pollution control map. At the same time, he offered no encouragement to MRC in its effort to gain legal status, reiterating in 1959 that "Nassau County will cooperate with one and all but will surrender its autonomy to no one." When the Council instituted a poll of its members to see whether they favored a move toward legal recognition, Patterson failed to return his ballot, declaring that he could not go along with "putting another overcoat of government on an already smothering taxpayer . . . [which might lead to] an obliteration of county boundaries."[10] In 1960, Patterson submitted a useful report dealing with regional control of water pollution and again refrained from taking a position on the legal future of MRC. By 1961, when the big push was made to gain tri-state recognition, Patterson no longer attended MRC meetings and showed no further interest in the work of his committee.

Patterson was not the only official whose suspicions could not be allayed. County Executive Michaelian of Westchester County, an active participant in MRC, expressed fear of the reaction of his Board of Supervisors to the interlocal agreement almost two years before he presented it to them for consideration, noting "the great resistance to a new agency or a new level of government which a great many people seem to think is what we are trying to set up with the MRC." Michaelian pointed out that his political leaders regarded the Council as a threat to the home-rule powers of Westchester cities, towns, and villages and looked upon the MRC legislation as the "opening wedge" for super-government.[11]

The Council listened to the comments of county executives Michaelian and Patterson but paid little attention to the warnings implicit in their respective words and deeds. Underestimating the hostility of suburban officials, who had been bred on distrust

[10] *Newsday*, October 2, 1959.
[11] Letter from Michaelian to Metzger, February 2, 1961, and minutes of executive board meeting, March 23, 1961.

of New York City and the "Tammany machine," MRC encouraged Democratic County Executive H. Lee Dennison of Suffolk County (Nassau's immediate neighbor on Long Island), to submit the MRC interlocal agreement to his Republican-controlled Board of Supervisors for ratification in the spring of 1962. An account of Suffolk's rejection of the agreement follows. It illustrates the opposition to which regional cooperation may be subjected by suburbanites, who prefer to cling to their traditions and existing institutions rather than face an unknown device which might lead to higher taxes or infringement of status.

The Suffolk County Story: "Rural Reactionaries Riding High"[12]

It will be recalled that Suffolk, along with Nassau, was one of four local governments which had refrained from taking a public stand in 1960 on the three recommendations for legal status, financial support, and the creation of a full-time secretariat that the Committee on the Future had proposed to the MRC general membership. County Executive Dennison had recently assumed office and felt that he needed time to study the matter. In October 1960, a feature article had appeared in the *Long Island Press*, highlighting opposition to the proposed MRC enabling legislation in New York State by neighboring County Executive Patterson, by Westchester Republicans, and by Suffolk's own Republican State Senator Elisha T. Barrett of Brightwaters, Chairman of the Joint Legislative Committee on Interstate Cooperation since 1951.

The newspaper article contained many misstatements: for example, it said that legal status involved "compulsory" membership for Suffolk and other suburban counties; that New York City would "hold the balance of power in the Council"; that the Council's creation would "break down county lines"; and that it was incumbent upon the Council members, "through taxation, to produce the money necessary to operate it." The article noted that Senator Barrett felt that "the Council would undoubtedly pass measures that would not be in the best interests of the coun-

---

[12] *Newsday*, editorial, May 16, 1962.

ties" (because New York City had sponsored the state legislation), and that he, Barrett, would oppose it, if reelected for another term.[13] Barrett has since been characterized as a "country-squire" type of suburbanite, who was inclined to be suspicious of "sophisticated" New York City politicians, particularly if they happened to be Democrats.[14] His previous experience with MRC may have confirmed, for him, the correctness of his views.

The MRC executive secretary sent a reasoned letter to the newspaper columnist correcting each of the misstatements in the article, but there is no record that his letter was published. The article set the tone for many of the arguments that were raised in Suffolk two years later when MRC again became a live issue.

No indication of further contact between Suffolk County and MRC is apparent until March 1962, when Lee E. Koppelman, then Planning Director for Suffolk, suggested to Lehman that County Executive Dennison, an interested observer of MRC activities, be asked to take a more active part in Council work. Because of Dennison's background as an engineer and planner, he was asked to serve on MRC's Traffic and Transportation Committee. A news release was issued by the County Executive's office soon after, pointing out that Dennison considered MRC an appropriate organization for the consideration of regional problems; that Suffolk, in its geographic isolation, had little to fear from "super-governmental interference in local affairs"; and that Suffolk would soon be asked to contribute its share toward support of this worthwhile operation. Dennison hammered away at these points during the next few months, in weekly newspaper articles and radio broadcasts, setting forth his reasons why "Suffolk Should Join [the] Council."[15]

In May 1962, MRC's executive secretary wrote a long letter to Arthur M. Cromarty, Chairman of the Suffolk County Board of Supervisors and also County Republican Chairman, informing

[13] John M. Greene, "GOP Opposed to Council Bill," *Long Island Press*, October 24, 1960.

[14] Interview with Lee E. Koppelman, Executive Director, Nassau-Suffolk Regional Planning Board, January 23, 1968.

[15] *Long Island Press*, March 4 and 13, 1962, and radio broadcast, April 18, 1962.

him of the Council's organization, plans, and programs. Lehman emphasized the Council's most "basic and fundamental policy, ... the maintenance of its non-political and bi-partisan nature," and pointed out that "it would be tragic" if Suffolk County residents were to be denied their voice in the future of the region.

There was little agreement on this prognosis of "tragedy." On the eve of the public hearing in Suffolk County on the resolution to join MRC, State Senator Barrett sent a telegram to Cromarty urging him to "avoid any entangling alliances with our all but bankrupt city neighbor. . . ." Suffolk's best interest, he felt, would be served by "cooperation without affiliation." State Assemblyman Perry B. Duryea of Montauk, Suffolk County, also sent a message that membership in the Council would be "detrimental" to the county. In his capacity as Long Island State Park Commissioner, Robert Moses advised against the creation of "any more super agencies. There are already examples of local cooperation that are good."[16]

Of the 150 persons in attendance at the Suffolk hearing, 35 received a turn to speak against MRC, including representatives of the Citizens Planning Council of Huntington, the Long Island Federation of Women's Clubs, Young Americans for Freedom, and the newly formed Committee to Protect Suffolk County from Metropolitan Regional Government. MRC supporters were three in number: Planning Director Koppelman; Mrs. Gustave Keane, former President of the Suffolk League of Women Voters; and Bernard Hillenbrand, Executive Director of the National Association of County Officials. Chairman Cromarty emphasized his beliefs in "home rule and in grass-roots government," labeled the Council "the first step toward total centralization of all government under a huge bureaucracy directed by political appointees," and charged that New York City "would like to take over control of Suffolk County . . . and make the Eastern seaboard one unit of government with appointed bosses responsible to no one."[17]

The result was never in doubt. The ten-man Board of Super-

[16] *Long Island Press*, May 14 and 15, 1962.
[17] *News Review*, May 17, 1962; *Long Island Press*, May 15, 1962; and *Newsday*, May 15, 1962, respectively.

visors voted unanimous rejection of the proposal for Suffolk to affiliate—and pay $6,640 as its share of MRC's annual expenses—on the basis that "the best interests of the County . . . will be served and promoted by not participating. . . ." County Executive Dennison, reported as "deeply disappointed" and "embarrassed" by the board's action, said he would no longer participate in MRC activities and relinquished his short-lived committee work.[18]

A number of factors might be suggested in explanation of the Suffolk defeat. Local pressures, politics, and personalities all played a part. Democratic County Executive Dennison had suffered another setback earlier in the day when the supervisors turned down his proposal to save money by eliminating branch offices of the County Motor Vehicle Bureau in Babylon, Huntington, and Patchogue. (Dennison had suffered a similar defeat two weeks before when the board voted unanimously to seek state aid for an engineering survey of the county's sewer needs, over his strenuous objections.) According to observer Koppelman, the vote was "as much against Dennison's leadership as against MRC."[19] Deputy County Executive Ann Mead, sympathetic to MRC and regional cooperation, was ill and did not attend the meeting. Moreover, the vote took place at a "public" meeting. Had it been otherwise (that is, in "executive" session), it is possible that the three Democrats on the board would have sided with Dennison. But the supervisors felt the pressure from the vocal public and voted accordingly.

Finally, Arthur Cromarty's influence should not be underestimated. He was a consistently outspoken foe of MRC over the years as well as a persistent advocate of local responsibility and local control. At joint hearings of the United States Senate and House Subcommittees on Intergovernmental Relations held in New York City one year later, he reiterated his opposition to MRC, stating: "Only the local official can accurately gauge the importance of a project and only a watchful eye can ferret out

[18] Suffolk County, Resolution No. 231, May 14, 1962. See also *News Review*, May 17, 1962, and *Newsday*, May 15, 1962.
[19] Memorandum from Prager to Lehman following a telephone conversation with Koppelman, May 15, 1962.

waste and corruption."[20] An influential political force in Suffolk County, he was a formidable opponent.

Failure by MRC to Do Its Homework

The record of the Suffolk public hearing indicates that MRC did not expect the strong resistance that it received from New York State officials. Nor had it made preparation to counter the "well-organized and well-prepared opposition"[21] of local officials and right-wing, conservative groups. Instead the Council relied on Dennison and Koppelman to "sell" regional cooperation and offered assistance only when specifically requested. When it began to look as if the public hearing might go against affiliation, the Council sent out a last-minute SOS to Hillenbrand to fly up from Washington and present the "county" point of view. Hillenbrand did an outstanding job, but by then it was too late.

A few days after the Suffolk defeat, the executive secretary expressed "shock . . . at this kind of response to cooperation among neighbors" and found it "depressing" to hear that New York City wanted to take over control of Suffolk. It was clear to him that MRC opponents were "dealing with something out of Fairyland, not reality."[22] It is uncertain whether the benefits of affiliation with an amorphous new agency such as MRC seemed equally "clear" to Suffolk's local officials, predisposed as they were against joining forces with "irresponsible" politicians from New York City who wanted to "annex . . . Suffolk and saddle [it] . . . with the city's vice, corruption and welfare problems."[23]

[20] U.S. Senate and House Committees on Government Operations, Subcommittees on Intergovernmental Relations, *Joint Hearings: Government in Metropolitan Areas (New York Metropolitan Region)*, 88th Congress, 1st Session (Washington: U.S. Government Printing Office, 1963), p. 134 (cited hereafter as *Joint Hearings: Government in Metropolitan Areas*). It is worthy of note that local corruption by Republican officials in Suffolk is presently under investigation by New York State and the Suffolk District Attorney's office. Apparently local officials have not been as "watchful" as they should.

[21] Memorandum from Prager to Lehman, May 15, 1962.

[22] Letter from Lehman to Dennison, May 17, 1962.

[23] Testimony of Arthur Cromarty, *Joint Hearings: Government in Metropolitan Areas* (1963), p. 135.

Although MRC prided itself on having set a "new example for the nation in the potentialities of regional cooperation,"[24] suburban officials, who had had no contact with the new agency, did not understand what it offered and rejected its point of view. In contrast to the opposition, which had circulated its views previously, MRC had never explored at all with the legislators the advantages of a regional council of local governments. (It was not, as the executive secretary suggested in a talk some weeks later, a "distortion of communication" as much as a *lack* of communication.)[25] The Council made no effort to point up the very severe urban problems with which Suffolk might be confronted in future years or to explain why MRC might be more useful to Suffolk in coping with the pressures of urban growth than the ad hoc cooperation between interested officials to which they were accustomed.

Certainly these problems which Suffolk would ultimately face were nothing "out of Fairyland." In 1960, MRC itself had prepared and distributed a chart of the population growth of the region's counties and municipalities from 1950 to 1960; this chart showed that Suffolk was the fastest growing county in the region, with a 141.5 percent increase in population over the ten-year period. In 1961, MRC had distributed a press release containing the official results of the 1960 census, which indicated that this population shift would place great strains on local governmental revenues and services. (MRC might have projected, as regional planners have done since, that this population growth would continue unabated; that Suffolk, with 922 square miles, had realized only one-third of its developmental potential; that taxes would climb as service demands increased; and that, if local governments failed to work together in meeting political demands in the future, state and federal governmental levels would be forced to intervene.)[26] It is by no means certain that this appeal—

[24] Address by Mayor Wagner to MRC membership, June 29, 1960.
[25] Address by Lehman to the League of Women Voters of New York City, May 24, 1962.
[26] In 1967, Suffolk County's population passed the one million mark, an increase of approximately fifty percent over the 1960 population of 667,-000. Planners estimate that nearly 400,000 new jobs will have to be created in Suffolk in the next twenty years, and a strong role is foreseen for gov-

or one similarly couched—would have made much of an impression on Suffolk's local officials or that, in view of Cromarty's tight control, they would have voted otherwise. But more people would have *understood* the reasons for support of MRC had a massive, sustained educational program been mounted to counteract local resistance to outside interference. With little or no information about the benefits of regional cooperation, defeat of the interlocal agreement was virtually inevitable. A negative vote, in keeping with traditional popular sentiment, was understandable, and might have been predicted.

One further word about the Suffolk defeat should be given. Suffolk County was a test case for the Council, with far-reaching repercussions. Suffolk's attempt at regional isolation, in conjunction with Nassau's hostile attitude, probably reinforced parochial attitudes of the Westchester Board of Supervisors and made it doubly hard for County Executive Michaelian to rally support for MRC in Westchester. The vote carried a warning for MRC as well. The Council knew it would be nearly impossible to sustain a regional organization without the support of Nassau and Suffolk counties. Approval by the remaining units of local government was crucial.

---

ernment in encouraging industry to move in. There is recent evidence that both Nassau and Suffolk have started to react to urban pressures. In 1965, a Nassau-Suffolk Regional Planning Board was created by joint action of the two boards of supervisors. It is an advisory planning agency with responsibility for the creation of a comprehensive plan under Sec. 701 of the Housing Act of 1954 as amended. In addition, the agency exercises review powers over all water, sewer, and open-space applications made in the two counties by any level of government.

IV

PUBLIC ATTITUDES: INDIFFERENCE

AND OPPOSITION

Public Apathy

Regional councils would be better able to combat ignorance, misinformation, and prejudice if there were wider public interest in their programs. However, metropolitan planners are faced with enormous public apathy toward intergovernmental cooperation. The term "regional cooperation" is abstract and does not evoke popular response. Nor is the idea sufficiently compelling to move people in the direction of changes which might involve uncertainty and risk. The concept of the "region" is equally remote. While the region may stand for a closely knit economic or geographic unit to the economist or transportation expert, it has no real meaning for the layman, whose major concern centers about his community. An individual citizen typically has little interest in "regional" problems unless they happen to affect his particular sphere of activity. He is even less likely to regard as urgent a problem which may require attention some time in the future.[1]

A different situation exists if a clearly recognizable and pressing need develops which, if left unresolved, would have an adverse effect on the region's inhabitants. In times of "crisis" (such as

[1] Bollens et al. find little awareness of metropolitan problems and needs even in the St. Louis metropolitan area, where there is great political, economic, and social interdependence between the citizens of the county and the city (*Exploring the Metropolitan Community*, p. 311). See also the findings of Hawley and Zimmer, in *Community Political Systems*, ed. Janowitz, I, 179.

water pollution in the Seattle area or the treatment of sewage in Syracuse), a proposal for change in existing governmental arrangements has a much greater chance of public acceptance.[2] In Suffolk County, New York, however, there was no sense of urgency about the passage of the MRC agreement. No specific situation existed (or was created) to arouse the people, and through them, the legislators, to act affirmatively. Communication consultants find that, in many cities where metropolitan reorganization has been defeated, "it has been presented as an antiseptic reform, untouched by selfish interests and inspired solely by the desire to progress with the times."[3] If a proposal like MRC is to gain popular approval, selective issues must be made important, with identifiable forces, contenders, and publicity. The citizen must be able to see what he has at stake.

This is probably asking too much of a voluntary organization. Short of creating a "villain" or an immediately recognizable danger, the council must anticipate difficulties in its attempts to achieve affirmative citizen participation in regional affairs. Basic to the educational process is the understanding that, in dealing with a local political entity, the council is dealing with people and groups with a strong sense of loyalty to their local communities and institutions. Efforts to secure efficiency and economy have been found to have a negligible impact on local points of view.

[2] See Martin, *Metropolis in Transition*, for a discussion of metropolitan action to ease the critical problem of water pollution in Lake Washington near Seattle (pp. 75–87). In Syracuse, New York, a metropolitan sewage-treatment plant was built when the sewage-disposal problem developed "crisis-like" proportions and public protest could no longer be ignored (Martin et al., *Decisions in Syracuse*, p. 102). For further discussion of public action following a "crisis," refer to Scott, *Two Notes on Metropolitan Research*, p. 17; Advisory Commission, *Factors Affecting Voter Reactions*, p. 19; Willbern, in *Metropolitan Issues*, ed. Birkhead, p. 55; Robert C. Wood, "The Contributions of Political Science to Urban Form," *Urban Life and Form*, ed. Werner Z. Hirsch (New York: Holt, Rinehart and Winston, 1963), p. 107; and Frank Smallwood, *Metro Toronto: A Decade Later* (Toronto: Bureau of Municipal Research, 1963), p. 35.

[3] Opinion Reporting Workshop of the Graduate School of Journalism, Columbia University, "Seminar on Effective Community Reporting," Pt. III, June 24–26, 1963 (draft copy), p. 21 (cited hereafter as "Seminar on Effective Community Reporting"). Refer also to Charlton F. Chute's recommendations for winning a campaign for charter reform, "Charter Campaigning," *National Municipal Review*, XLV (December 1956), 537–540.

The council must realize the deep interest that the neighborhood dweller has in preserving the character and quality of his living environment and the representation of this interest by local officials. The conflict between the city and town must be recognized as such and deliberate steps taken to explore ways in which common objectives may be emphasized.[4]

It is worthy of note that, at about the same time as the Suffolk defeat, RPA found that a large proportion of the region's "educated activists," who participated in a study of prospective living conditions in the New York metropolitan region, supported metropolitan planning and MRC because they understood the need for coherent development of the region.[5] If the Council actually believed that the establishment of regular channels of communication and collaboration between elected officials would help local communities withstand state and federal intervention into matters which are regarded as local affairs, it clearly did not find means to convince the interested citizen of this.

Public Hearings: A Diversity of Opinions

It is particularly important for a council of governments, which depends on voluntary support for financial contributions and implementation of its programs, to seek a high degree of public visibility. Public hearings can be used as one way of bridging the gap in communications between the council and the public and may also furnish a means of developing a plan for united action.[6] This is the path MRC followed in 1958 when its Committee on

[4] For further discussion of this point, refer to Fordham, *University of Pennsylvania Law Review*, CV (February 1957), 441; Martin et al., *Decisions in Syracuse*, pp. 155, 218–221; and Adrian, *Public Administration Review*, XXI (Summer, 1961), 150.

[5] Regional Plan Association, *Public Participation in Regional Planning: A Report of the Second Regional Plan* (1967), p. 29.

[6] Vernon speaks of "two views of reality": that of the "expert," who is troubled by wasteful, unplanned land use, the little regard shown for open space, new suburban slums, and shifting transportation patterns; and that of the "people" living in the New York region, who feel that they are enjoying more comfortable lives than their grandparents did and have only a vague awareness of future problems (*Metropolis 1985*, pp. 284–285). See also Advisory Commission, *Factors Affecting Voter Reactions*, pp. 17 and 30–31.

the Future sought public recommendations for the Council's future course of action. Four public hearings were scheduled in different sectors of the region, and public officials, civic groups, political scientists, and special-interest groups were invited to testify. Three questions were considered in the main: whether to continue the Council as a voluntary organization, whether to seek statutory recognition, or whether to recommend some form of regional government. The suggestions made during the course of these hearings are given here in some detail. They furnish a good indication of public reaction to the Council as it then existed, as well as an indication of how this sentiment might develop in the future.

The first hearing was held in Stamford, Connecticut, on November 18, 1958. A few speakers favored statutory authorization for MRC: W. H. Wheeler, Jr., President of Pitney Bowes, supported any effort to strengthen MRC and broaden its fields of interest; Professor Troy Westmeyer of New York University, representing the Stamford Joint Committee on Housing, favored a reduction in the number of local governments and creation of a new governmental arrangement; Professor Robert C. Wood, then a member of the M.I.T. faculty, regarded the Council's "continued development as the best means of providing the necessary public policies in a democratic manner . . . [and urged] firm statutory authorization for the Council's operations"; and Charlton F. Chute, then Director of the Institute of Public Administration, thought MRC "should be given governmental status, a budget and a trained staff, and be authorized to prepare a redevelopment program" for the metropolitan area.[7]

Most of the representatives of local civic groups—including the president and director of the Community Action Committee of the Stamford League of Women Voters; the general manager of the Conde Nast Press, Greenwich; the executive vice-president of Stamford–Greenwich manufacturers; the president of the Stamford Chamber of Commerce; a member of the legislative committee of the Greenwich Representative Town Meeting; and

[7] Public hearing conducted by the Committee on the Future of the MRC, Stamford, Connecticut, November 18, 1958. Robert Wood's views were expressed in a telegram to the chairman of the committee.

the first selectman of Greenwich—favored continuation of MRC as a voluntary organization without statutory recognition.[8] More outspoken opinions were offered by members of the Stamford Mayor's Advisory Council and the East Stamford Taxpayers Association, deploring MRC's possible effect on the already over-burdened tax load, and by Stamford's superintendent of parks and trees, who warned that continued emphasis on the statutory crea-tion of "regional government would spell the end of the MRC. . . . Even the talk . . . has been enough to scare off selectmen and mayors of the small Fairfield towns and cities."[9]

The second public hearing held by the Committee on the Future of the MRC took place in Newark, New Jersey, one week later. At this hearing Professors Benjamin Baker and Bennett M. Rich of Rutgers University spoke in favor of MRC as an official governmental agency with the necessary legal status and a full-time research staff, whereas the president of the New Jersey Association of Freeholders, the executive director of the Greater Newark Development Council, the research director of Mercer County, and the Board of Chosen Freeholders, Somerset County, thought that the move to create a permanent metropolitan gov-ernmental structure was premature and preferred to see MRC continue in its present form.[10]

At the third public hearing, held in White Plains, New York, on December 9, 1958, William D. Carlebach, First Deputy Com-missioner, New York State Department of Commerce, urged creation of a "federation . . . with teeth," and William N. Cas-sella, Jr., then Senior Associate with the National Municipal League, recommended tools for the Council of "legal status . . . , research staff . . . and sufficient operating powers . . . including

[8] *Ibid.*, statements of Mrs. Jesse Orlansky, Mrs. Arthur W. Viner, Joseph Chanko, Dean Brossman, John Beck, Donald H. MacKensie, and Thomas Kerrigan, respectively.

[9] *Ibid.*, testimony of Harry Cooke and Frank Daly, and letter from Ed-ward A. Connell to Mayor Wagner, November 17, 1958, respectively.

[10] Statements presented at the public hearing conducted by the Com-mittee on the Future of the MRC, Newark, New Jersey, November 25, 1958, by Joseph S. Holland, Henry W. Connor, and Percy F. Jowett, respectively. The Board of Chosen Freeholders, Somerset County, ex-pressed its views by letter to Maxwell Lehman, December 19, 1958.

arrangements for mandatory referral of data by the units of the area." Among those advocating the Council's continuance as a voluntary organization were John Mead, Supervisor of Lewisboro, Westchester County; F. Richard Wolff, President of the Westchester County Realty Board; and Colby Kalloch, First Vice-President of the Westchester County Association.

The New York City public hearing, held on January 13, 1959, was the best attended of all and presented the same division of opinions over the degree of authority that should be given to the Council. Some participants argued that MRC be limited to planning authority at the outset. Luther Gulick, then President of the Institute of Public Administration, emphasized that "cooperation needs effective machinery for teamwork" and urged legal sanction of MRC by interstate compact and the addition of staff, so that it could function as a "program-developing, cooperation-arranging and policy-defining organization" for the region. Harold R. Osborne, then President of RPA, favored full legal status for MRC and the addition of a small, full-time staff for research, planning, and analysis of regional problems. This recommendation was supported by representatives of many local civic groups, including the Women's City Club, League of Women Voters, Citizens Budget Commission, City Club of New York, Commerce and Industry Association, Citizens Housing Council, New York City CIO Council, and by the editor of *Architectural Forum*.[11]

Others argued for broad authority for MRC in addition to planning. James Felt and Goodhue Livingston, Jr., of the New York City Planning Commission, Louis Glickman, President of the Association of Real Estate Syndicators, and Professor Charles Stonier of Hofstra College favored legal status and granting to MRC the additional power of review over existing regional agencies and those to be created in the future. Professor Martin

[11] Statements presented at the public hearing conducted by the Committee on the Future of the MRC, New York City, January 13, 1959, by Mrs. Henry Crosby West, Mrs. Earl Johnson, Harold Riegelman, Simeon Goldstein, Ralph Brooks, Roger Starr, Morris Iushewitz, and Douglas Haskell, respectively. See also letter to the committee from Byard Williams, Chairman, Committee on Housing, Community Service Society, January 26, 1959.

Dworkis of New York University, representing the Citizens Union, and Bentley Kassal, New York State Assemblyman, favored a strong MRC with operating powers, and Professor Paul Studenski recommended study of legislation needed for the establishment of an effective metropolitan government. Minority opinions were offered by William Dietley, representing the New York Chamber of Commerce, and Professor Joseph F. Maloney of Fordham University in favor of continuation of MRC as a voluntary body. A letter opposing any change in status was received from a private citizen named Henry Such Smith, a persistent advocate of "leadership" but not "leadership institutions" in the New York metropolitan region.

Response to Hearings: A Failure of Communications

The hearings ended in early 1959 and MRC embarked on its tortuous route—via state legislative enactment—to secure statutory recognition of its efforts. There was little further contact with civic groups or local representatives until three years later, when the question of MRC status was presented to the local legislative bodies of the region for determination. This hiatus may have had unfortunate consequences for MRC and its attempt to secure favorable consideration of the interlocal agreement. Much support and good will were manifested by a large number of community leaders during the course of the hearings. After a prolonged gap in time, MRC could no longer capitalize on this support in the same way it might have previously.

Maintenance of contact with local leaders might also have permitted the Council to hear the views of potential opponents. Members of local legislative bodies were singularly silent during the time of the public hearings, many not having been asked to testify—or attend. If MRC wished to hear comments from a broad spectrum of community interests, it would have been interesting and useful to call on more of the people's elected representatives. Not only would this have given MRC an insight into some of the arguments that would be raised subsequently; it might also have provided local legislators with a firsthand encounter with MRC supporters, who were outnumbered and outspoken at public meetings in later years. State legislators, who represented the communities whose advice was being sought, were also absent from the hearings. Since statutory recognition of MRC was one of the items under consideration for the future, it might have been wise to enlist the views of the representatives who would be called on to support this legislation in the state capitals.[12]

On the other hand, many questioning voices *were* heard at the hearings, but the points they raised were not answered. Some of these comments were symptomatic of public attitudes that would plague the Council in future years. Frank Daley of Stamford, for example, was concerned about the eventual payment of dues and questioned the need for another "tax-collecting" organization. Similar concern about overlapping and conflicting dues payments between counties and cities was subsequently manifested elsewhere but was never clarified satisfactorily by MRC.[13]

Another participant, Professor Maloney of Fordham University, suggested that "elected officials from minority parties of New York City, Nassau and Westchester . . . [be admitted to membership in MRC] because metropolitan regional problems necessarily involve political complications in their solutions." Maloney pointed out that the only representative from New York City in MRC at that time was a Democrat and the only Nassau representative at that time was a Republican: "In both instances the minority parties could become political obstacles to implementation of the Council's agreements or unmentionable but real obstacles to the freedom of action required by Council members."[14] This question of broader representation also returned to haunt the Council. The concept of a nonpartisan MRC was satisfactory in theory, but Westchester and Suffolk Republi-

[12] In reviewing the reasons for the defeat of a proposal for metropolitan integration in the St. Louis metropolitan area, Bollens et al. suggest that "the existence of a broadly based citizens' committee that has participated in all stages of the studies gives reasonable assurance of a knowledgeable, motivated group to promote the action program once the research is completed" (*Exploring the Metropolitan Community*, p. 166).

[13] Public hearing, Stamford, Connecticut, November 18, 1958. This question of dues payments will be explored further in Chap. VII, pp. 154–157.

[14] Public hearing, New York City, January 13, 1959. For further discussion of this question, refer to Chap. VI.

cans, schooled in partisan political battles, voted along party lines and evidenced little patience with theoretical nonpartisanship.

A further question, which has been raised previously in these pages, concerned the amount of authority the Council might wield in future years. Clayton Knowles of the *New York Times* sparked general discussion of this point by reporting in early September 1958 that "a study of the question [of the Council's future] . . . could lead to a recommendation for the establishment of a new layer of government over existing local governments in the tri-state region."[15] An MRC press release of October 20, 1958, announcing a hearing to consider "the possibilities of 'regional government' in the metropolitan area," contributed to the uncertain atmosphere. As Edward Connell of Stamford pointed out, the announcement frightened local officials before the hearings even started. Connell was then a member of the MRC Committee on Recreation and Land Use and had spent a lot of time gathering data from Fairfield County towns and cities for a joint RPA-MRC study of park, recreation, and open space. He felt that MRC's "greatest accomplishment" lay in the area of "regional thinking" it had engendered and that it was "ridiculous to discuss the creation of a superimposed government when the traditions—political and otherwise—are considered."[16]

This concern for home rule was shared by others. The hearings indicated that an overwhelming number of the nonprofessional speakers outside of New York City favored continuation of the Council on a voluntary basis. Had MRC paid closer attention to those who testified in Stamford, White Plains, and Newark—other than the "experts"—it would have had a clearer conception of the need to clarify its intentions for the benefit of the general public.

Finally, mention should be made of a letter which MRC received from Louis Greenbaum, Chairman of the Mayor's Advisory Committee in Stamford, some weeks before the first hearing was held. Greenbaum pointed to the "vagueness in our minds" with reference to the testimony to be offered at the hearing, stemming from the finding that "very few of the people who will

---

[15] *New York Times*, September 3, 1958, p. 21.
[16] Letter from Connell to Wagner, November 17, 1958.

be asked for an opinion as to the 'Future of the MRC' have enough knowledge about the MRC on which to base an opinion as to the utility of its continuance." This lack of briefing seems to have been a continuing problem. Some years after the hearings, the Citizens Budget Commission attributed MRC's lack of success to a "failure of officialdom to convey the full story to the people of the individual communities and to the region as a whole."[17] The Council seemed to look upon the hearings as an overwhelming mandate of its predetermined course of securing legal status, and showed little evidence of willingness to profit from this one opportunity it had for genuine communication and feedback with residents outside New York City.

Assistance from the Press

MRC may have failed to avail itself of all the opportunities presented by public hearings, but it was conscientious in its attempts to gain public attention through contacts with newspapermen and the issuance of press releases. The physical location of MRC in the Office of the City Administrator—a few short blocks from City Hall, New York City; the fact that the Mayor of New York was chairman of MRC; and the ready availability of newspaper reporters in the City Hall newsroom contributed to an easy relationship with members of the metropolitan press and furnished a ready outlet for the Council's steady stream of news releases. The effect of these is uncertain. There is little agreement among urban observers about the effectiveness of the newspapers in creating changes in public attitudes. There is, moreover, little consistency in attitudes among the metropolitan newspapers themselves toward regional matters and proposals of metropolitan reorganization. However, a friendly newspaper can be a considerable help in the selection of priorities and issues for consideration and, under certain circumstances, may help to pave the way for acceptance of new proposals.[18]

[17] *Joint Hearings: Government in Metropolitan Areas* (1963), p. 312.
[18] For a detailed presentation of the role of the mass media in the making of political decisions, refer to Robert A. Dahl, *Who Governs? Democracy and Power in an American City* (New Haven and London: Yale University Press, 1961), pp. 256 and 267; Norton E. Long, "The Local Com-

In the New York metropolitan region, the *New York Times* has shown great concern for regional planning and regional problems. Both in its news coverage and in its editorial policy, the paper has been a consistent supporter of MRC since the Council's creation. Thus, the *Times* found the original idea of a regional conference in 1956 "well worth while," termed the Council "the metropolitan hope" in 1960, deplored the Council's untimely death in 1964, and applauded all attempts in recent years to "revive the regional council."[19] Other New York City newspapers have also supported regional cooperation, though none as persistently as the *Times.*[20]

News media outside New York City have been divided in their concern for regional problems and MRC. During the period when MRC was most active, they displayed a wide range of attitudes—from outright hostility toward MRC on the part of the Westchester–Rockland chain of newspapers to expressions of support from *Newsday* on Long Island, the *Record* in Bergen County, and the *Home News* in New Brunswick, New Jersey. The latter was outstanding in its efforts on the Council's behalf.

---

munity as an Ecology of Games," *American Journal of Sociology*, LXIV (November 1958), 261; Chute, *National Municipal Review*, XLV (December 1956), 540; Greer, in *Metropolitan Issues*, ed. Birkhead, p. 26; Martin et al., *Decisions in Syracuse*, p. 314. Lennox L. Moak is generally critical of newspapers in metropolitan areas because of their focus on city problems to city dwellers and local problems to local dwellers ("Some Practical Obstacles in Modifying Governmental Structure to Meet Metropolitan Problems," *University of Pennsylvania Law Review*, CV [February 1957], 615). On the other hand, the Opinion Reporting Workshop at Columbia University finds that urban and suburban newspapers are developing a new regional approach, which is cutting across the old geographical circulation concepts ("Seminar on Effective Community Reporting," Pt. I, p. 13). For a more specific discussion of the role of the press in affecting the outcome of proposals for metropolitan reorganization, refer to Chap. VI, n. 75.

[19] *New York Times*, editorials, May 24, 1956, p. 30; February 25, 1960, p. 31; May 15, 1964, p. 42; April 15, 1966, p. 38; and July 27, 1967, p. 34. Forbes B. Hays's study of RPA indicates that this organization is likewise pleased with the extent of the *New York Times* coverage of its activities (*Community Leadership: The Regional Plan Association of New York* [New York: Columbia University Press, 1965], p. 117).

[20] E.g., "21 Counties Pulling Together," *Herald Tribune*, September 4, 1958, p. 16; "Work Together," *Journal American*, September 7, 1958, p. 13.

In December 1960, Hugh Boyd, *Home News* publisher, invited all daily newspaper editors and publishers in the New Jersey area covered by MRC, as well as the editors and publishers of all weekly newspapers of more than 5,000 circulation in the area, to be the newspaper's guest at lunch and participate in a round-table discussion of MRC's aims and objectives. Mayor Wagner served as moderator and his panel members included Karl Metzger, Director of the Middlesex County Board of Chosen Freeholders; Griffith E. Harris, First Selectman of Greenwich, Connecticut; Kristen Kristenson, Mayor of Yonkers, New York; Frank X. Graves, Director of the Passaic County Board of Chosen Freeholders; and Arthur W. Vervaet, member of the Bergen County Board of Chosen Freeholders. Writers, editors, and general managers of sixteen different New Jersey newspapers were present and heard about MRC's plans for attaining legal status.

Newspaper comment following the meeting was flattering and complete, with feature stories in many local papers. Typical headlines were "Council Seen as Solution: Held Weapon against Supergovernment," "Regional Council Clarifies Purpose," "Regional Unit Assures Towns of Home Rule," "Bergen Eases Stand vs. Regional Council Status."[21] Among the noteworthy results of the meeting was the reaction of Freeholder Arthur Vervaet of Bergen County, who was reported to have advised Mayor Wagner that "Unquestionably there is . . . a need for cooperation . . . within municipalities and counties." This was interpreted as a "considerable shift in attitude" from that expressed in February 1960, when Bergen cast the only dissenting vote against the Council's plan to seek legal status.[22] Publisher Boyd felt that a great deal

[21] *Daily Home News* (New Brunswick), *Newark Evening News*, *Paterson Evening News*, and *Newark Star Ledger*, December 7, 1960, respectively. Other local newspapers with feature stories included the *Plainfield Courier News*, *Record* (Bergen County), *Red Bank Register*, *Bayonne Times*, *Jersey Journal* (Jersey City), and *Evening News* (Perth Amboy).

[22] Robert Comstock, "Bergen Softens Regional Stand: Need for Cooperation Recognized by County Representative," *Record*, December 7, 1960. The *Record*, which has had a consistently favorable editorial policy toward MRC, was singled out by the Opinion Reporting Workshop at Columbia University as a dramatic example of the changes that are taking place among suburban newspapers. Its circulation more than doubled between 1952 and 1963, and the focus of its news coverage changed from being purely local to regional and more general. ("Seminar on Effective Community Reporting," Pt. I, p. 12).

of interest in this "round table idea" had been demonstrated, and offered his services in trying to interest newspapers in Connecticut and Westchester to conduct similar sessions.

MRC expressed interest in the project but scheduled no further sessions in other sectors of the region. Because of the consistently unfriendly editorial policy against MRC in the Westchester press (which will be discussed further in Chapter VI), a joint offer from publisher Boyd and Executive Secretary Lehman might well have been turned down. On the other hand, Harold Riegelman of the Citizens Budget Commission was able to approach Edward Hughes, Vice-President and Editorial Director of the Westchester newspaper chain, some years later and have a fruitful discussion with him concerning MRC's objectives and its possible threat to home rule in Westchester. Unfortunately, this meeting was not held until some time after the Westchester Board of Supervisors had cast a negative vote against MRC affiliation. Again, the Council was unable to follow through on what might have developed into a profitable and useful public relations activity.

Relations with Civic Organizations: Regional Plan Association

MRC recognized early in its development that its effectiveness as a voluntary organization would be greatly enhanced if it could gain the support and help of civic groups and business leaders in identifying regional problems and mapping possible courses of action. The logical group to work with in this way was RPA, which has been attempting to alert citizens to the need for a region-wide approach to developmental policies for almost forty years. A recent study of RPA indicates that MRC was warmly received by the older regional organization.[23] RPA had long called for cooperation among the various governmental units comprising the metropolitan region, and it was pleased to witness the development of a regional focus among elected officials. A joint study of park, recreation, and open space in the region did much to cement relationships between MRC and RPA, and it also alerted local officials to their recreational and open-space needs.

[23] Hays, *Community Leadership*, p. 114.

When MRC started to seek advice as to its future plans in 1958, RPA's executive committee authorized its president to appoint a committee on metropolitan governmental affairs which would prepare a report on governmental organizations in the New York metropolitan region, with special reference to MRC. An eight-man committee, chaired by Professor Wallace S. Sayre of Columbia University, found that MRC "represents the important and promising beginnings of a leadership institution indispensable to the growth, prosperity and well-being of this Tri-State Metropolitan Region." The report suggested that MRC acquire full legal status as a regional agency and develop its organization by adding a "small, full-time, talented and experienced staff." The committee felt that the advantage of full legal status for MRC would be fourfold: increased stature, increased responsibility for regional matters, continuity of work, and eligibility to receive federal, state, and municipal grants. RPA's board of directors endorsed the recommendations and publicly congratulated the Council "on the pioneer work which it has been able to do as an informal and volunteer group of elected officials."[24]

RPA continued to lend encouragement over the years. The Sayre report was widely read and served as a guide for the later efforts of the Council to achieve legal status and staff. When New York State failed to pass specific legislation for MRC, RPA helped to prepare enabling legislation in Connecticut and New Jersey and sought help from its members to urge passage in both states. John Keith, Vice-President of RPA, served on MRC's Technical Advisory Committee and helped to draft the interlocal agreement in accordance with the terms of the enabling legislation. RPA did what it could to gain support for the interlocal agreement among the region's local governments.

RPA had high hopes for MRC in its formative years as the official metropolitan regional agency to which RPA and other citizens' groups "might present their proposals."[25] In 1959, it

[24] All of the quoted material in the foregoing paragraph comes from the statement of RPA to the Committee on the Future of the MRC, New York City, January 13, 1959.
[25] Text of the report on the future of MRC by the Special Committee on Metropolitan Governmental Affairs of RPA, *New York Times*, January 9, 1959, p. 16. See also RPA *News*, No. 861, February 19, 1960.

looked upon MRC as the appropriate group to develop and carry out new proposals in the field of commuter transportation, recommending that the Council be given the task of developing consistent programs for meeting the needs of metropolitan growth, including "responsibility to advise any and all of the agencies and authorities providing regional facilities or services for the Tri-State Metropolitan Region."[26] As the transportation problems of the region mounted, and MRC's preoccupation with legal status developed into the Council's major activity, RPA's expectations of MRC's regional role diminished accordingly. In 1961, RPA called for the establishment of a tri-state transportation committee to undertake comprehensive long-range studies of the region's transportation needs, and hoped that this committee and MRC might work closely together in implementing regional plans. RPA also sought—and received—MRC support in the creation of a public regional commuter agency to ensure continuation of rail commuter operations within the metropolitan region.[27]

On the whole, RPA and MRC had a "fruitful relationship" with each other.[28] At the zenith of this relationship, MRC's executive secretary reported to his members that RPA had been an "unstinting help" in enlarging public orientation in regional matters. RPA returned the compliment some years later when its president found that MRC's backing was "instrumental" in achieving establishment of the Tri-State Transportation Committee.[29] Despite minor irritations which developed out of personality differences between the leaders of the two groups, RPA expected to work closely with the Council once it gained legal status and a

[26] RPA, memorandum to Mayor Wagner and to Governors Meyner, Ribicoff, and Rockefeller, concerning "Commuter Transportation," February 10, 1959.

[27] Outline of RPA statement to MRC on "Commuter Transportation Problems in the New York Metropolitan Region," February 27, 1962.

[28] Letter from John P. Keith to James Schrader, Senior Planner, American Society of Planning Officials, December 31, 1962.

[29] Report of executive secretary to MRC membership, June 29, 1960, and outline of RPA statement to MRC, February 27, 1962, respectively. In the latter statement, Walter D. Binger, then Chairman of RPA's Transportation Committee, expressed the hope that MRC would use its "public influence and political strength" to secure a public regional commuter railroad agency.

staff of its own. When MRC succeeded in incorporating as a legal body in 1966, the two organizations again worked on a joint study—of natural resources and waste disposal in the metropolitan region.

Relations with Civic Organizations: Citizens Budget Commission

The Citizens Budget Commission, a private organization concerned primarily with the finances and management of New York City, played a supportive role in behalf of MRC as well. Harold Riegelman, counsel to the Commission, proposed establishment of a voluntary Metropolitan Council of Municipalities as early as 1955, and the Commission endorsed Wagner's proposal to create MRC when this was made. At the same time, the Commission strongly encouraged the establishment of a parallel organization of voluntary civic agencies to channel information from elected officials to the general public and to improve the prospects of action on regional problems.[30]

In May 1960, the Citizens Budget Commission convened representatives of twenty-eight civic and trade associations in the metropolitan area to join together as a Metropolitan Assembly of Civic Organizations. This group met again in February 1963, when the Commission—in conjunction with RPA—arranged a special luncheon meeting to acquaint the Assembly with the work, objectives, and potential usefulness of MRC. The meeting was well attended and publicized, but the help was not as useful to MRC as it might have been at an earlier date. MRC members were now discouraged, and the little time they devoted to MRC was spent in defending themselves against inaccurate and irre-

[30] Harold Riegelman's original proposal for creation of a Metropolitan Council of Municipalities was made at a Citizens Budget Commission luncheon, January 12, 1955. See also Citizens Budget Commission bulletins: "Problems of Metropolitan New York—A Challenge for Leadership and A Challenge to Leaders," September 12, 1955; "Fiscal Implications of the Growth of the Metropolitan Region of New York," January 23, 1956; "Trend toward Metropolitan Action," May 18, 1956; statement of Harold Riegelman at public hearing of the Committee on the Future of the MRC, New York City, January 13, 1959; and letter to the editor, *Herald Tribune*, September 26, 1962, p. 27, deploring irresponsible attacks on MRC by candidates for public office.

sponsible charges from conservative splinter groups. One month later, the attempt to secure legal status was abandoned.

In 1965, the Citizens Budget Commission, continuing its support of MRC, recommended that the Council engage in a survey of the total water needs of the region. The *New York Times* picked up the story and, in an editorial titled "Water for Metropolitan Areas," suggested that the protracted drought in the tri-state area furnished an excellent opportunity to revive MRC's usefulness.[31] This particular "crisis" arrived too late—MRC's chairman was no longer holding elective office and his successor, Mayor John V. Lindsay, had more demanding problems to attend to initially than MRC.

A view of the record indicates that MRC failed to take full advantage of the help that was available from existing regional organizations. In 1959, for example, the need for civic support was discussed—as it had been on earlier occasions—and the executive secretary proposed creation of a *new* regional civic organization to publicize the Council's work. At this time, it was strongly suggested by a long time friend and supporter of MRC, William N. Cassella, Jr., of the National Municipal League, that MRC call on RPA, the only civic organization with a well-established regional interest, to play the key role in civic support for MRC and to have other groups join with RPA in a cooperative civic effort. Disregarding this advice, the executive secretary continued to refer to a new "civic arm for the Council," and used the meeting in 1960 of the loosely knit Metropolitan Assembly of Civic Organizations as evidence of the "growing citizen interest in MRC."[32] Each time the executive secretary referred to sponsorship of a rival citizens' organization, it caused grave concern at RPA and created unnecessary tensions between the two organizations. MRC had only one full-time professional employee, and he had little time to devote to public relations. To attain the greatest measure of exposure—at a time when public understanding was most needed—it would have been more useful to build on existing civic organizations rather than attempt to create a new one.

[31] *New York Times*, November 15, 1965, p. 36.
[32] Report by the executive secretary to MRC membership, June 29, 1960. Cassella's suggestion concerning "Civic Organization Support for MRC" was made in a memorandum to the executive secretary, April 14, 1959.

Had MRC worked more closely with RPA and other groups, perhaps its efforts to reach important segments of the public would have been more profitable. MRC's major contact with the mass media of television, for example, took place in March 1963, after the abandonment of the effort to secure legal status for the Council.[33] The attempt to offer Westchester residents a true picture of MRC's aims and objectives, through the intervention of the Westchester County League of Women Voters, was made after the Westchester Board of Supervisors voted against membership in MRC.[34] The services of Colonel Riegelman as "amicus curiae" in the Council's imbroglio with the Westchester newspaper chain came after the Westchester press no longer regarded MRC as a threat to local home rule. Thus, these potentially constructive moves were uncoordinated and tardy; major efforts to reach the public via RPA and similar organizations were not made.

The Sinister Attack

Not all civic organizations were sympathetic to the objectives of MRC. From the very beginning, the Council was subjected to attack by groups who fear that regional cooperation is the first step to "metro," which is regarded as some sort of dastardly plot to do away with government by elected representatives. In 1959, MRC was singled out to be the subject of the *Dan Smoot Report*, a "radical right" weekly newsletter published in Dallas, Texas.[35]

---

[33] David Shefrin, Director of News, WABC-TV, commentary on "The Big News," March 20, 1963. The MRC executive secretary also appeared on television to debate MRC's merits with Mrs. Joan Tierney of Bergen County some time in mid-winter, 1963.

[34] A letter from Mrs. Martin J. Brennan, then President of the League of Women Voters of Westchester County, to Maxwell Lehman indicated that the League's "policies, procedures, and criteria in relation to adopting a current agenda program" precluded it from including a study of MRC in its program (May 10, 1963). However, a "fact sheet" on MRC was distributed by the Westchester County League as a public service in May 1964.

[35] This characterization of *Dan Smoot Report* is derived from a study of extremist groups made by the Anti-Defamation League of B'nai Brith in 1964, and printed under the title, "Danger on the Right."

The *Report* portrayed MRC as an organization created by RPA and chaired by Wallace Sayre that provided "government by non-elected experts . . . [who wield] more power over the people than the governments [federal and state] themselves have." To Smoot, the Sayre report for RPA was "a classic example of propaganda for metropolitan government which has been seeping into the public consciousness for several years."[36]

If the public was not conscious of the dangers inherent in MRC, self-appointed observers, particularly in New Jersey, stood ready to awaken it. Henry Such Smith, mentioned previously as the author of a crank letter to the New York City public hearing of the Committee on the Future of the MRC, was pleased to find that his apprehension of "the loss of local and states' rights," which would follow legal status for MRC, was shared by Smoot, "a Texan with FBI experience."[37] Mrs. Joan Tierney, speaking for the Ridgewood Unit of Republican Women, advised the Northwest Bergen Inter-Community Committee, a citizens' group with members from thirteen northwest Bergen towns, that MRC was "evil" because it was "coercive . . . and vested with unlimited powers to tax, employ and spend."[38] Mrs. Tierney was such a persistent and tireless speaker that Freeholder Vervaet of Bergen spent a considerable amount of time in defense of MRC and had to make repeated requests for legal opinions with respect to the Council's organization, powers, and constitutionality.

The attacks mounted in intensity in late 1962 and early 1963 as New Jersey communities began to consider affiliation with the Council as dues-paying members. The Bergen County Young

---

[36] "Metro Government," Part I, *Dan Smoot Report*, V (April 13, 1959), 115. In Part II, published the following week, a jaundiced look was taken at Dade County, Florida, and Toronto, Canada, both of which were allegedly supported and run by "1313" in Chicago (V [April 20, 1959], 128). The term "1313" refers to the building at 1313 East 60th Street, Chicago, Illinois, which serves as headquarters for many public agencies and organizations of public officials interested in governmental improvement and administrative reform. "Anti-metro" groups throughout the nation have used "1313" to refer to a "giant cell" which is attempting to undermine local government and impose some kind of bureaucratic "super-state."

[37] Letter from Smith to Lehman, June 20, 1959.

[38] "Vervaet Defends Regional Council," *Herald News* (Passaic), December 6, 1962.

Republican Club passed a resolution opposing ratification of a "compact" to bestow regional planning powers on an organization that would ultimately destroy local boundaries and create large urban areas governed by appointed officials. The club later published a 37-page *Report on the MRC*, scholarly in appearance but inaccurate in spelling and factual material, which again raised the specter of supergovernment "by appointed officials."[39] Frederick W. Kuechenmeister, club President and author of the report, was later named Republican Chairman for Bergen County. This was a further blow to MRC and its hopes for passage of the interlocal agreement.

The Pro-Constitution Association (which evolved from the former Taft-for-President Club of Union County, New Jersey, for the purpose of "supporting the constitution and opposing socialist, communist and all leftist influences") picked up the battle cry and strongly urged the Board of Chosen Freeholders in Union County not to "relinquish their authority and local government" in favor of MRC.[40] *The Patriot*, a newsletter termed "New Jersey's Voice for Constitutional Freedom" (and likewise dedicated to the defeat of Socialist–Communist influences), represented MRC as the first step to "UNESCO working at all levels to establish a new form of area government in a centralized unit."[41] So that this warning should not be missed, the editors made a tape of the message and had it played at a Masonic Fellowship meeting and at other gatherings.

A new group called the "Tri-State Conference on Community Problems" held a rally in a large Bergen auditorium and invited citizens to learn about "the basic change in the structure of our government and possible threats to individual rights and com-

[39] Bergen County Young Republican Club, *Report on the MRC* (March 25, 1963), p. 16. (Possibly the only accurate statement about MRC to be found herein was an indictment of MRC's public relations efforts—"its failure either to inform or educate the general public as to its goals and objectives" [p. 17].) See also "Young GOP Raps Planning Contract," *Newark Evening News*, January 25, 1963.

[40] Letter from John H. Wisner, Jr., Chairman, Pro-Constitution Association, to Jay A. Stemmer, Board of Chosen Freeholders, Union County, New Jersey, February 23, 1963.

[41] *The Patriot*, No. 17, February 27, 1963. For those who wanted further information about MRC, the editors recommended a subscription to the *Dan Smoot Report*.

munity identity that may result from Bergen's membership in the MRC." MRC's assistant executive secretary, who was among the hundred or so people present, reported that he was informed that MRC was "financed and directed out of '1313' in Chicago ... [by] a group of 'pseudo-intellectual carpet baggers' who want to take over the functions of the elected heads of the local governments."[42] The Tri-State Conference subsequently distributed handouts containing diatribes against MRC to the Morris County Young Republicans who met at Morris Plains, New Jersey, in May 1963.

All of the anti-MRC speakers urged their listeners and readers to "write and make telephone calls" to preserve local government, and they did.[43] They also distributed spurious copies of the interlocal agreement and the *Dan Smoot Report*, and created general confusion in the minds of the public, including those sympathetic to MRC.

The former mayor of Plainfield wondered if the interlocal agreement voted on and ratified by Plainfield and Union County was the same document given to other members. The incumbent mayor questioned if MRC would cause Plainfield to be governed by New York and Connecticut laws, and was it possible to withdraw from an "interstate compact" (or was an act of Congress necessary)?[44] A reader asked the *Home News* for assurance that the New Jersey enabling legislation for MRC would not "place under a dictatorship the approximately 16 million people residing in this metropolitan area, by eliminating the County Board of Freeholders and making elected municipal officials subservient to an appointed metro-regional director."[45] The Board of Freeholders of Union County was so confused by mounting opposi-

---

[42] Letter to "Friends" from Tri-State Conference on Community Problems, March 13, 1963. The report of the Bergen meeting is given in a memorandum from Prager to Lehman, March 27, 1963.

[43] Notes by Prager on meeting of Morris County Young Republicans, Morris Plains, New Jersey, May 13, 1963. *The Patriot* also advised its readers to "fight this [MRC] like the plague" (No. 18, March 13, 1963).

[44] See letters from Prager to former Mayor Richard P. Dyckman, March 5, 1963, and from Lehman to Mayor Robert C. Maddox, March 13, 1963.

[45] *Sunday Home News*, March 10, 1963. In assuring the reader that MRC was "no supergovernment," the editor pointed out that he "still regarded the MRC as one of the brightest hopes for orderly planning . . . in the fast moving days ahead. . . ."

tion to alleged supergovernment, New York City takeover, entrapment in Connecticut problems—and so concerned with their own political futures—that they were badly shaken. After years of easy cooperation between MRC and Union County (and its cities of Elizabeth, Rahway, Linden, and Plainfield), Union County was ready to reconsider its previous vote on MRC, originally taken in August 1962.[46]

The extremists from Bergen, Union, Essex, and Morris counties, New Jersey, became increasingly aggressive and turned out in force for public hearings held in New York City in June 1963 by the Subcommittees on Intergovernmental Relations of the Senate and House Committees on Government Operations. The demonstrators, a group of about fifty middle-aged men and women, representing "conservative groups opposed to coercive illegal master plans and state and federal intervention," alternately applauded and groaned at the testimony of state and local officials, and one of them went so far as to yell "liar" at Senator Edmund S. Muskie, the Senate Subcommittee Chairman.[47] The Tri-State Conference on Community Problems termed the hearings "Operations Sellout" because of its inability to be heard and distributed pamphlets attacking MRC as Soviet-styled invisible government. A number of "Selected Communications from Private Groups and Individuals in the New York Metropolitan Region," which appear in the report of the joint hearings, bear witness to further uncomplimentary remarks.[48]

Significance of Extremist Efforts

New Jersey was not the only place in the region where extremist groups found fertile soil for distribution of crank pamphlets and misleading information. In 1959, Rockland County, New York,

[46] Minutes of public meeting, Union County Board of Freeholders, April 1, 1963. See also *Newark Evening News*, April 15, 1963.

[47] MRC *Bulletin* (June 1963), and letter from Lehman to Patrick Healy, Executive Director, American Municipal Association, June 20, 1963.

[48] *Joint Hearings: Government in Metropolitan Areas* (1963), letters from Bergen County Conservative Club, pp. 310–311, and Jockey Hollow, New Jersey Conservative Chapter of Young Americans for Freedom, p. 317, and statement of Ridgewood Unit of Republican Women, p. 323.

was reluctant to give its seal of approval to MRC's decision to seek legal status because of the concern of its Board of Supervisors with the contents of the *Dan Smoot Report*. In 1960, the Women's City Club of Forest Hills, New York, submitted a resolution in opposition to "Metro" to the New York City Federation of Women's Clubs because of similar concerns. And antimetro correspondence flourished in Darien, Greenwich, and Stamford, Connecticut, each time proposals of charter revision, urban renewal, and regional planning were announced.[49]

By the time MRC proposals were presented to Suffolk and Westchester, the antimetro groups were well rehearsed and well organized. (They were also treated with more tolerance by the local boards of supervisors than by the Congressional subcommittees.) Once the two important New York counties had voted against affiliation with MRC, New Jersey freeholders became increasingly hesitant about supporting an organization which other communities had refused to join.

As the lines of opposition stiffened in New Jersey, familiar questions were raised with regard to the powers the Council might wield in future years. On the one side, the Council faced the right-wing groups, who raised the bogie of supergovernment, and timid legislative officials, who, reinforced by the extremists, opposed formal membership because of alleged vagueness in the Council's charter dealing with formal powers.[50] On the other side, it had to contend with the *Newark News*, which wondered if MRC would become "another costly exercise in futility ... [leading to] another bureaucratic featherbed." A similar concern was expressed by Mayor Graves of Paterson, New Jersey, who de-

---

[49] Letter from Richard S. Childs of the National Municipal League to Mrs. Claude Williams, Forest Hills, New York, attempting to clear up misinformation in "Resolution No. 4" passed by the Women's City Club of Forest Hills; letter from Dominic Del Guidice, Executive Director, Citizens Action Council for the Improvement of Stamford, Connecticut, to Prager, February 3, 1965, enclosing antimetro correspondence published in the *Darien Review*, August 10, 1961; letters from Leslie T. Hand, Greenwich, Connecticut, to *Village Gazette*, Old Greenwich, Connecticut, and to the Subcommittees on Intergovernmental Relations, *Joint Hearings: Government in Metropolitan Areas* [1963], p. 316).

[50] "Freeholder Opposed to Regional Council," *Record*, March 12, 1963, and "Between Hesitancy and Paralysis," *Record*, March 14, 1963.

plored MRC's lack of "financial background and know how," and felt that it should have more authority and power to enforce its decisions.[51] The Council thus found itself caught between two opposing points of view: some charged it would remain weak as a political force and would be able to make no decisions worthy of commanding respect; others feared that the Council would do too much and looked upon supergovernment as a likely prospect. Constant references to the interlocal agreement, and reminders that it bestowed no "operating functions," served to satisfy neither side.

Opposition from extremist groups made the Council's job more difficult. Not only did it have to carry on its day-by-day operations and try to orient the public with respect to vague goals and activities—a difficult enough task—but it now had to fight a continuous rear-guard action against many groups whose attacks were venomous and irrelevant. Responding to the lies, insinuations, false pamphlets, and spurious handouts became a full-time occupation for hard-pressed Council personnel. The attempt to stifle the voices of the "hate groups" had an interesting side effect, however, in that it provided the Council with more sustained publicity over a six-month period than it had received previously. No longer was knowledge of the Council limited only to newspaper editors or civic leaders. In responding to the accusations that were forthcoming from all sides, MRC answered more inquiries, wrote more letters, and addressed more civic groups than it had done before. The concept of a regional partnership of individual communities became more concrete as the public was compelled to take sides.[52]

While there is little doubt that the harassing attacks slowed down the Council's activities, MRC had embarked on its down-

[51] "Nobody Loves It," *Newark Evening News*, March 23, 1963, and *Joint Hearings: Government in Metropolitan Areas* (1963), p. 55, respectively.

[52] Other regional councils, in common with various other agencies of state and local governments, have suffered from similar harassing attacks. See "Extremists Derided for Fear of 'Super Metro Government,'" *Washington Post*, December 12, 1963, p. B-4; H. G. Pope, "New Peas in an Old Shell Game," *Public Administration Service* (January 1960); and Advisory Commission, *Factors Affecting Voter Reaction*, p. 15.

ward course before the attacks became overwhelming. The Council had been in business for six years by 1962 and was already showing signs of weakness. The extremist groups fed into the hands of those who found it expedient on other grounds—parochial, personal, political—to oppose the Council's continued existence. To overcome all of these, MRC needed a broad base of support, private and public. Help from the public sector remains to be explored.

V

INTERGOVERNMENTAL RELATIONSHIPS

Competing Regional Organizations

A voluntary council must not only find ways to overcome the traditional antipathy of many groups of people and local governments; it must also anticipate the reactions of existing agencies concerned with area-wide problems and learn how to deal with them. Individual authorities, special districts, commissions, and boards show a marked tendency toward preoccupation with their own programs and jurisdictional bailiwicks, and wish to preserve traditional values and processes—as they see them. They are apt to regard new proposals as a threat to specialized points of view, and can develop into powerful adversaries unless proper liaison is established.[1]

Resistance is likely to increase when a new agency shows indications of developing into a full-scale threat to existing spheres of influence. MRC created lasting animosities among some of the important regional agencies by raising divisive and controversial issues soon after its establishment—in seeming disregard of the impact these issues would have upon many of the older regional institutions.

Mayor Wagner set the tone for curbing the power and role of existing authorities in an address to Council members in February 1958. Advising that MRC's future activities might well include

[1] For further discussion, refer to Gulick, *The Metropolitan Problem and American Ideas*, p. 114; Sayre and Kaufman, *Governing New York City*, particularly pp. 294–305; and Martin et al., *Decisions in Syracuse*, p. 155.

coordination of interstate activities then in existence, he suggested that the Council "act in a supervisory or governing capacity" for any new bi-state or tri-state agencies which might be created. Elaborating on this theme, Wagner asked MRC members in June 1958 to consider the use of MRC as a "central point of reference" to bring together and correlate all data about regional activities. Since the Council appeared to be the sole regional agency with a broad outlook on regional problems, he proposed that the "fragmented regional organizations" in the metropolitan area "report" to it on a regular basis.

Luther Gulick lent his weight to these proposals in October 1958 in an address to the annual conference of RPA. Pointing out that the Council had the "duty" to recommend action on urgent regional problems, he suggested that all state and local operating agencies in the metropolitan area be required "by law" to inform and consult with MRC before making decisions about metropolitan matters. Karl Metzger, Chairman of the Committee on the Future of the MRC, publicly agreed in *his* speech to RPA members that the role of the authorities must be reexamined. The MRC executive secretary emphasized this point in an address to the Women's City Club a few months later, calling attention to the lack of coordination among the many independent authorities in the region which were not answerable to the people served.[2]

All of these points—that MRC should act as coordinator for all regional activities, that all special-purpose regional agencies should report regularly to the Council, and that MRC should participate in any new interstate agency which was established— were clearly and loudly enunciated by the MRC chairman at each semiannual Council meeting between 1959 and 1962. At the same time, Mayor Wagner attempted to assure the various agencies then operating in the region that MRC had no desire to "take over" or compete with them. "On the contrary, the cooperative impulse which activates this Council applies in our deal-

[2] Gulick, "Our Emerging Metropolitan Crises: Whose Responsibility?," October 8, 1958; Metzger, "Government in Tomorrow's Region: Prospects for Coordination among 550 Municipalities," October 8, 1958; Lehman, "The Metropolitan Region Gets Together," December 2, 1958.

ings with these other agencies too."[3] To some of the authorities, however, these words might have appeared less than reassuring. The Council frequently acted as if it wished to develop into the principal governing body of a new regional agency—composed of elected officials—which would take over some important operating functions for the region, including transportation, recreation, regional planning, water supply, and air- and water-pollution control.[4]

PORT OF NEW YORK AUTHORITY.—A review of MRC's relations with the Port of New York Authority, which operates bridges, tunnels, airports, piers, and other facilities in the New York–New Jersey area, shows little "cooperative impulse" toward other regional agencies. By the time MRC came into existence in 1956, the Port Authority was experiencing sharp criticism from many quarters for its failure to assume some financial responsibility for measures leading to a solution of the rail-commuter crisis in the New York region. Resisting these pressures, the Authority claimed that assuming transit deficits would compromise its credit structure. In 1954, a bi-state Metropolitan Rapid Transit Commission had been created by New York and New Jersey to engage in a comprehensive study of transit facilities in the New York region. Attempting to maintain its freedom of action in finance and planning, the Port Authority provided the Commission with $800,000 in return for a "Memorandum of Understanding," which provided for joint control of the study by the Port Authority and the Commission, and limited the scope of the study to the New Jersey–Manhattan sector of the region.[5]

[3] Address to MRC members, February 19, 1958. Mayor Wagner delivered other messages dealing with coordination of regional activities on June 16, 1959, February 23, 1960, February 28, 1961, and February 27, 1962.

[4] The key to MRC's attitude vis-à-vis other regional agencies can be found in the executive secretary's remarks to Columbia University students, April 8, 1958, cited in Chap. II, p. 27.

[5] Much of the background material dealing with the Metropolitan Rapid Transit Commission and the Port of New York Authority is based on Doig's account, *Metropolitan Transportation Politics*, particularly Chap. IV, "The Study Commission and the Port Authority." It should be noted that the "Memorandum of Understanding" limited the Port Authority's responsibility in dealing with problems of rail transit and similarly limited

After extensive deliberation, the Metropolitan Rapid Transit Commission issued a final report in 1958, recommending that a permanent bi-state rapid-transit district be established by interstate compact to subsidize existing commuter services and build additional facilities. The report assigned no financial responsibilities to the Port Authority for improving trans-Hudson rail transit, but placed the entire financial burden of transit deficits on local communities. Immediate legislation was requested for establishment of the district.

In contrast to the Port Authority and most of the major civic associations in New York City, which welcomed the possibility of new means of commuter transportation, MRC reacted sharply against the proposed new cooperative effort between New York and New Jersey. Originally, the Council urged that specific action on S. 50 (the New Jersey bill providing for an interstate compact to create a bi-state transit district) be deferred on the ground that it was "defective in scope and structure." Reporting to MRC members in February 1958, the Council's Traffic and Transportation Committee made it clear that any undertaking in the field of regional transit should not be performed by another—perhaps competing—regional agency, when MRC itself already existed and contained "the necessary governmental machinery." (If the Council's structure and legislative authorization needed changing to comply with its added responsibilities, the Council would be willing to consider such changes.) Council members also objected to the proposed selection of members of the transit-district council by county officials, with no voice or representation from the cities of the area. Furthermore, they were hesitant to use local tax resources to aid the railroads, and preferred that the states and/or the Port of New York Authority assume financial responsibility.[6]

---

the study commission's role in the field of highway planning. There was no provision for an overall evaluation of total trans-Hudson movements. Doig's book indicates that the final proposal which emerged from the study was consistent with the views, preferences, and goals of the Port of New York Authority.

[6] MRC memorandum concerning legislation for a bi-state transit district, 1958. The Council wanted further study and deliberation preceding the preparation of "soundly conceived, realistic legislation" for submission to

When the New Jersey legislature rejected the alternative of further study, the Council sent letters and telegrams to leaders of the New Jersey Assembly and Senate and to Governor Meyner, advising them of MRC's "strong and decisive" and unanimous opposition to S. 50. MRC's executive secretary testified against the bill before two New Jersey Assembly committees in November 1958, taking issue with the bill's proposed allocation of financial deficits, its bi-state structure, its limited geographical scope, and its single consideration of rail-transit problems. The bi-state transit bill was defeated in the New Jersey legislature in December 1958. MRC and its member communities in northern New Jersey claimed credit for having administered the death blow.[7]

MRC's opposition to the bi-state transit bill set the stage for its direct confrontation with the Port of New York Authority. The latter had supported the transit district as sound policy for meeting the region's rapid transit needs. By virtue of its financial contribution to the study leading to the proposals of the Metropolitan Rapid Transit Commission, the Authority felt that it had complied with its obligations to the problems of commuter transportation in the region.[8]

MRC adopted a different point of view. Lehman's testimony before the two New Jersey legislative committees singled out the Port Authority (as well as the Triborough Bridge and Tunnel Authority) as a target for legislative action, suggesting that further study be made of the ways in which the "revenue-producing transportation facilities" might contribute to the transit burden. A letter to MRC members reiterated in clarion tones the Council's "established policy" of working toward integration

---

the next year's legislative sessions. See also the resolution of MRC's Traffic and Transportation Committee, February 5, 1958, and memorandum from Lehman to City Administrator Charles F. Preusse, March 3, 1958.

[7] The letters and telegrams were sent out on June 11, 1958. See also Lehman's testimony before the New Jersey State Assembly Committee on Federal and Interstate Relations and the Highway Committee, Trenton, New Jersey, November 24, 1958; and the report of MRC's Traffic and Transportation Committee, February 19, 1959.

[8] Doig, *Metropolitan Transportation Politics*, pp. 176 and 242. See also Danielson, *Federal-Metropolitan Politics*, p. 21.

of rail and highway planning and the creation of a tri-state transportation agency—under MRC auspices—to coordinate existing
approaches to traffic and transportation problems.[9] These statements seem prematurely militant for an organization in the early
stages of its development. The four public hearings to discuss the
future direction of the Council were then taking place, and MRC
still lacked staff, financial support, and legal authority. It might
have been wiser for the Council to plot its own future course
before it ran the risk of incurring opposition from well-established
regional agencies.

If the Port Authority did not yet have sufficient reason to consider MRC an immediate threat to its own independent status,
it could not shut its ears to the frontal attack which was forthcoming from another quarter. In October 1958, Mayor Charles
S. Witkowski of Jersey City, the outspoken Chairman of MRC's
Traffic and Transportation Committee, addressed RPA members
on the subject of governmental responsibility for the improvement of commuter transportation in the metropolitan area.
Reminding his listeners that the Metropolitan Rapid Transit
Commission should have avoided deficit financing by means of
a "pooling of revenues of bridges, tunnels and transit in the area,"
he pointed out that this possibility was never considered because
of the Port Authority's influence over the results of the study.
Witkowski found it clear that the "Authority wants to take no
part in solving the region's commuter problems," adding, "[It]
sure got its money's worth." These were even stronger words to
hurl against an influential state-created regional body. MRC was
now moving toward an inflexible position from which it would
be increasingly difficult to retreat.

Witkowski proposed consideration of MRC as the proper organization to provide a realistic approach to problems of regional
transportation, and other observers concurred with his assessment of the Council's role. The technical advisory group to the
MRC Traffic and Transportation Committee felt that MRC policy decisions must be "imposed" on the independent authorities
presently operating transportation facilities in the region and that

[9] MRC's letter to member communities was sent on December 19, 1958.

MRC should be given "the necessary political power . . . to require the Port Authority to operate and finance all its facilities" in accordance with a regional plan.[10]

A further suggestion for rearranging existing lines of political control was made at the hearing of the Committee on the Future of the MRC in New York City in January 1959 by Commissioner Goodhue Livingston, Jr., of the City Planning Commission. Recommending that the Port and Triborough authorities be reorganized as new agencies under MRC jurisdiction, he felt that they should be required, at the very least, to report to MRC to ensure public responsibility and coordination of policy. At the same time, Luther Gulick endorsed legal status for the Council so that it might function as a "policy-defining agency" for the region vis-à-vis other groups. The Sayre report for RPA also called on MRC to assume an "official advisory role" to any regional agency established in the transportation field, "with particular responsibility to review and evaluate all proposals for the improvement of the Region's mass transportation facilities."[11]

Encouraged by these expressions of support, MRC's belligerent attitude toward the Port Authority continued unabated. At each semiannual meeting, the Traffic and Transportation Committee reiterated the need for coordination of "the existing piecemeal approaches" by a new regional transit agency, integration of rubber and rail mass transit, and sharing of commuter deficits among all jurisdictions of government, including the Port Authority. In February 1960, the Council adopted a resolution for submission to the New Jersey and New York legislatures calling for an examination and investigation of the functions, responsibilities, and

[10] Notes on meeting of the technical advisory group to the Traffic and Transportation Committee of MRC, October 24, 1958. At this time, the advisors included Salomon J. Flink, economic consultant to the New Jersey General Assembly; Charles E. Stonier, Associate Professor, Hofstra College; Lawrence M. Orton, member of the New York City Planning Commission; Joseph Lieper and Allen K. Sloan, Transportation Division, New York City Planning Commission; and Henry Cohen and Leslie Slote, with the Office of the City Administrator, New York City.

[11] Statements made at the public hearing, January 13, 1959. Livingston urged that two new authorities be created—a regional transport authority to handle transportation on highways and railroads, and a "genuine" port authority to look after port installations and airports.

activities of the Port Authority. (This resolution received strong support from Mayor Wagner as "the most solid and practical proposal made so far.") Grudging acquiescence was given by the Council to the Port Authority's proposal to purchase and modernize the Hudson and Manhattan Railroad, provided that the Authority would not be thereby given "absolute power" to determine the extent and conditions of its actions in this area.[12]

In view of MRC's difficulties in establishing its own position as a regional study and planning group, it is not easy to rationalize its unnecessary posture of overt antagonism toward intrenched interests in related functional fields. It was one thing to urge that the financial burdens of commuter services be shared by governments other than those of the localities. It was quite a different matter to urge the dismantling and reorganization of an influential regional agency—established by interstate compact between two powerful states—by a voluntary group which was engaged in an all-out effort to secure legal status in those two states. MRC erred in permitting itself to become the vehicle whereby other regional officials—for whatever reasons—attacked the virtually unlimited freedom of action by the Port Authority. By using these expressions as support for its own adversary position, the Council created animosity that persisted to 1967.

On the basis of MRC assertions, agencies operating in related fields had cause to fear that the Council would eventually receive mandatory authority to veto plans of any other governmental agency not conforming with its view of what was best for the region as a whole. Had MRC become more prominent, it would probably have become involved in the more difficult area of interjurisdictional disputes between agencies in an attempt to relate programs in one functional field to those in another. The record indicates, however, that the membership showed little support of MRC's potential role as a coordinator of regional authorities. Although a number of New Jersey communities in 1960 expressed reservations about the specific operations of the Port Authority, they did not feel MRC was in any position to intervene. Since the Council was in an "early developmental stage with only token

[12] Minutes of Traffic and Transportation Committee meetings, January 16, 1959, February 19, 1959, February 23, 1960, and February 28, 1961.

powers and very sketchy member loyalty,"[13] a slower and more tactful approach in trying to establish its own position in the region might have been more effective.

INTERSTATE SANITATION COMMISSION.—MRC's relations with the Interstate Sanitation Commission, a New York–New Jersey–Connecticut agency established in 1935 to abate air and water pollution in the New York harbor area, displayed similar aggressive intent. After studying the interstate aspects of the problem of air-pollution control in 1958, MRC's Air Pollution Committee concluded that the Commission "provides at best only a very limited approach to the solution of the regional problem of air pollution control," and that MRC was the "most effective medium" for coordinating existing efforts. One year later, a somewhat milder approach was used. The committee recommended that a new "Air Pollution Control Compact" proposed by the Interstate Sanitation Commission be passed with the proviso that the new air-pollution commission be directed to report its activities directly to MRC as well as to the states. The Council continued to consider the possibility of reconstituting the Commission as an executive agency of the Council.[14]

Following a discussion with the Interstate Sanitation Commission in 1961, MRC adopted a more conciliatory attitude and urged passage of legislation which would give the Commission coordinating powers with respect to interstate air-pollution problems between the states of New York and New Jersey. This latter move was apparently insufficient to overcome the suspicion that had developed. When MRC was seeking funds to prepare a comprehensive water-pollution source and control map for the tri-state area in 1962, it requested the Commission to subsidize its publication. MRC suggested that such a map would help local administrators identify and control pollution sources and would tie in nicely with the Commission's program for achieving the best use of district waters. The Commission, on the other hand, indi-

---

[13] Memorandum from Frank Smallwood, temporary staff member, MRC, to Lehman, August 12, 1960.

[14] Minutes of meetings of Air Pollution Committee, January 8, 1958, and February 19, 1959, and memorandum from Leslie Slote to Lehman, September 25, 1958.

cated that the map would probably duplicate maps already published under its own auspices, and denied the request.

TRIBOROUGH BRIDGE AND TUNNEL AUTHORITY.—Relations with Robert Moses, Chairman of the Triborough Bridge and Tunnel Authority, which operates bridges, tunnels, roadways, garage facilities, and commercial buildings within the five boroughs of New York City, followed a similarly uneven course. They seemed to start out smoothly enough. Wagner praised the leadership of "such outstanding public servants" as Bob Moses (and Austin Tobin, Executive Director of the Port of New York Authority) to RPA members in October 1956, but warned MRC officials that "new solutions were necessary" to counteract the palliatives offered by special-purpose agencies.[15] Moses was equally guarded. He felt that Wagner's idea of stimulating further discussion with regard to metropolitan planning was a good one "provided definite, limited, realizable objectives and not empty gestures, noble generalities and revolutionary schemes of regional supergovernment are the purposes." Executive Secretary Lehman welcomed Moses' cooperative comments and assured him that MRC was not just a "meeting group . . . [but] prepared to take specific action on specfic matters."[16]

MRC's assertions with respect to its own role as a regional coordinator must have caused Moses a good deal of uneasiness in the many local and state offices which he held in addition to his post with the Triborough Authority.[17] In 1958, he called a meeting of a "Metropolitan Regional Recreation Conference" to

[15] Wagner's remarks were made on October 22, 1956, and December 11, 1956, respectively.

[16] Letters from Moses to former Governor W. Averell Harriman of New York, June 20, 1956, and from Lehman to Moses, November 15, 1956.

[17] Moses' other posts were Commissioner of the Department of Parks of New York City, City Construction Coordinator, member of the City Planning Commission, Chairman of the Mayor's Committee on Slum Clearance, head of the Office of Planning and Construction of the City Office of Civil Defense, member of the New York City Youth Board, President of the Long Island State Park Commission, Chairman of the State Council of Parks, President of the Jones Beach State Parkway Authority and of the Bethpage (Long Island) Park Authority, and Chairman of the New York State Power Authority (Sayre and Kaufman, *Governing New York City*, p. 341).

demonstrate publicly that "competent officials" working together could best solve regional problems "except where special-purpose agencies (like the Port of New York Authority) might be needed for limited purposes." By 1962, Moses saw MRC as a threat to his own programs, and his enmity was firm. When Suffolk County, New York, was considering affiliation with MRC as a dues-paying member, Moses, in his capacity as Long Island State Park Commissioner, strongly recommended that Suffolk refrain from joining "a superior overriding metropolitan government . . . [where] local jurisdictions would be surrendering considerable power and control."[18]

By virtue of his many appointive positions with New York States as well as New York City, Moses possessed great influence in both places. When MRC tangled with him—as well as with the Port of New York Authority and the Interstate Sanitation Commission—it entered into direct competition with state-oriented and state-created agencies. As an organization of local communities, in which the local interest was predominant, MRC was faced with the potential rivalry of the three states from the very beginning. The Council may have felt that it would be self-defeating to support these state-supported alternatives and this may explain, in large part, the hostile attitude of the fledgling group toward the powerful "metropolitan giants."[19]

On the other hand, premature assertion of its own role, at the expense of other regional participants, was unrealistic since this role could not be implemented. Doig's account of *Metropolitan Transportation Politics and the New York Region* clearly demonstrates the ineffectiveness of MRC and the local governments in the transportation field and the comparative advantages enjoyed by the state political institutions.[20] Local communities were unable and unwilling to accept the heavy cost of financing remedies for the commuter-transit problem. They did not even agree about the urgency of the problem. The state governments were finan-

---

[18] Letter from Moses to Arthur Cromarty, Chairman, Suffolk County Board of Supervisors, May 10, 1962. Moses' address to recreational officials was delivered at Bear Mountain, New York, May 8, 1958.

[19] Wood, *1400 Governments*, Chap. IV.

[20] Pp. 141–146, 228–229, 243.

cially capable, but they were not likely to put up the necessary funds and then relinquish control to the localities. In point of fact, how did the states respond to MRC?

State Assistance to Metropolitan Areas

It is generally agreed that there are few purely "local" problems in metropolitan areas, and that the states must take a more active role in developing rational policies for urban growth.[21] Since local governments are creatures of the state, and can exercise only those powers specifically granted to them, the states are in a pivotal position with respect to local government and politics. For many reasons, including financial incapacity, statutory and constitutional restrictions, and state bias in favor of rural areas—aggravated by inequitable representation of urban centers in state legislatures—the states have been insufficiently responsive to the needs of metropolitan areas.

Recommendations for state leadership in alleviating metropolitan problems cover a host of activities, including state support for urban-oriented programs, a significant rise in state expenditures for urban development, state assumption of functions where costs impinge unequally and unevenly on the local communities, establishment of minimum-performance standards with regard to functions affecting more than one local community, guidance and technical assistance to local officials, and more comprehensive planning at the state level—along less functionally oriented lines.[22]

[21] See, for example, the Commission on Intergovernmental Relations, *Message from the President of the United States Transmitting the Final Report of the Commission on Intergovernmental Relations, Pursuant to Public Law 109, 83rd Congress* (Washington: U.S. Government Printing Office, 1955), p. 52; Advisory Commission, *Governmental Structure*, pp. 24–25, *State Constitutional and Statutory Restrictions upon the Structural, Functional, and Personnel Powers of Local Government* (Washington: U.S. Government Printing Office, 1962), p. 66, and *Alternative Approaches*, p. 38. See also Studenski, *National Civic Review*, XLIX (October 1960), 9; Martin, *ibid.*, LII (July 1963), 367; and Bollens, *The States and the Metropolitan Problem*, particularly Pt. III.

[22] For specific suggestions, see the authors mentioned in n. 21 to this chapter. Refer also to Harvey E. Brazer, "Some Fiscal Implications of Metropolitanism," *Metropolitan Issues*, ed. Birkhead, p. 80; Henry C. Hart,

It is also urged that the states take a more active part in facilitating interlocal planning and cooperation, and grant local officials the necessary authority to form councils of governments. Until now, the states have played a relatively limited role in fostering cooperative regional approaches to urban problems, particularly when compared to the strong federal encouragement of recent years.[23]

MRC and the Three States

The review in Chapter II of some of the obstacles which impeded MRC's development into a legally authorized body highlights the difficulty of establishing a regional council in a metropolitan area which comprises portions of three states. Each state is subjected to different environmental pressures, is committed to different philosophies of expenditures and revenues, and pursues varying policies with respect to the local governments within its borders.[24] During the years that MRC was struggling to make its

---

"The Dawn of a Community-Defining Federalism," *Annals*, CCCLIX (May 1965), 154; William G. Colman, "The Role of the Federal Government in the Design and Administration of Intergovernmental Programs," *ibid.*, p. 34; Gulick, *The Metropolitan Problem and American Ideas*, p. 164; and Alan K. Campbell, "States at Crossroads," *National Civic Review*, LV (November 1966), 554.

[23] In its *1967 State Legislative Program*, the Advisory Commission finds that two methods are useful for the creation of councils of governments: the passage of special acts by the state legislature creating the council, or the passage of general enabling acts that permit local units of government to undertake jointly any action they are empowered to perform on their own. A third statutory approach, authorizing local governments to join together for the specific purpose of forming and operating councils, is also suggested (1966, p. 367). As of September 22, 1967, the *News Service to Regional Councils* (No. 3) reports that nine states—Washington, Oregon, Minnesota, Connecticut, Maryland, Arkansas, Ohio, North Carolina, and Tennessee—have specific enabling legislation for councils. (Michigan has since passed the Urban Cooperation Act of 1967, which provides a broad grant of power to local governments to make interlocal agreements or to form councils.)

[24] See Wood, *1400 Governments*, pp. 26 and 110; and Alan K. Campbell and Seymour Sacks, "Administering the Spread City," *Public Administration Review*, XXIV (September 1964), 148, for discussion of some of the variations in policies among the states in the New York metropolitan region.

influence felt, the three states showed little enthusiasm for the cooperative, local approach offered by MRC. While these states were urban-oriented for the most part, their efforts toward helping local communities adjust to new urban responsibilities were dominated by functional considerations rather than by a concern for metropolitan integration. (To expect otherwise is felt to be unrealistic. State legislators have been found to respond to the same values and pressures which influence local political leaders, and to think in terms of their own particular needs—which end on their borders—rather than in terms of regionally valuable objectives.)[25]

Mention has already been made of New York State's passage of legislation in 1957 authorizing local units of government to enter into cooperative arrangements in certain specified fields with adjacent units in other states. Its enactment represented the high-water mark in cooperative dealings between MRC and the Joint Legislative Committee on Interstate Cooperation, sponsoring body for the legislation and New York's official legislative agency in the matter of federal and state and interstate relations.

Elisha Barrett, Chairman of the Joint Legislative Committee, informed MRC that interlocal agreements permitted by the 1957 act might be useful for dealing with some of the aggravating problems in the New York metropolitan region such as teen-age drinking. A meeting on interlocal cooperation was scheduled by the Council of State Governments in 1958, at the request of the Joint Legislative Committee, and Barrett pointed out then, as he did thereafter, that the New York enabling legislation was appropriate for MRC purposes in securing legal status. When MRC

[25] For a thorough analysis of New York's activities in the functional fields of highways, health, education, and pollution, see Harold Herman, *New York State and the Metropolitan Problem* (Philadelphia: University of Pennsylvania Press, 1963), pp. 184 ff.; and Martin et al., *Decisions in Syracuse*, particularly pp. 35 and 223. Some discussion of the political perceptions of state legislators, which condition their attitudes toward urban policies, is given by Herman, *New York State*, p. 178; Winston Crouch, "Conflict and Cooperation among Local Governments in the Metropolis," *Annals*, CCCLIX (May 1965), 61; Charles R. Adrian, "State and Local Government Participation in the Design and Administration of Intergovernmental Programs," *ibid.*, p. 37; and Martin, *The Cities and the Federal System*, pp. 77–79.

chose to submit its own legislation, Barrett indicated concern about the creation of a possible new metropolitan power center, dominated by New York City, and became increasingly hostile toward MRC. In 1962, Barrett read "with alarm" a news article announcing plans for an inventory of the region's water supply to be undertaken by the MRC Committee on Water Supply, and advised Nassau County Executive Eugene Nickerson, Chairman of the committee, that Suffolk County, Nassau's neighbor and Barrett's home district, had "since early in the century" been making every effort to protect its water supply from the "grasping efforts of New York City." Barrett warned Nassau to guard its own water "by every means" and, above all else, "to avoid regional plans."[26] Barrett sent a similar warning to the Suffolk Board of Supervisors on the eve of the public hearing on the resolution to affiliate with MRC.

Once this avenue of communication with the state legislature was closed off, the Council maintained an extremely informal relationship with other state agencies. It amounted to little more than keeping them informed of MRC activities and inviting them to participate in the semiannual membership meetings. During MRC's first ten years, there was no administrative framework within any of the three state governments for dealing with regional problems. The Office of Local Government created by New York State in 1959 served as a clearing house of information for local communities, but it displayed little interest in encouraging the development of new approaches for handling area-wide problems. There is no evidence that MRC had any direct contact with it or with similar agencies then existing in New Jersey or Connecticut.[27] MRC felt that the states should be more sensitive to

[26] Letter from Barrett to Nickerson, June 28, 1962, referring to a news article in the *Long Island Press* of June 20, 1962.

[27] For a further description of the role of the New York Office of Local Government, see Campbell, *National Civic Review*, LV (November 1966), 559. See Bennett M. Rich, *The Government and Administration of New Jersey* (New York: Thomas Y. Crowell, 1957), pp. 355–359, for a discussion of the Division of Local Government and the Local Government Board of New Jersey. MRC had no contact with these two agencies or with the Connecticut Development Commission or regional plan agencies in Connecticut. For present institutional arrangements within the three states, refer to Chap. IX, pp. 206–207.

the needs of metropolitan areas within their borders, and deplored the fact that state development programs with regional implications were not coordinated with similar studies in the other two states and did not include the participation of *all* of the region's officials.

State Representation on MRC

MRC's chairman made frequent reference to the establishment of some form of direct contact between MRC and the three state governments at the semiannual meetings, and members of the executive board and functional committees did the same. Additionally, the Sayre report for RPA, which served as a guide for the Council's effort to secure legal status, and RPA itself urged that state representatives participate directly in MRC activities— either as voting or nonvoting members.[28] In spite of repeated discussions of the need for joint state-local effort, no steps were taken to ensure that the states would have a built-in role in the Council's deliberations. State representatives were included only upon the insistence of New Jersey in 1962, when it became absolutely necessary to uniformalize the provisions of the enabling legislation passed by the three states. MRC's interlocal agreement, drawn up in conformity with the enabling legislation, provided state agencies and authorities with the privilege of the floor, without vote, at all Council meetings.

Thus, it was not until February 1962 that Mayor Wagner suggested that state representatives be brought into MRC "on a more direct permanent basis" since so much of the Council's work involved the state governments. This arrangement might have been more productive had it been effected at an earlier date. Con-

---

[28] See Wagner's address, "Problems of the Metropolitan Area," to the American Municipal Association, November 28, 1955; agenda of MRC steering committee meeting, April 17, 1957; Wagner's address to MRC members, May 27, 1957; agenda of executive board meeting, January 8, 1958; minutes of MRC special meeting, April 7, 1959; and Wagner's remarks to Regional Plan Conference, October 7, 1959. See also Report of the Special Committee on Metropolitan Governmental Affairs of RPA, and RPA memorandum from John P. Keith to C. McKim Norton, then Executive Vice-President of RPA, December 15, 1961.

ceivably, it might have made the state legislatures more receptive to the MRC enabling legislation in the first instance (thus permitting the whole legal process to take less time) and to other legislative proposals emanating from MRC and its member components. However, Wagner's statements over the years indicated that he and his colleagues had hoped to play the dominant role in establishing regional policy in the New York metropolitan area without interference from other levels of government. While they wished the states to "confer with the Council on all matters having regional implications,"[29] they did not seek the kind of intervention that would give the states control over the making of regional decisions. By 1962, the recurring transportation crises had made it abundantly clear that neither MRC nor the local governments—acting singly or collectively—could furnish the necessary solutions without direct state assistance. When Wagner finally made his suggestion to MRC members, the Council's internal position was unstable and its relations with the states were poor.[30]

Governors' Reactions Toward MRC

Because no regular channels of communication with state personnel had been developed, MRC's contacts with the three states depended in great measure upon the personality and the political conviction of the person holding the top elected office. Governor W. Averell Harriman of New York assured the Council in 1957 that his administration was ready to cooperate in every way possible and offered help if a statutory framework for MRC were sought. Governor Nelson A. Rockefeller, who succeeded Harriman in 1958, expressed a different point of view. Rockefeller declared himself "convinced that state government is the logical leader of intergovernmental cooperation . . . [rather than] super-

[29] Wagner, address to Regional Plan Conference, October 7, 1959. For further background on Wagner's feelings about state participation, refer to his letter to Governor Hughes of New Jersey, Chap. II, p. 37.

[30] See Wagner's public charge at the annual meeting of the American Municipal Association that the Council was "hamstrung by . . . the state governments" in its efforts to solve regional problems (*New York Times*, August 28, 1962, p. 18).

governments that dry up local initiative,"[31] and he never mentioned MRC by name nor attended a meeting when invited. Neither did Lieutenant Governor Malcolm Wilson or Secretary William J. Ronan.

Governor Robert B. Meyner of New Jersey had a strong sense of the state's role in dealing with regional problems and adopted an ambivalent attitude toward MRC. While he expressed support of cooperation among local governments, he had a negative reaction toward an agency which he considered unnecessary and which made no provision for state supervision and review. In MRC's clash with the Port of New York Authority over the proposals of the Metropolitan Rapid Transit Commission, Meyner supported the Authority, because it removed political and financial pressure from his own administration in meeting the mounting costs of rail transit. When the MRC bill was pending in New Jersey, he withheld his signature until the very end of his term in office and then vetoed it.[32] His successor, Governor Richard J. Hughes, expressed a strong belief in encouraging cooperation among municipal and county governments, and was instrumental in gaining passage of the enabling legislation for MRC. Governors Abraham A. Ribicoff and John N. Dempsey of Connecticut were sympathetic and cordial throughout.

Creation of a Tri-State Transportation Committee

The governors' reactions toward MRC's recommendations for the creation of a regional transportation agency for the metro-

[31] *Joint Hearings: Government in Metropolitan Areas* (1963), pp. 295–296. In the same work, see also the testimony of Francis X. O'Rourke, Supervisor of Eastchester, New York, who quoted Lieutenant Governor Malcolm Wilson as advising members of the Board of Supervisors of Westchester County, at the time that ratification of MRC's interlocal agreement was pending, to "guard well . . . home rule in towns, cities and villages as government close to the people is the best government" (p. 283).

[32] Refer to Chap. II, p. 36, for Governor Meyner's veto message. Refer also to letter from Governor Meyner to the public hearing of the Committee on the Future of the MRC, Newark, New Jersey, November 25, 1958. For Meyner's views of the transit district proposed by the Metropolitan Rapid Transit Commission, see Doig, *Metropolitan Transportation Politics*, p. 179.

politan area were indicative perhaps of their attitudes toward
MRC itself. Once the proposal for the bi-state transit district was
defeated in late 1958, MRC reiterated its long-held position that
the problem of mass transit was basically regional, requiring cooperative effort across state lines. (It was at this time that RPA
recommended adding representatives of the governors and state
legislatures to MRC to strengthen the Council for its role in
undertaking a "fundamental reappraisal of the region's transportation institutions").[33] MRC, in turn, suggested the development
of a transportation panel with representation from five governmental bodies: New York, New Jersey, Connecticut, New York
City, and MRC.

In February 1959, the three governors conferred with Mayor
Wagner about the disintegration of the region's commuter rail
facilities. Rockefeller, who was looked to for leadership by the
other participants, opposed creation of a regional agency, calling
for individual action by each state "on a coordinated basis."
Rockefeller's attitude was so negative and his rejection of a tri-
state agency so outright that they appeared to be a deliberate affront to MRC.[34] Some months later, a four-man group, consisting
of Mayor Witkowski of Jersey City, County Executive Michaelian of Westchester, First Selectman Herbert E. Baldwin of
Westport, Connecticut, and Maxwell Lehman, was named by
MRC to meet with the governors and urge formation of an effective tri-state transportation agency. Following the meeting,
the executive secretary reported to MRC's executive board that
Governor Ribicoff "accepted MRC's tri-state approach"; Governor Meyner "was willing to go along with the plan if the other
governors agreed to it"; and Governor Rockefeller "favored a
piecemeal approach to the transportation problem, preferring to
deal first with items affecting New York State."[35]

Unwilling to encourage local participation in regional ap-

[33] RPA, memorandum to Mayor Wagner and to Governors Meyner,
Ribicoff, and Rockefeller, concerning "Commuter Transportation," February 10, 1959.

[34] *New York Times*, February 9, 1959, p. 11, and February 11, 1959, p. 1.
It might be noted that Rockefeller received strong endorsement of his
position from Austin Tobin of the Port Authority, who resisted involvement in any phase of the program.

[35] Minutes, MRC executive board meeting, October 18, 1960. Danielson's
account of the positions of the various participants indicates that Wagner

proaches, the states embarked on unilateral short-term programs
to meet the mounting transportation pressures in the New York
region.[36] Largely as a result of the interpersonal relationships that
developed out of the handling of the periodic crises, and because
of the prodding efforts of RPA and MRC, a Tri-State Transportation Committee was created by the three governors in August 1961 to engage in studies and make recommendations for
meeting the region's immediate and long-term transportation
needs.[37]

Local Participation in Tri-State

As part of the Tri-State program, each governor and the mayor
of New York City was asked to designate members of "local cooperating committees" to provide local liaison and exchange of
information and personnel with the committee.[38] In New Jersey

---

was committed to a minor financial role for the localities, a strong federal
role, and a tri-state approach; Meyner was uncommitted, except for his
desire to keep New Jersey free from financial burdens; Ribicoff wanted
action; and Rockefeller wished state leadership to be exercised (*Federal-
Metropolitan Politics*, p. 53).

[36] For discussion of the short-sighted and minimal action undertaken by
the states, refer to Danielson, *ibid.*, pp. 75, 78, 92, and 186; and Doig,
Metropolitan Transportation Politics, particularly Chap. IX, "State Leadership and Partial Solutions," and Chap. X, "Patterns of Conflict and Cooperation."

[37] Representatives of New York and New Jersey worked closely together to maintain operation of the Hudson tubes, an interurban railroad
operating between New York and New Jersey; the two states subsequently
passed legislation authorizing the Port of New York Authority to acquire,
operate and rehabilitate the Hudson and Manhattan Railroad system. Interstate staff committees from New York, Connecticut, Massachusetts, and
Rhode Island were active in persuading the Interstate Commerce Commission to guarantee millions of dollars in additional loans to keep the New
York, New Haven and Hartford Railroad running. In addition, a bi-state
agency was established to coordinate commuter rail programs in Albany
and Trenton.

[38] The three governors explained that this arrangement was provided so
that individual communities might "contribute" to the comprehensive program and "plan realistically for their own development" (*New York
Times*, September 28, 1961, p. 29). For further discussion of this point,
see memorandum to Tri-State Transportation Committee and Local Cooperating Committees from William J. Ronan, Tri-State Chairman,
January 5, 1962; and Tri-State Transportation Committee, *Prospectus*
(April 1962), pp. 10–11.

and New York, these committees consisted of the heads of each county government in the region; in Connecticut, the chief executives of leading cities in the southwestern part of the state were named. The mayor of New York City designated five department heads to serve as members of his local cooperating committee. Each member of the local cooperating committees was asked to furnish a liaison representative, in the form of a top staff planner or engineer, to the staff of Tri-State. Tri-State was also to work closely with a "technical advisory group" consisting of staff representatives of state, county, city, and federal agencies participating and assisting in the program.

While this formal arrangement would seem to have furnished adequate representation to the region's local governments, in actuality Tri-State maintained no contact with local officials. The technical advisory group convened frequently at meetings which local planners were free to attend, but the local cooperating committees met once for an early briefing and did not meet again— until the summer of 1967. Rather than "encourage the vital interests of the local communities which want to determine their own destinies," as Tri-State's Chairman William J. Ronan alledged it wished to do,[39] Tri-State excluded local interests from its activities, with the exception of a local governmental representative from each state and representatives from New York City who served on the technical advisory committee.

Paradoxically, so far as its own competitive position in the region was concerned, MRC joined RPA in encouraging efforts by the states to create a stronger tri-state agency to handle the planning and operation of the region's commuter railroads. A Tri-State Transportation Commission compact was drawn up in 1963, providing for the establishment of an interstate planning commission, with representation from the states, the federal gov-

[39] William J. Ronan, "The Tri-State Transportation Committee," in *Metropolitan Problems: As Presented by Eight of America's Recognized Experts* (Madison, New Jersey: Drew University, 1963), p. 54. Doig's comments with reference to local participation on Tri-State are instructive: "The new body was not a means for involving local representation in transportation policy-making . . . but primarily a mechanism through which the state capitals would cooperate on mutual problems in the New York region" (*Metropolitan Transportation Politics*, p. 229).

ernment, and New York City. The compact was adopted by the legislatures of the three states in March 1965. (The objections of New Jersey legislators were finally met by depriving the agency of all operating functions and confining it to a planning role.)[40] Tri-State's most recent publication shows a current membership of seventeen commissioners: four from New Jersey (one appointment is still pending), five from New York, five from Connecticut, and three federal representatives. The chairman of the New York City Planning Commission and the mayor of New Haven, Connecticut—both state appointees—presumably represent the interests of the localities.[41]

As late as 1963, Wallace Sayre could suggest that the choice still might be made in the New York metropolitan area between a regional planning agency dominated by the local governments and one directed by the states.[42] By 1965, the region's local governments no longer had a functioning mechanism to represent their communities, and Tri-State had emerged as the official planning body for transportation and land use. In failing to acknowledge an appropriate role for state governments, MRC had isolated itself from existing power centers and programs at the state level. This tended to create a regional vacuum into which the states were able to move with their own agencies.

But the regional situation is far from stabilized. Now that MRC has become a legal body for the first time in its history, a new look will have to be taken (in the final chapter) at a possible accommodation of the interests represented by Tri-State and MRC. The states have strongly asserted their powers in the New York metropolitan region, including the provision of new services. In addition, a number of suggestions have been made with respect to changes in the membership of Tri-State to make it more representative of local interests. However, further discussion of

[40] Part of the reason for the legislative hesitation in New Jersey stemmed from fear that the state would have to help subsidize the New Haven railroad and assist in other New York–Connecticut transportation problems (*New York Times*, March 10, 1965, p. 43).

[41] Tri-State Transportation Commission, *Regional Forecast 1985* (December 1967).

[42] Sayre, "The Metropolitan Regional Council," in *Metropolitan Problems*, p. 73.

emerging regional relationships cannot be undertaken at this point without first directing attention to the third level of government with a stake in metropolitan development. The federal government has been a relatively silent partner in this discussion up to this point, but the silence is illusory. Programs emanating from the federal level have had a pervasive influence upon the pattern of governmental arrangements in the New York metropolitan region.

Federal-Local Relations

Collaboration between the federal government and the localities is not a new phenomenon, despite the lack of direct constitutional relationship. The great expansion of federal programs during the New Deal era acted as a stimulus to the growth of a new set of relationships which provide direct national-urban contact in many fields including housing and urban renewal, open space, transportation, civil defense, airport construction, health, welfare, and hospital construction. Financial assistance from the higher governmental level in the form of grants-in-aid for specific programs has become an important vehicle of intergovernmental cooperation; as urban problems continue to mount, "cooperative federalism" is likely to become even more significant in the American scene.[43]

The increased scope of the national government since World War II has been accompanied by a greater concern with intergovernmental relations as well as a greater interaction among governmental levels. The Commission on Intergovernmental Relations (the Kestnbaum Commission), established by Congress

[43] For a detailed discussion of different aspects of intergovernmental relations in the United States, refer to entire issue of *Annals*, CCCLIX (May 1965), particularly Colman, pp. 24–30; Hart, pp. 147–156; Daniel J. Elazar, "The Shaping of Intergovernmental Relations in the 20th Century," pp. 1–22; and Alan K. Campbell, "National-State-Local Systems of Government and Intergovernmental Aid," pp. 94–106. An excellent summary of federal participation in metropolitan development is provided in Robert H. Connery and Richard H. Leach, *The Federal Government and Metropolitan Areas* (Cambridge: Harvard University Press, 1960); and in Graves, *American Intergovernmental Relations*, particularly Chap. XIX, "Federal-Local Relations," and Chap. XXIII, "Cooperative Federalism."

in 1953, offered many specific recommendations regarding the allocation of functions between the national government and the states, as did the Commission on Organization of the Executive Branch of the Government (the first Hoover Commission) before it. One of the notable results of the Kestnbaum report was the creation by Congress in 1959 of a permanent bi-partisan body of twenty-six members, the Advisory Commission on Intergovernmental Relations, to give continuous study to the relationships among governments at all levels. Since its creation, the Commission has performed valuable service in reviewing different aspects of the complex federal system and making recommendations for cooperative action to meet the needs of an urbanized society.

The Advisory Commission, in common with many other observers of urban affairs, has been outspoken in its recommendations for a review of all federal programs directed toward urban development, so as to promote policy coordination at the federal level and avoid further fragmentation of local governmental units in the metropolitan areas.[44] Steps to implement these recommendations have recently been undertaken. One such step has been the creation of the federal Department of Housing and Urban Development, which brings together all federal assistance programs to urban areas; another is the growing use of "performance requirements" in federal grant-in-aid legislation, through which the national government is trying to ensure that federally aided projects are properly related to each other and to the needs of the local areas to which they are applicable.[45]

An increasing number of federal-grant programs have been

[44] E.g., Advisory Commission, *Periodic Reassessments of Federal Grants-In-Aid to State and Local Governments* (Washington: U.S. Government Printing Office, 1961), pp. 8–11, *Impact of Federal Urban Development Programs on Local Government Organization and Planning*, prepared in cooperation with the Subcommittee on Intergovernmental Relations of the Committee on Government Operations, U.S. Senate (Washington: U.S. Government Printing Office, 1964), p. 2, *Governmental Structure*, p. 43, and *Metropolitan Social and Economic Disparities*, p. 45.

[45] For further discussion, refer to Crouch, *Annals*, CCCLIX (May 1965), 69; and U.S. Senate, Committee on Government Operations, Subcommittee on Intergovernmental Relations, *The Effectiveness of Metropolitan Planning* (Washington: U.S. Government Printing Office, 1964), pp. 99–113.

designed to encourage comprehensive planning at the metropolitan level. The 1954 amendments to the Housing Act of 1949, which authorized planning assistance under its 701 program, marked the first time that financial aid was offered to planning agencies which engaged in area-wide analyses and planning activities. Since that time, federal grants have been contingent upon comprehensive planning activities in a number of functional fields, including the acquisition and development of open space and recreational areas (Federal Housing Act, 1961), highway projects (Federal Aid Highway Act of 1962), transit facilities and equipment (Urban Mass Transportation Act of 1964), and basic water and sewage facilities (Housing and Urban Development Act of 1965, and others).

Federal Aid to Councils of Government

In 1965, federal assistance for comprehensive developmental programs in metropolitan areas was made available to groups such as councils of governments. Section 1102(c) of the Housing and Urban Development Act (Public Law 89–117) amended the federal Housing Act of 1954 by authorizing grants of up to two-thirds of the estimated cost to organizations of public officials representing the political jurisdictions within a metropolitan area. These grants were to assist such organizations in undertaking studies, collecting data, developing regional plans and programs, and engaging in other activities necessary or desirable to the solution of regional problems. While a number of regional councils (notably the Association of Bay Area Governments and the Metropolitan Washington Council of Governments) had participated in federal-grant programs in the past, the 1965 provision was enormously important in focusing public attention on the particular approach to urban problems provided by councils of elected officials.

Councils of governments were given another federal stimulus in 1966. In further encouragement of metropolitan planning activities, section 204(a) of the Demonstration Cities and Metropolitan Development Act (Public Law 89–754) required all applications made after June 30, 1967, for federal grants or loans for any one of thirty-nine specified projects in metropolitan areas to be ". . . submitted for review (and comment)—to any areawide agency which is designated to perform metropolitan or regional planning for the area." Of special importance to councils was the provision calling for the designated review agency to be, ". . . to the greatest practicable extent, composed of or responsible to the elected officials of a unit of areawide government or of the units of general local government within whose jurisdiction such agency is authorized to engage in such planning." By providing councils with the potential function of regional review and co-ordination of local applications for federally aided programs, the federal government increased the strength of councils within their respective metropolitan areas. By late 1967, more than 50 councils of governments had been designated as review agencies in the 233 standard metropolitan statistical areas of the country.[46]

Section 205 of the Demonstration Cities Act takes an additional step toward metropolitan coordination in its offer of financial incentives—in the form of supplementary grants up to 20 per-cent—for federally assisted programs of metropolitan develop-ment which conform to a regional plan. While these monetary inducements have not yet been funded by Congress, it seems evident that the federal government is now insisting on joint planning and cooperation by cities and towns in the metropolitan areas. By virtue of the recent provisions calling for representative area-wide bodies and mandatory area-wide review, state and local governments have received fair warning of the need to plan major services on a regional basis if federal grants are to be forth-coming.[47]

[46] These figures come from *News Service to Regional Councils*, No. 3, September 22, 1967, and No. 5, October 31, 1967. Other review agencies are planning commissions, state planning agencies, transportation study groups, and county governments.

[47] For further consideration of the federal impact upon local govern-mental structure, see Norton E. Long, "The Role of State Government in Regional Development," *The State's Biggest Business—Local and Re-gional Problems*, Policy Papers for the Connecticut Commission to Study the Necessity and Feasibility of Metropolitan Government (January 1967), p. 52; Victor Jones, "State, Local and Federal Relations in Governing Metropolitan Connecticut," *ibid.*, pp. 81–95; and the authors cited in Chap. IX, nn. 6 and 14.

The effect of the recent federal legislation on the use of councils of governments as review agencies is not yet clear. While the federal government appears to consider councils of elected officials as the most suitable agencies for the performance of comprehensive regional planning under the Demonstration Cities Act, it is not certain what type of metropolitan review agency will emerge in the future. The United States Bureau of the Budget, which presently administers section 204, defines an "areawide agency" as an official body which is empowered to perform comprehensive planning (in a metropolitan area), an organization of public officials representative of the political jurisdictions in a metropolitan area, or an agency which is designated by the governor (or governors, in metropolitan areas which cross state lines) to perform comprehensive planning.[48]

The Federal Government and the New York Metropolitan Region

The impact of recent federal legislation in the complex New York metropolitan region is even less certain. A current analysis of the implications of federal review requirements finds that New York is so different from all other metropolitan areas that "any regional review procedure must be tailored to it individually."[49] In the recent past, Region I of the Department of Housing and Urban Development (with headquarters in New York City) has displayed considerable interest in fostering new working re-

[48] U.S. Bureau of the Budget, Circular No. A-82 Revised, "Coordination of Federal Aids in Metropolitan Areas under Section 204 of the Demonstration Cities and Metropolitan Development Act of 1966," December 18, 1967. Refer also to earlier circulars, No. A-80, "Coordination of Development Planning for Programs Based on Multijurisdictional Areas," January 31, 1967, and No. A-82, dealing with the same subject as No. A-82 Revised. Administrative responsibility for section 204 of the Demonstration Cities Act was originally assigned by the Bureau of the Budget to the Department of Housing and Urban Development (HUD). In the appropriation bill for HUD for the fiscal year 1968, the Bureau of the Budget regained this responsibility.

[49] Robert G. Smith, "Implications of the Federal Requirements for Regional Review in the New York Metropolitan Region," New York City, October 1967, p. 5. Unpublished report for Professors in Public Agencies Program.

lationships between the local governmental units and the states, as well as among the local communities themselves in the joint performance of area-wide functions.[50] Faced with a variety of conflicting political institutions, the federal government seems to be inclined to offer financial aid to both state and local agencies and encourage them to work out arrangements for effecting area-wide coordination.

The federal government has given financial support to the Tri-State Transportation Commission since its creation. Established in partial response to the Federal Aid Highway Act of 1962, which required all federally aided highway projects in urbanized areas to be based on a comprehensive transportation planning process after July 1, 1965, Tri-State has received highway-planning aid from the United States Bureau of Public Roads and planning and mass-transportation grants from the Department of Housing and Urban Development (HUD). Federal membership on Tri-State currently includes representatives of HUD, the Federal Aviation Agency, and the Department of Transportation. Tri-State has been designated on an interim basis as the official regional review agency for the New York metropolitan area for all functional fields covered by the Demonstration Cities Act. Because of the size and complexity of the region, and the involvement of three states, each of which is concerned with different problems and programs, state planning offices and county planning agencies are employed by Tri-State in the regional review procedure.

At the same time, in view of its conviction that local governments, along with the states, should be represented on a regional planning body, HUD is also supporting MRC. Mention has already been made in these pages that MRC reconstituted itself as a legal body in late 1966 in order to qualify for financial planning assistance under the 1965 act. MRC submitted an application for federal funds in May 1967 and received a grant of $100,000 in

[50] E.g., Capitol Region Planning Agency, Governmental Functions Committee, *Governmental Organizations for the Capitol Region*, (October 1967), pp. 3.3–3.5. It should be noted that the New York metropolitan area extends into two of HUD's regional offices: Connecticut and New York are in Region I, and New Jersey is in Region II (with a central office in Philadelphia).

March 1968. This federal assistance marks a milestone in the history of MRC; it is the first time that MRC has received formal recognition from the federal level of government since its establishment in 1956.

Federal Response to MRC Prior to 1965

In the past, MRC has had an intermittent and unstructured relationship with the federal government. Its contacts with the federal field offices, from which it received information on a variety of matters, were helpful for the most part. Because of time, distance, and lack of direct personal contact in the nation's capital, its relationships with Washington were spasmodic and uncertain. During its period of greatest activity, the Council attempted to exert pressure with respect to a number of federal programs before many different agencies, including the Senate Commerce Subcommittee, the Senate Housing Subcommittee of the Banking and Currency Committee, the Senate Appropriations Committee, the House Banking and Currency Committee, and the Federal Aviation Agency.[51] MRC corresponded with the federal Department of Health, Education and Welfare in an unsuccessful attempt to secure funds for a comprehensive program for water-pollution control in the tri-state metropolitan area. It also sought to have a new federal water-pollution laboratory and research facility (provided for in the Federal Water Pollution Control Act of July 1961) established in the New York metropolitan area. The Council was unsuccessful in this effort as well; such a laboratory was authorized to be constructed in Boston, Massachusetts, and it encompasses the New York metropolitan area as part of the Northeast region.

There is no evidence to suggest that MRC's stand on regional matters has had any effect on federal legislation. Much has depended on the particular circumstances surrounding the Council's intervention and the allies with which it was aligned. In most

[51] E.g., MRC opposed legislation that would weaken the regulatory powers of the Federal Power Commission over the price of natural gas to be sold in interstate commerce, it sought a review of state and local rail taxes, it campaigned for improved mass-transportation services and increased aid for open-space acquisition in urban areas, and it requested an evaluation of proposals concerning a new airport in the region.

of its public appearances, the Council was represented by either Robert Wagner or Maxwell Lehman in their dual roles as New York City Mayor and City Administrator as well as MRC Chairman and Executive Secretary, respectively. Congressional and bureaucratic reaction to their statements was likely to have been based more on their primary job obligations than on their Council positions. One of the few noteworthy instances in which MRC received satisfaction from a federal agency came when the United States Budget Bureau agreed to maintain the statistical definition of the New York–Northeastern New Jersey metropolitan area. In this instance, MRC received powerful support from the Port of New York Authority, RPA, Congressman James C. Auchincloss of New Jersey, Senators Jacob K. Javits of New York and Clifford P. Case and Harrison A. Williams, Jr., of New Jersey, and members of county planning boards.[52]

All of the Council members were anxious to see MRC expand its activities as a regional spokesman, particularly in terms of articulating regional needs at the Washington level. It was specifically recommended that the Council go further in establishing contacts with other spokesmen for metropolitan programs such as the United States Conference of Mayors, the American Municipal Association, the National Urban League, and the National Municipal League, and assume a leadership position in making the urban voice heard nationally.[53]

Joint Hearings, 1963

MRC had an opportunity to elicit federal support for its regional role in June 1963, when the Senate and House Subcommittees on Intergovernmental Relations, chaired jointly by Senator Edmund S. Muskie and Representative L. H. Fountain, held three days of joint hearings in New York City on the subject of "Federal-State-Local Relationships in the Metropolitan Region." The hearings were part of a series of field surveys conducted to identify the basic problems confronting the various levels of governments in metropolitan areas, and to secure information that would be

[52] See manual, "Measures of Metropolitan Growth," September 22, 1959, prepared jointly by MRC, RPA, and the Port of New York Authority.
[53] Memorandum from Smallwood to Lehman, August 12, 1960.

useful in drafting federal legislation relating to intergovernmental cooperation. Subcommittee members were interested in MRC primarily as an example of efforts to solve metropolitan problems; by highlighting divergent viewpoints from representative officials of state, county, and local governments in New York, New Jersey, and Connecticut, Senator Muskie was hopeful that Congress and the public would gain a *clearer* view of the difficulties created by the emergence of metropolitan regions throughout the country.

The results could not have been farther from the intent. The subcommittees expected a certain amount of controversy to emerge during the course of the testimony, but the number of conflicting and hostile viewpoints that developed about MRC far exceeded expectations. Confusion centered about the kind of decisions that would be made by the Council, the nature of the opposition, the powers that the Council sought, the categories of membership, and its effect on home rule.[54] The result was that many of the Congressmen had difficulty understanding the particular approach to urban problems which MRC represented, and were confused in much the same fashion as the general public.

Subcommittee members were unsure whether MRC was a supergovernment as charged by its opponents, or a valuable advisory forum as its supporters contended. There were no clearcut political lines to guide them. Both Westchester County Executive Edwin Michaelian, a Republican, and Nassau County Executive Eugene Nickerson, a Democrat, testified in favor of the Council. Three Westchester Republican supervisors differed flatly with Michaelian, their Republican County Chairman. (Only the Conservative Party was consistent in its opposition.) Without a solid institutional base of support from federal, state, or local governments, MRC was in a disadvantaged position in defending itself.

A New Pattern of Governmental Arrangements

The regional picture has, of course, changed considerably since 1963. With the creation of HUD, MRC now has a strong poten-

[54] *Joint Hearings: Government in Metropolitan Areas* (1963), pp. 32, 37, 38, 40, 95, 182–185, 203, and 249.

tial ally in representing the New York metropolitan view before Congress and the federal agencies in Washington, and in helping its members comply with federal requirements affecting metropolitan areas. The states, too, are on the move and have established new institutional arrangements to deal with metropolitan areas in their midst. In addition, the states have interjected themselves massively into the regional transportation arena and may do the same with respect to other functional fields. The Tri-State Transportation Commission has become the coordinating layer between the states and the localities. It is ironic that, by contributing to the formation of this new agency, MRC helped to ensure the presence of a competing organization that would make its own existence precarious.

Intervention by other levels of government has thus been instrumental in reshaping the region that a reconstituted MRC must face. Another look will be taken at current governmental patterns in the New York metropolitan area in the concluding chapter; at this stage of our study it would be premature to consider the implications of recent developments. The Council which was created in 1956 was confronted with a different political field and different power centers, and many of these contributed to the failure of the initial attempt. A further look must now be taken at more of the early problems since they presage the kind of pressures with which any council of governments—with or without federal backing—must deal in order to survive.

VI

POLITICAL OBSTACLES

No Political Guidelines

MRC's experience with competing regional agencies indicates that voluntary councils must carefully consider the political limits of the programs they can undertake. The region is not a mechanical structure, but an enormous complex of individual and group relationships. It is not easy for an informal planning group, engaged in the complexities and demands of its day-to-day activities, to develop support from the activists, or the people in the community who make the decisions. Each council must be flexible and expert enough to accommodate itself to the particular environment in which it exists. The approach must be geared to local needs and must include an intimate knowledge of the limits of acceptability. These considerations are unusually important, and complicated, in the New York metropolitan region, where the political environment encompasses an infinite number of shifting decision centers, including those of the federal government, three state governments, and 1,500 local governments.[1]

The preceding chapter notes the absence of political forces at the state level agitating for regional reform. With a diffusion of

---

[1] Refer to Scott, *Two Notes on Metropolitan Research*, p. 16, for discussion of the many variables which bear on the making of decisions in metropolitan areas. For accounts of differences in the decision-making frameworks of the various governments in the New York metropolitan region, see Campbell and Sacks, *Public Administration Review*, XXIV, (September 1964), 141–152; and Sayre and Kaufman, *Governing New York City*, pp. 710–716. In Wood's opinion, "the assembling of a coalition of effective political figures" in the New York metropolitan region is "perhaps the most formidable obstacle to changing the structure or the philosophy of the region's governments" (*1400 Governments*, p. 193).

power and political party members at varying governmental levels, neither of the political parties had much integrating influence. For the greater part of MRC's first ten years, there was a constant clash of interests between the Republican-controlled New York State legislature and Democratic-dominated New York City. There was further conflict, and partisan differences, between New York City and many of the surrounding communities.[2] Even where the political affiliation was the same, however, the influence of the political party was not controlling. Increasing urbanization has caused the traditional city-suburban conflict to become more severe, and the central city party has come to be more and more regarded as a threat to local security.[3]

Moreover, in the New York metropolitan region, party organizations of three states are involved, and there is no party uniformity or attention devoted to the issue of regional cooperation. At the joint congressional hearings, political party lines were ignored as opposing views were taken by fellow party members. Even in those instances where community-wide goals were espoused by important political figures, local party leaders saw little profit for themselves in supporting reform which might disturb the pattern of party politics. In the absence of intelligent deliberation of issues and policies at the local level, regional cooperation often became subject to factional attack, with debate revolving around personalities and irrelevant considerations rather than focusing on cooperation itself.[4]

Wagner the Image of MRC?

Mayor Wagner's actions in suggesting and supporting MRC have

[2] In contrast with this, Martin and his colleagues find that the Republican party organization, dominant in both the city and suburban governments in the Syracuse metropolitan area, has been a potent influence in encouraging metropolitan action. In addition, Republican state legislators have been in close contact with Republican legislators in Syracuse and have generally given them and their proposals a warm reception in Albany (*Decisions in Syracuse*, p. 155). For further discussion of the same point, see Herman, *New York State*, p. 179; and Willbern, in *Metropolitan Issues*, ed. Birkhead, p. 59.

[3] For confirmation of this point, see Bollens (ed.), *Exploring the Metropolitan Community*, p. 83; and Martin et al., *Decisions in Syracuse*, p. 229.

[4] E.g., following a visit in 1960 to Edward Carey, Director of the Board of Freeholders of Hudson County, Frank Smallwood pointed out that "a

been termed acts of "considerable imagination and boldness."[5] But his retention of the post of MRC chairman from 1956 to the mid-1960s caused hard feelings which were damaging to the Council itself. Because of the social and economic pressures besetting the central city, Wagner viewed regional problems from a different perspective from the state governments and did not hesitate to criticize the "crippling . . . overlordship of [New York] State over the cities."[6] Since Wagner was the most important political figure of the region as well as the personification of the regional approach, it was inevitable that MRC become involved in the city-state fight. In 1962, Wagner made the situation a little tougher for the Council than it might have been by writing a magazine article for the Sunday *Times*, forecasting that the New York City of the future would be a "supercity," requiring a "supergovernment to which all local governments in the area— along with the three state governments of New York, New Jersey, and Connecticut—will have to yield some of their present authority."[7]

Publication of this article by the MRC chairman also alarmed suburban communities whose concept of the "public interest" differed from that of the central city.[8] In fielding the many questions that arose concerning Mayor Wagner's lengthy tenure as chairman, the assistant executive secretary of MRC explained that the composition of the board of directors had remained static since 1957 because the members were considered "temporary"

---

major problem in Hudson County—MRC relationships was Mayor Witkowski of Jersey City." Carey felt that Witkowski "was ruining Jersey City" and was hesitant about getting involved with any group in which Witkowski was active (Smallwood, MRC, Interview Data No. 3, August 3, 1960).

[5] Sayre, in *Metropolitan Problems*, p. 67.

[6] *Joint Hearings: Government in Metropolitan Areas* (1963), p. 27. For further discussion of the traditional cleavages between the central cities and the states in the New York region, refer to Danielson, *Federal-Metropolitan Politics*, p. 186.

[7] "Forecast of New York in 2012 A.D.," *New York Times Magazine*, October 7, 1962, p. 47. See also statement by William Cassella that "many upstate people consider MRC a publicity gimmick for Robert Wagner and Edwin Michaelian" (record of a telephone conversation with Prager, December 11, 1962).

[8] For further discussion of this point, see Banfield and Wilson, *City Politics*, p. 46, and other authors mentioned in Chap. III, n. 4.

pending formal legal status for MRC. Once ratified, the new interlocal agreement would limit the term of executive board members to one year.[9]

A number of advisors to MRC suggested periodically that prolongation of this "temporary" situation might serve as a stumbling block to popular acceptance. George Deming, then with the Conference on Metropolitan Area Problems, wondered if Wagner's continuation as chairman might not be regarded as "self-serving," and William Cassella, of the National Municipal League, proposed that Wagner should "make a public statement offering to step down as chairman . . . when the interlocal agreement is finally ratified and that the executive secretary should do the same. (However, the statement should guarantee New York's money and participation as usual.)"[10] Frederick Zimmerman of Hunter College noted that "murmurs for a rotating chairman" had been heard more than once, and wondered if New York City insisted on retaining the leadership because it was contributing most of the funds.[11] The minutes of a meeting of advisors who were called together in 1964 to discuss MRC's reorganization note specific agreement on limiting the tenure of the chairman in the new charter, so that the job might be open to all. It was further agreed that the executive secretary should be an employee of MRC and paid by the Council itself.[12]

While there seems to be general agreement that MRC needed a rotating chairman, many observers currently disagree about whether anyone else would have been willing to accept the post. W. Bernard Richland, former legal counsel to MRC, and Edwin Michaelian, former Vice-Chairman of MRC, doubt whether anyone else would have been able to serve as chairman while New York City was maintaining the secretariat. On the other hand, John Keith of RPA and Leslie Slote, former Senior Management Consultant in the Office of the City Administrator, feel that a new chairman could have been found had the position definitely

[9] Letter from Prager to Richard P. Dyckman, Plainfield, New Jersey, March 5, 1963.

[10] Telephone conversation between Prager and Cassella, December 11, 1962.

[11] Telephone interview with Zimmerman, February 16, 1966.

[12] Minutes of meeting of September 10, 1964.

been made available.[13] Reconstruction on the basis of past recollections is hazardous; the important point is that member governments needed reassurance concerning their fear of domination by New York City and this was not furnished.[14]

Determination of a proper role for a central city in a council of governments is not easy or precise. When MRC was reconstituted as a legal entity in 1966, Mayor John V. Lindsay of New York City was designated Chairman, and Mathias L. Spiegel, then First Deputy City Administrator, assumed the post of Executive Secretary. Lindsay did nothing to allay the fears of suburban communities by asserting, in his initial speech as MRC Chairman, his hope of establishing "a working relationship [between New York City and the outlying areas] to develop concepts and policies which have the force of *law* behind them" (italics mine). When Lindsay spoke, in addition, of "the region's responsibility to the core city," his words took on added significance, coming as they did shortly after passage by the New York legislature of the commuter tax which was levied on the region's suburban communities.[15]

On the other hand, it is essential that the central city play an important role in the new MRC, and New York City has demonstrated its recognition of this need. The city was one of the first members to pay its annual dues for 1967–68, a cash contribution of $40,000, and this acted as a stimulus for governments outside New York City to follow suit.[16] Had the region's central city

[13] Interviews with Richland, September 26, 1967; Michaelian, April 12, 1966; Keith, April 22, 1966; and Slote, May 5, 1966. Both Keith and Slote felt that Karl Metzger would have accepted the post had it been offered at an appropriate time.

[14] In this connection, note Martin's description of the Salem, Oregon, city manager, "father" of the Mid-Williamette Valley Council of Governments, who consistently refused to take any action which might result in fear of domination by the city of Salem over the surrounding communities. To Martin, the manager's novel conception of himself as a citizen of the region as well as the city was in large measure responsible for the success of the Council in Salem (*Metropolis in Transition*, p. 37).

[15] Address to MRC members, June 20, 1966. For further discussion of New York City's position in relation to MRC, see Chap. IX, pp. 217–218. See also Hanson, *Metropolitan Councils of Governments*, p. 20.

[16] Lindsay said, "We can't expect local governments of the region to come in unless New York City puts its money on the line" (*New York Times*, October 29, 1966, p. 31).

failed to set an example for its parochially minded neighbors, MRC could not have been relaunched with any hope of success. The new by-laws of the Council, adopted March 3, 1967, limit the terms of MRC's board of directors to one year, and provide for the annual election of chairman and vice-chairman. A new executive director of MRC was named in January 1968, and the Council moved out of the City Administrator's office to a new location in the city.

Shifting Membership

In sharp contrast to the long tenure of Mayor Wagner as MRC Chairman were the relatively brief terms in office of other members of MRC's executive board. In 1962, the Council's executive board of nine members received three newcomers as a result of local elections. By 1966, only three of the 1962 officers remained on the board, and County Executive Michaelian was the only holdover from the 1960 executive board. There were seven changes in the MRC roster of membership in November 1967, and four new vacancies were created on the executive board.

This turnover in membership was a continuing problem. The November 1959 MRC *Bulletin* listed eight changes in representation on the Council as a result of the 1959 elections. (Of the seventeen member units which had held elections for their top elective positions, eight did not reelect their incumbents.) The November 1961 *Bulletin* listed another three representatives who replaced existing members. At the April 1964 membership meeting, the executive secretary felt compelled to devote the greater part of his remarks to an account of the history, guiding principles, accomplishments, and future plans of the Council, since the 1963 elections had caused a turnover of more than one-third of the chief elected officers of the region.

The shifting membership caused severe disruption to Council programs. The results of the November 1963 elections were particularly acute, since MRC lost a number of devoted, hardworking friends. Foremost among these was Griffith Harris, former First Selectman of Greenwich, who lost his bid for the Republican nomination because of the question of MRC affiliation. Harris had been in office for six years and was very active in MRC committee work, particularly in the field of recreation and land use. His replacement by a right-wing Republican meant the end not only of Greenwich involvement in MRC but also of close MRC-RPA collaborative effort on the open-space needs of the region.[17] Another staunch supporter of the concept of regional cooperation, Karl E. Metzger, Chairman of the Committee on the Future of the MRC during the long, trying period that the Council attempted to secure legal status, decided to relinquish his post as Chairman of the Board of Freeholders in Middlesex County, New Jersey, in 1963, in order to devote full time to his position as Secretary of Rutgers University.

The large number of new officials presented by local elections necessitated continuing educational efforts by MRC. Some newly elected officials knew MRC only as an attempt at supergovernment and a violation of home rule. Others were unconcerned about regional cooperation and were not likely to regard it as a major issue if, indeed, they wondered about it at all. The indoctrinating efforts had to be geared to a wide range of divergent attitudes since MRC communities were headed by officials of sharply dissimilar competence and training. In 1966, for example, the director of the Board of Freeholders in Passaic County was the owner of a chain of bakeries, the mayor of Morristown was a stockbroker, the director of the Monmouth Board of Freeholders owned a yacht basin, and the mayor of Plainfield, New Jersey, was a full-time insurance attorney who practiced in Newark. All of these men were part-time office holders, who met with their fellow Council members an average of once a week.[18]

Because of the short terms and relatively heavy turnover of the region's officials, there was little evidence among them of a

[17] For a detailed description of the MRC Recreation and Land Use Committee, see Chap. VIII, pp. 188–192.

[18] The office holders described here are Joseph Lazzara, J. Raymond Manahan, Joseph G. Irwin, and Robert C. Maddox, respectively. Job descriptions were furnished by Prager, April 7, 1966. For further discussion concerning the varying attitudes of public officials, refer to Robert W. McCulloch, "Intergovernmental Relations as Seen by Public Officials," *Annals*, CCCLIX (May 1965), 128.

feeling of metropolitan consciousness. Council members had their primary positions to maintain, with obligations to their own constituencies. When Council membership became a political liability at election time, as it did to six MRC members in 1962, regional cooperation commanded little, if any, overt support.[19]

A voluntary council must convince dissimilar public officials of the potential benefits to be gained from regional partnership. During the early 1960s, this was an unrewarding assignment since the Council was engaged in little constructive work. The present political climate should make the task easier, now that the federal government is requiring joint effort for a large number of metropolitan programs. Recent observers presently find a greater interest in regional organizations among local officials.[20] If MRC becomes a more prestigious organization and mounts programs of tangible worth, the advantages of membership will be self-evident.

Local Legislative Bodies:
A Failure of Political Communication

If cooperative relationships between local governments are to lead to meaningful programs, *all* of the members of local governing bodies must be involved, as well as the chief elected officials who are members of a voluntary council. In the New York metropolitan region, county boards of supervisors play a

[19] In 1962, the mayors of Hoboken, Jersey City, Linden, and Morristown, New Jersey; New Rochelle, New York; and Stamford, Connecticut, felt that regional cooperation was so controversial an issue that they did not present the interlocal agreement to their respective legislative bodies until after local elections had been held. This tactic delayed consideration of the agreement in these communities by almost a year, and, in turn, it delayed consideration by Hudson County, New Jersey, which was willing to vote for ratification only if Jersey City did so first. For an excellent analysis of the difficulties in developing metropolitan viewpoints among public officials, refer to Hanson, *The Politics of Metropolitan Cooperation*, pp. 70–71.
[20] *News Service to Regional Councils*, No. 6, December 26, 1967. Also refer to Royce Hanson, "Councils of Governments and the Demise of Service Regionalism," address delivered at the annual conference of the American Society for Public Administration (ASPA), Boston, Massachusetts, March 29, 1968.

large role in formulating metropolitan decisions. Because of the structure of the boards, the members represent towns and cities according to geographical boundaries, and tend to examine proposals in terms of costs and benefits to their own communities. While all legislative bodies display this tendency to some degree, it has been said that "the representative base of the Board of Supervisors has the effect of elevating local loyalty to the status of the primary political virtue."[21] The characteristically negative attitudes of local legislative bodies are likely to be reinforced by pressure from civic groups, taxpayer groups, associations of public officials and employees, and extremist groups, when any of them feels that their specific interests in the status quo are challenged.[22]

A conspicuous failure of communication became evident in the cooperative effort in the New York–New Jersey–Connecticut region at the time of ratification of the proposed interlocal agreement. Up to this time, MRC had prided itself on having done its best to "observe the niceties of democratic procedure, full discussion, open debate, and sensitivity to the needs of local elected officials."[23] However, when the interlocal agreement was submitted to the local legislative bodies for ratification, they proved reluctant to act and were especially subject to the arguments of opponents. Many of the elected executive officials, active themselves in MRC and strongly supporting its work, had failed to communicate word of their involvement to the legislative officials of their local communities. In some cases, even where the mayor or the county head was directly engaged in regional activities, his local council or board of supervisors was hardly aware of MRC's existence.

The Council had engaged in no effort of its own to involve

[21] Martin et al., *Decisions in Syracuse*, p. 225. (Now that the Supreme Court has ruled in *Avery* v. *Midland County*, 390 U.S. 474 [1968], that if county, city, and town governments elect their representatives from single-member districts, the districts must be substantially equal in population, the membership of local legislative bodies will no longer be able to remain as described herein.)

[22] See the Advisory Commission, *Factors Affecting Voter Reactions*, p. 20, for further discussion of this point.

[23] Interview with Lehman, April 19, 1963. The remainder of this paragraph is derived from his comments as well.

the legislative officials either. An invitation from MRC in June 1962 to the supervisors of the cities and towns of Long Beach, Glen Cove, Hempstead, and Oyster Bay, all members of the Nassau County Board of Supervisors, to attend an MRC meeting and observe the Council in action, was the first time direct contact was made with local members of legislative bodies. Unfortunately, the meeting to which they were invited did not take place until nine months later, by which time MRC affiliation had already been voted down by their Westchester and Suffolk counterparts. At the March 1963 meeting, the executive secretary conceded that MRC had made a "serious error" in originally setting itself up as an organization of communities represented by their elected chief executives: "The Council should also have included the legislative branch of government."[24]

To remedy the inadequate briefing of legislative officials, a meeting was scheduled for December 1963, under the sponsorship of Paul Screvane, then President of the New York City Council, to which all of the members of all of the legislative bodies in the region were to be invited. This was planned as an all-day session, with discussions on the outstanding regional problems by panels which would be evenly balanced politically, geographically, and in the proportion of city to county representatives. After-dinner speeches were to center around the topic of "Federal Aspects of Regional Cooperation" with participation by senators from the three states, five of whom had expressed themselves in favor of metropolitan cooperation.[25] Unfortunately, plans for the meeting were terminated due to a general lack of

[24] Minutes of MRC membership meeting, March 19, 1963. Charlton Chute, Professor of Public Administration at New York University, regards the exclusion of legislative officials from MRC activities as a "fatal blunder" (interview, August 24, 1966). The sending of letters of invitation to Nassau officials was in line with a recommendation made earlier by William Cassella that Nassau municipalities ought to be approached singly for membership in view of the hopelessness of securing ratification of the interlocal agreement by the Nassau Board of Supervisors (December 11, 1962).

[25] Senators Clifford P. Case and Harrison A. Williams, Jr., of New Jersey, Kenneth B. Keating and Jacob K. Javits of New York, and Abraham A. Ribicoff of Connecticut. Senator Thomas J. Dodd of Connecticut never took a public stand on MRC.

interest within the New York City administration, and it was never held.

It is clear that regional cooperation must cultivate the good will, understanding, and assistance of local political leaders if it is to be successful. This involves, at the very minimum, communicating with legislative bodies and keeping them continuously informed. Preferably, legislators should be encouraged to participate freely in regional activities.[26] It seems worthy of note that Lowell B. Weicker, who defeated MRC supporter Griffith Harris for the Republican nomination for First Selectman of Greenwich—after having characterized MRC as an "attempt at supergovernment dominated by New York City"—came to the MRC meeting in April 1964 and stated publicly that he would not object to joining if the Council were to revise its by-laws and intentions as announced.[27] Another regional council, the Mid-Willamette Valley Council of Governments, modified its compact to provide that legislative bodies of the respective governments should name representatives to the Council. A commissioner who had been critical of the Council's organization and procedure was appointed to membership in the administrative committee (Salem's equivalent of MRC's executive board) and became a supporter of the Council.[28] Perhaps legislative officials in the New York area might have reacted more favorably had

[26] See discussion by Crouch, *Annals*, CCCLIX (May, 1965), 67; and Citizens Research Council of Michigan, "Research Brief on Selection of Representation to Serve on Major Policy Bodies," mimeographed (Detroit, 1966), pp. 1, 2, and 12.

[27] *Stamford Advocate*, April 27, 1964, p. 1. See also Hanson's account of the experience of Dr. Thomas Wilson, member of the County Council of Montgomery County, Maryland, who was opposed to membership in the Metropolitan Washington Council of Governments. When prevailed upon to participate in Council activities (simply because Montgomery County's membership was paid between March and July 1963), he became "favorably impressed" with the Council's work and decided he wished to preserve Montgomery County's membership. When the issue of withdrawal came up before his local body for a final vote, Wilson voted with the Democratic minority against his Republican colleagues in favor of retaining membership (*The Politics of Metropolitan Cooperation*, p. 57).

[28] Martin feels that this change in organization was influential in engendering new support for the Salem Council (*Metropolis in Transition*, p. 35).

MRC been willing to modify its mode of operation at a sufficiently early date to make a difference.

Westchester: Unbalanced Participation in MRC

The lack of communication between legislative and executive branches of government was particularly striking in Westchester County, where the executive branch participated actively in work of the Council and the Board of Supervisors was singularly uninformed. In 1958, Westchester representation on MRC committees included the county executive who was a member of the executive board and of the Traffic and Transportation Committee; the assistant to the county executive, likewise a member of the Traffic and Transportation Committee; the county director of planning, who served as secretary of the Housing and Redevelopment Committee; the Westchester parkway police chief, member of the Traffic and Transportation Committee; the county recreation superintendent, member of the Recreation and Land Use Committee; and the county public works commissioner, on the Water Supply Committee. Two more county officials, the general superintendent of the Westchester Park Commission and the Westchester health commissioner, gained membership on the Recreation Committee and the Air Pollution Committee, respectively, a short time later. Other MRC members from Westchester, but not part of the county government, included the city manager and mayor of Yonkers, and the mayor, corporation counsel, and a councilman from White Plains, all of whom were members of different committees. This participation continued unabated: in 1962, for example, Westchester attendance at a general MRC membership meeting included the foregoing county officials plus eight additional staff members.

In 1963, however, County Executive Michaelian admitted to the joint congressional hearings that: "Perhaps the Council by its own operation created its own problem. Members of the legislative branches of member municipalities should have been invited to participate. . . ." Michaelian regarded MRC membership as desirable and deplored the fact that he could not "sell this to the people because the supervisors themselves did not understand the motives of MRC. . . ."[29] Certainly, some of the Westchester supervisors seemed unaware of MRC's aims and objectives in their testimony before the congressional subcommittees. Eastchester Supervisor Francis X. O'Rourke, for example, explained that the majority of the Westchester Board of Supervisors was opposed to MRC because of the great "suspicions and distrust . . . in surrendering to a group of 'experts' our delegated powers as elected officials in a particular subdivision of government. . . . Since the elected officials, particularly in Westchester County, . . . would [not] have time to attend MRC meetings, . . . the entire operation of MRC would be under the executive director."[30]

It is interesting to note that, in 1966, Michaelian no longer advocated participation in Council activities by members of his Board of Supervisors. At this time, he thought: "Where legislators wield executive powers in their own towns and legislative powers in the County, they will [inevitably] display a lack of interest [in County affairs]." From Michaelian's point of view as County Executive, many of the supervisors had "deep-rooted prejudices against MRC. . . . 'I'm going to run my town my own way' was the typical attitude," and it would have remained thus, even after MRC participation. He felt that supervisors with a more progressive philosophy would have supported MRC in any event.[31] Michaelian's change in point of view over the years may be a reaction to the present composition of the Westchester Board of Supervisors, which has demonstrated great resistance to some of his most cherished proposals, including the matter of its own reapportionment.

Political Opportunism: The Westchester Story

Although MRC attempted to be free of partisan political considerations in its policy determinations and actions, it could not always operate in nonpartisan fashion. A council must constantly

[29] *Joint Hearings: Government in Metropolitan Areas* (1963), pp. 165–166 and 171.

[30] *Ibid.*, p. 285.

[31] Interview with Michaelian, April 12, 1966.

test the political atmosphere by talking with elected officials, familiarizing itself with local newspapers, observing local political trends, and timing action accordingly. MRC's unwillingness to enter the political arena, and its failure to recognize the factional political battles into which its own cause might be drawn, played a large part in its inability to maintain itself as a functioning organization. An illuminating example of professionalism versus partisan political action is furnished in the case of Westchester County, which follows.

Westchester County, a suburb of New York City noted for its rural character, upper middle-class population, and resistance to the outward movement of people and industry from New York, became a charter member of MRC in 1956. James D. Hopkins, then Westchester County Executive, drew up a joint policy statement and a proposal for continued action at the first MRC meeting. When Hopkins resigned to accept an appointment as a judge, his successor, Edwin G. Michaelian, took an active role in Council affairs. The position of Vice-Chairman of MRC was created in February 1960, and Michaelian assumed the post and helped to draft the interlocal agreement. Michaelian first proposed the matter of MRC affiliation in his annual message to his Board of Supervisors in April 1962, stating in part: "There are many problems common to all levels of government that do not recognize geographical boundaries. . . . The MRC . . . is an example of governmental cooperation at the top area level. This body is not a supergovernment nor is it so intended. . . . We do not wish to lose our identity as an individual county with our own right of self-determination . . . and become part of a huge metropolitan complex or the City of New York."

In June 1962, the County Executive requested approval from his Board of Supervisors "to contract to continue as an active, participating and contributing member of the New York Metropolitan Regional Council." In his request, Michaelian pointed out that the secretarial and staff work had been carried on by members of the staff of the mayor of New York City from 1956 to the present. He suggested that beginning in 1963 the county should contribute to the MRC budget an amount not to exceed $.01 per resident of the county as per the 1960 census of 808,891 residents, or approximately $8,090. Michaelian indicated that the county might voluntarily withdraw from participation any time it wished. Failure to pay a member's share toward the Council's budget would be tantamount to withdrawal. If the Council showed signs of developing into a "super or new layer of government," Michaelian said, "Westchester should and would withdraw."[32]

At the public hearing held in September 1962 on the proposal to have Westchester join MRC, eight speakers denounced the Council "as a stepping stone to socialism, communism, fascist dictatorship and ultimate abolition of all home rule." Mayor Milton A. Gibbons of Tuckahoe told the Board of Supervisors that "consolidation of local offices, abolition of county lines and elimination of officials is the plan. . . . Step by step the plan is to continue until this reaches the state levels and the state constitutions, then eventually the national level and the national constitution."[33] Only two persons spoke for MRC, Mrs. Jewel Bellush of Pelham, Professor of Political Science at Hunter College, and John Keith of Hartsdale, presently Vice-President of RPA. The small turnout was "disappointing" to at least one member of the board, and interested persons were asked to express their opinions to the supervisors.[34] Such opinions were expressed at a rally held two weeks later under the sponsorship of "The Committee for the Preservation of Home Rule," where about fifty persons called on the Board of Supervisors to vote down any involvement in metropolitan regional government, "a socialistic move potentially involving the confiscation of private property."[35]

Political pressure centering about MRC mounted in Westchester between September 1962 and March 1963. A news article appearing at the end of September described the "growing sentiment" among members of the Board of Supervisors, both Republicans and Democrats, to refuse the county permission to join

[32] Letter from Michaelian to the Board of Supervisors of Westchester County, June 4, 1962.

[33] Merrill Folsom, "Regional Unit Called Dictatorial as Westchester Debates Joining," *New York Times*, September 11, 1962, p. 35.

[34] *Tarrytown Daily News*, September 12, 1962. The board member in question was D. Anthony Attisani, Democrat, from New Rochelle.

[35] *Reporter Dispatch* (White Plains), September 28, 1962.

MRC, which could "lead to a clash between Michaelian and the Board."[36] By November, affiliation with MRC was termed "the hottest issue before the Westchester Board of Supervisors."[37] Republican supervisors expressed relief when an appropriation for MRC dues was not included in the new county budget. Thus a showdown was temporarily averted between those opposed and those in favor. To veteran reporter Milton Hoffman, this appeared to be one of the few times that the Democrats, with eleven members on the forty-five member board, "could swing the vote either way."[38]

In February, Harrison Republicans agreed unanimously that "we in Westchester do not want to be swept under the rug by New York City."[39] A few days later the 11th Ward Republican Club in Yonkers voted a resolution against joining. During most of this time the issue remained tied up in the Budget and Appropriations Committee of the Board of Supervisors, which was composed of nine Republicans and three Democrats. Either a deadlock or a seven-to-five vote either way was predicted for the Budget Committee, "provided that the Democrats line up against the Michaelian administration."[40]

At the end of February, the Budget Committee of the Board of Supervisors recommended by a six-to-five vote (the twelfth member was absent) that the board authorize Westchester County to join MRC on a formal dues-paying basis. In submitting its report (called the "Berman report" after the Chairman of the Board of Supervisors), the proponents of MRC (all Republicans) suggested two amendments to the interlocal agreement to meet objections raised by the anti-MRC forces. Three Democrats joined with two Republicans to cast the minority vote and to submit their own recommendations, known as the "O'Rourke report," after the Republican Supervisor from Eastchester, Chairman of the Budget Committee. This latter report pointed out that, since changes in the agreement were contemplated, a

[36] *Tarrytown Daily News*, September 29, 1962.
[37] *Reporter Dispatch*, November 7, 1962.
[38] *Ibid.*
[39] *Reporter Dispatch*, February 21, 1963.
[40] Milton Hoffman, "County Nears MRC Showdown," *Reporter Dispatch*, February 23, 1963.

new public hearing would be necessary before the final vote was taken or the agreement would be illegal. The county attorney's opinion was to be sought on this matter.

The final vote was to be taken by the Board of Supervisors in a week. Each side felt that it had about nineteen votes; the remaining members were "fence-sitters." It was claimed that "tremendous political pressures" were being brought against Republican members, with Michaelian's prestige "riding on the vote." The Democrats reported "getting calls from the strangest places. . . ." As the deadline grew near, Hoffman wrote, "Probably no other issue in this decade has split the Republican party as has MRC."[41]

A legal opinion from the corporation counsel of Yonkers that the city of Yonkers was not properly a member of MRC gave opponents on the Board of Supervisors "new ammunition and possibly new strength."[42] In a letter sent in reply to a question raised by a Democratic member of the board, the counsel advised that, while the Common Council of Yonkers had approved the provisions set forth in the interlocal agreement establishing the MRC (in April 1962), the city had not complied with all the provisions of the New York State General Municipal Law. Also, Yonkers had ratified before New Jersey had approved the enabling legislation. The counsel's ruling was significant because the Yonkers block of twelve supervisors, six Republicans and six Democrats, could hold the key to the vote in the board on March 4th, three days hence.

At this time there was a dispute in the Board of Supervisors over whether a simple majority or a two thirds vote of the forty-five members was needed for passage of the bill. Opponents maintained that, since budget funds were involved, at least two-

---

[41] Milton Hoffman, "MRC Advocates Win 1st Bout," *Reporter Dispatch*, February 26, 1963. The other quotations in this paragraph come from the same article.

[42] *Herald Statesman* (Yonkers), March 1, 1963. Later in March 1963, the Yonkers Common Council asked the city manager to direct the corporation counsel to prepare the necessary legislation to make Yonkers a full partner in MRC. The legislation was referred to the Committee of the Whole of the Common Council and was never reported out.

thirds of the supervisors must approve. Tension mounted as Leonard Berman, Republican from Mount Vernon, ruled that twenty-three out of forty-five votes were needed to settle the board's resolution to join. Even if some supervisors were ill or absent, a majority of the total number was necessary. According to surveys made by local newspaper reporters, eleven supervisors had made public statements against the Council, with seven in favor.[43] The vote was shaping up as a "photo-finish climax," which was likely to be settled by a few votes in either direction.[44] The Democrats still had not committed themselves as a party. Five were against MRC as a formal agency, and the other six, all from Yonkers, had not taken a definite stand.

The Westchester Vote

On March 4, 1963, the Board of Supervisors rejected affiliation with MRC on a formal dues-paying basis after four hours of bitter debate. Over 100 people, the largest audience ever to attend a Board of Supervisors meeting, were present and applauded all persons opposed to MRC. Personal denunciations were made against Maxwell Lehman, John Keith, Wallace Sayre, and others. Only two supervisors, Rudolph P. Berle of Scarsdale and Mizell Wilson of White Plains (both Republicans), deplored the arguments being made and attempted to use a reasoned approach in explaining their positions.[45]

Parliamentary maneuvering resulted in numerous ballots. With three supervisors absent, two of whom were known to be in favor of MRC, proponents of MRC sought originally to recommit the matter to the Budget Committee on the basis that no legal ruling had yet been made as to whether or not a public hearing was necessary because of the two amendments proposed in the Berman report. The motion to recommit was lost by a tie

[43] *Ibid.*

[44] *Reporter Dispatch*, March 4, 1963.

[45] Milton Hoffman, "Supervisors Veto MRC Plan," *Reporter Dispatch*, March 5, 1963. Also see memorandum from Prager to Lehman concerning the vote by Westchester Board of Supervisors, following a conversation with James Steed, Assistant to the County Executive, March 5, 1963.

vote of twenty-one to twenty-one. Proponents then sought to have the matter tabled, and this failed by a vote of twenty-three to nineteen. The board next voted on whether to accept the Berman report (the majority vote of the Budget Committee, supporting MRC), and this lost thirty-eight to two. (According to supervisor Berle, this was not a vote against MRC as such, but rather an indication of unwillingness to act without a public hearing, or a ruling that a public hearing was not necessary.) The fourth vote, on whether to accept the O'Rourke report (the minority report of the Budget Committee, and a clear-cut rejection of formal participation in the Council), won by thirty-two to seven. This vote was also misleading. It could have been interpreted as opposition to MRC or as opposition to MRC under the original agreement without amendment. (To supervisor Berle, it could not be regarded as a decisive vote against formal participation in MRC, "since the motive for a vote might well relate only to the content of the unamended agreement.")[46]

Internecine Slaughter in Westchester

Had the first motion to recommit the majority report received one more affirmative vote, MRC would probably have remained alive in Westchester. Since two of the three missing supervisors were ill and unable to attend (the third missing board member died on the day the vote was taken), Berle and Hoffman believe that the defeat was, in large part, due to fortuitous circumstances. From his vantage point, the county executive claimed that he "did not want to make it a partisan measure and push it through."[47] (It might be questioned, however, whether Michaelian's estimate of his political influence in this particular matter might not have been somewhat overrated.)

Party discipline broke in Westchester as the twelve or so Re-

---

[46] Rudolph P. Berle, "Review of MRC 'Fight,'" *Scarsdale Inquirer*, March 21, 1963. Berle felt that the vote on the motion to recommit the majority report, which ended in a tie, was "the more significant measure of the opinion of the Board on this question."

[47] Interview with Michaelian, April 12, 1966.

publicans who opposed Michaelian found themselves on the same side with the Democrats on every vote against MRC. "Of all the people who were definitely committed (one week before) to vote for MRC, only one person actually voted for it."[48] White Plains Republicans had voted previously to join MRC on behalf of their city, but only two of their three supervisors on the county board voted in favor of MRC. The rejection appeared to be a personal affront to the county executive as "a number of supervisors expressed the belief that the display of independence will put Mr. Michaelian on guard that they are not rubber stamps for administration plans."[49]

The *New York Times* attributed much of the opposition to "political opportunism: Supervisors seeking higher posts were said to believe that Mr. Michaelian might retire soon as the county executive or as the Republican chairman. It was also suggested that one or two county commissioners were about to retire and that this inspired a grasping for leadership under the popular home-rule banner."[50] The *New York Daily News* reported in its columns: "You wouldn't believe it department: . . . The eyebrows were raised . . . because Michaelian's very own palace guard voted it down. The action is interpreted by many as a weakening of Michaelian's iron grip. . . . [Michaelian] is said to covet the title role of a suburban Robert Moses, in planning the metropolis of the future. . . . Michaelian's defeat has heartened critics of his administration."[51] The MRC defeat was the first major setback suffered at the hands of the Board of Supervisors by the county executive, and it affected their relationship thenceforth. Michaelian resigned as Republican County Chairman in September 1963, and relinquished his Vice-Chairmanship of MRC when the Council was incorporated in 1966. In January

[48] Memorandum from Prager to Lehman, quoting remarks of James Steed, March 5, 1963.

[49] Milton Hoffman, "Future of MRC Will Be Decided at Meeting of Full Membership," *Reporter Dispatch*, March 7, 1963.

[50] Merrill Folsom, "Regional Council Surviving Attack," *New York Times*, April 7, 1963, p. 76.

[51] "County Lines, Westchester Section," *Daily News*, April 7, 1963, p. W2.

1964, Supervisor Francis X. O'Rourke, who led the move against MRC, was elected Chairman of the Board of Supervisors.[52]

Like Michaelian, New York City Democrats also wanted to avoid becoming "embroiled in what might become a purely partisan battle."[53] When they realized—at the eleventh hour—the ominous pattern of the vote that was shaping up in Westchester, Lehman called William H. McKeon, then Chairman of the Democratic State Committee, to ask his assistance in speaking to William F. Luddy, Westchester's Democratic County Chairman, about lining up votes for MRC. In reporting to Lehman on his conversation with Luddy, McKeon wrote: "There is some problem but he is going to work it out. . . ." A further communication from Lehman to McKeon warned that: "It would be particularly embarrassing if the Democratic minority in Westchester were to be lined up in opposition to the MRC, since Bob Wagner is the founder, chairman, and a strong proponent of metropolitan cooperation; and since President Kennedy has strongly endorsed the idea of regional cooperation." Lehman was not asking for a "strong" endorsement of MRC by the Democratic minority of Westchester, but just that the Democrats, "on the merits alone, act favorably" when the interlocal agreement came up for consideration by the Board of Supervisors.[54]

Lehman was unsuccessful. The eleven Democrats voted together as a bloc each time against MRC, declaring publicly that they would not vote for a full-time staff for MRC when the Board of Supervisors did not have a research staff of its own. They criticized Michaelian, too, charging: "After many years of being accused of being mainly interested in, and dictated to, by

[52] For further discussion, see Merrill Folsom, "Schisms Disrupt Westchester GOP; Maneuvering Is Intensified for Control of Party," and "Politics A-Boiling in Westchester," *New York Times*, December 12, 1965, p. 54, and April 17, 1966, p. 71 respectively. Folsom points out that the schism between Michaelian and a combine of some Republican leaders stemmed partly from his advocacy of a stronger MRC and partly from his rejection of leaders from Yonkers and Greenburgh for high county posts.

[53] Letter from Lehman to William H. McKeon, February 14, 1963.

[54] Letters from McKeon to Lehman, February 8, 1963, and from Lehman to McKeon, February 14, 1963.

the powers from New York City, it is ironic that it is our county executive who is espousing that cause."[55]

The evidence indicates that political opportunism was involved in Democratic as well as Republican ranks. The city of Yonkers, which was controlled by the Democrats, had voted to join MRC previously, but its Democratic supervisors on the county board were unanimously opposed. The Greenburgh Democrats had issued a fifteen-point platform in September 1962 supporting the entry of Greenburgh and Westchester to MRC, but they too voted against joining. A vote against MRC was felt to be a blow to Michaelian's power and prestige, and MRC was held to be the "sacrificial cow."[56]

Miffed also that the minority party was not contacted until two weeks before the vote, the Democrats saw an opportunity to get "the Tammany label off their backs."[57] Some local supervisors saw the Council as the first step toward consolidation of the region and elimination of their own jobs, and claimed to be suspicious of New York City's one vote on the Council. Mention should be made that, shortly before the MRC vote, Michaelian proposed a change in the structure of the bipartisan Westchester Board of Elections that would have had the effect of eliminating Luddy's post as Election Commissioner. Some Democrats considered this an "unwise move" on Michaelian's part, and Luddy claimed that he was reluctant to engage in "political blackmail."[58] Michaelian, on the other hand, stated that Luddy was jealous of the county executive's good relationship with the Wagner administration and has "always been uncooperative."[59]

In this fashion, MRC, which assiduously avoided all political involvements, with its executive board memberships and commit-

---

[55] *Reporter Dispatch*, March 5, 1963.
[56] Interview with William F. Luddy, April 4, 1963.
[57] *Ibid.*
[58] *Reporter Dispatch*, March 7, 1963, and interview with Luddy, April 4, 1963.
[59] Interview with Michaelian, April 12, 1966. According to Michaelian, when his appointment as a representative of the county level of government to the Advisory Commission on Intergovernmental Relations was up for renewal in 1960, Luddy was instrumental in blocking Michaelian's reappointment in spite of Wagner's approval.

tee chairmanships carefully allocated among Republicans and Democrats, found itself the victim of a crude kind of local political maneuvering. Had MRC been able to reach the Democratic faction, perhaps the results might have been different. But the message was not sent sufficiently soon; nor was it made sufficiently strong. The politicians voted just as they wished—in the negative. The only voices that came through were those of the extremists, which were loud, strident, and emotional.

Opposition from Right-Wing Conservatives

Defeat of MRC in Westchester was a victory for the right-wing groups as well as for local politicians. The *Westchester Conservative*, a monthly publication published by the Westchester branch of Young Americans for Freedom, had cautioned: "If the planners cannot sell the idea of one-worldism nationally, they can trap us into it by means of metropolitan government."[60] Gordon Miller, Republican majority leader of the Board of Supervisors, told of being awakened at 2 A.M. by a flashlight shining into his bedroom. When he went to the window, a stranger passed him some anti-MRC literature that "was so violently to the right that it made Barry Goldwater appear to be a radical leftist."[61] The literature not only repeated the familiar arguments about "terrible 1313," but it also accused the federal government of forcibly moving Negroes into formerly all white neighborhoods to tighten what the literature described as national dictatorship.

Even after the MRC defeat by the Board of Supervisors, the attacks continued. The Tri-State Conference on Community Problems moved to Westchester from New Jersey and distributed a one-page handout warning, "Beware of Metro: Operation Sellout." Mrs. Joan Tierney commuted from Glen Rock, New Jersey, to warn American Legionnaires and their friends about MRC, "its many dangers and its ties with the national group pro-

---

[60] *New York Times*, April 7, 1963, p. 76.
[61] *Ibid*. See also "Long Reach on MRC Issue," *Reporter Dispatch*, March 5, 1963.

moting one-world socialism."[62] These were the same "hate groups" which had plagued MRC elsewhere, and their irrelevant arguments were accepted by the Young Men's Republican Club of Westchester and circulated widely by Conservative Party members and local newspapers.

The Macy Chain of Newspapers

No account of the MRC defeat in Westchester would be complete without some mention of the part played by the local press. Because of the prolonged strike of New York City newspapers from December 1962 to April 1963, Westchester readers received much of their information about MRC from the Westchester County Publishers, Inc. Known informally as the "Macy chain," this organization consisted of ten newspapers in Westchester and Rockland counties (eight dailies in Westchester, one daily in Rockland, and one weekly in Bronxville, with a total average daily circulation of approximately 180,000 in 1963), all under the editorial direction of the Vice-President, Edward J. Hughes. Between the time of the public hearing in September and the final vote in March, newspaper comment with respect to MRC was vitriolic. Originally sympathetic to *informal* cooperation among local governments, the newspapers mounted a steady barrage of editorial propaganda against bureaucratic power and takeover by New York City as soon as the Council showed signs of developing into a formal agency.[63]

When Michaelian requested an annual contribution to the MRC budget from the Board of Supervisors, editor Hughes opposed being led through "any legalistic backdoor into a governmental monstrosity, which may . . . weaken the distinctive and independent character of Westchester and impose . . . unwar-

---

[62] *Westchester Conservative*, Vol. II, Issue 8, August 28, 1963. Handouts were distributed by the Tri-State Conference on Community Problems on July 20, 1963.

[63] In 1956, the *Reporter Dispatch* found Mayor Wagner's invitation to public officials to come to New York City to discuss regional problems to be an "excellent idea" ("Friendly Hands Across the Bronx Border," May 28, 1956).

ranted and insupportable economic burdens."[64] In commenting on the disapproval of MRC evidenced by those opposing it, the *Tarrytown News* saw real "substance" in the fear that the "development of regional bodies could lead only to . . . erosion of the powers of the people and their directly elected officials."[65] Deriding government by "experts," the *Reporter Dispatch* warned that payment of dues might lead to "non-responsive, non-elected, . . . all-powerful government."[66] When MRC received an endorsement from the Westchester Village Officials Association, the Macy chain found the endorsement "questionable" and "politically motivated."[67]

The newspapers continued to emphasize the editorial director's long-standing conviction that MRC should remain as presently constituted, and "not be given an expensive organizational formality which inevitably must generate a demand for bureaucratic power. . . . Surely in a public hearing spokesmen for the people of Westchester made it abundantly clear that they don't want [MRC]."[68] An editorial deplored efforts of the county administration to "pressure" key members of the board into joining MRC, and suggested that "this matter is far too important to the ultimate best interests of Westchester County to be used as a pawn in a political power play."[69] The newspapers also provided generous space in the columns set aside for "Letters from Our Readers" for diatribes against "the over-all scourge of . . . metropolitan government."[70]

Once MRC was voted down and Westchester's right to determine its own future was secure from "short-sighted involvement

[64] "Let's Be Permanently Sure," *ibid.*, June 8, 1962.

[65] *Tarrytown News*, September 12, 1962.

[66] *Reporter Dispatch*, September 29, 1962.

[67] *Ibid.*, October 23, 1962.

[68] *Ibid.*, October 27, 1962, and February 9, 1963.

[69] "They Should Vote as They Believe," *ibid.*, February 15, 1963.

[70] Letter from John A. Granlund, "Metropolitan Council Draws Heavy Fire," *Reporter Dispatch*, February 21, 1963. See also four-column letter titled "Citizens Are Being Brainwashed over Metro" from Eloise F. Cardwell, Secretary, Committee for the Preservation of Home Rule, *Reporter Dispatch*, November 3, 1962, and letter titled "Dade County 'Metro Plan'—Shows Why It's Dangerous" from Richard Krikhan in the New Rochelle *Standard Star*, February 27, 1963.

in a hastily defined agency," the papers turned their attention to the Tri-State Transportation Commission, "a new instrument of supergovernment . . . [whose programs would] supersede and nullify any conflicting 'land use' plans."[71] At the same time editor Hughes urged his readers to elect as town supervisors those who looked "with skepticism on schemes for 'regional plans,' 'supergovernment' and 'cooperation' with big cities."[72] Only at the time of the water shortage in the Middle Atlantic region did the newspapers deviate from their long-established positions and advocate that Westchester do some planning in cooperation with New York City and the three states to safeguard its water supply for the future. (They even took some members of the Board of Supervisors to task for displaying "precocious and parochial" attitudes in shunning "intelligent teamwork" on water conservation and other issues.)[73] When MRC was incorporated as a legal entity in 1966, the papers resumed their critical stance, warning readers of possible "loss of home rule, local autonomy, and dictation by a non-accountable federally subsidized agency for the principal benefit of New York City."[74]

The specific effect of the newspapers in influencing the attitudes of members of the Board of Supervisors is uncertain in view of the many other factors which have been described here. However, it is probable that the prejudices of the editorial board of the Westchester newspapers *did* reduce the readers' level of information and understanding and may have influenced their receptiveness to the notion of a formalized MRC. Certainly, the press's suspicions against any change in governmental arrangements provided fresh ammunition to those groups who were most active in opposition and may well have reinforced the fears of those in doubt. Only when the newspapers felt that a regional

[71] *Herald Statesman*, March 6, 1963, and *Reporter-Dispatch*, March 12, 1963, respectively.

[72] *Reporter Dispatch*, November 2, 1963.

[73] ". . . And Plan for the Long Pull," *ibid.*, June 19, 1965, and "A Strangely Nonsensical Attitude," *ibid.*, June 25, 1965.

[74] *Reporter Dispatch*, June 22, 1966. The chain of newspapers owned by Westchester County Publishers, Inc., was sold to Gannett Publishers in 1964, and is now known as Westchester–Rockland Newspapers, Inc. The editorial policy toward MRC has remained unchanged.

problem was an immediate threat to Westchester's own welfare did they find it convenient to promote attitudes of concern toward regional planning.[75]

MRC Rebuttal: Too Little, Too Late

During this same period of time, MRC and its friends attempted to set the record straight. A "staunch Westchester ally" was found in George B. Case, Village Trustee and Chairman of the Planning Board of Tarrytown, New York, who tried to correct the distortions in the Macy chain editorials and in the attacks made by various groups.[76] He introduced a resolution in support of MRC at a meeting of the Westchester Municipal Planning Federation for presentation to the Board of Supervisors, and he was influential in having a similar motion passed by the Westchester Village Officials Association. The Women's Club of White Plains devoted one of the issues of its monthly magazine to a brief, favorable description of the Council, and Mayor Richard S. Hendey's annual message to his city council in White Plains set forth the reasons why White Plains enjoyed formal membership in MRC.[77] The Office of the County Executive issued a report for general distribution in February 1963 pointing out "MRC accomplishments," and the MRC secretariat wrote a few letters and articles correcting the most glaring inaccuracies

[75] Bollens and his colleagues find that the suburban press has a great influence on local issues and that "the position they take may well be crucial in determining the outcome of metropolitan reorganization efforts" (*Exploring the Metropolitan Community*, p. 86). On the other hand, interviewing surveys conducted by the Opinion Reporting Workshop of Columbia University in Nashville, Tennessee, where the voters approved a proposal for city-county consolidation, "disclosed virtually no one who said he had shifted his view . . . because of the stand of the newspapers." But in Dayton, Ohio (where a proposal to consolidate lost) and in Miami, Florida (where a proposal won), interviewers felt that the newspapers had a "considerable influence on the outcome" ("Seminar on Effective Community Reporting," Pt. III, p. 16).

[76] Memorandum from Prager to Lehman, October 25, 1962, on the subject of the interlocal agreement. See also "Letter to the Editor" from Case, *Reporter Dispatch*, October 27, 1962.

[77] "What is MRC?," *Club Dial* (January 1963), and *Reporter Dispatch*, January 8, 1963.

that were being perpetrated about the Council.[78] These did not always have the desired effect. A four-page telegram sent to O'Rourke as Chairman of the Budget Committee of the Board of Supervisors was later used by O'Rourke to prove that if Westchester joined MRC, "appointed officials will tell elected officials what to do."[79]

The executive secretary of MRC reported in February 1963 that "nobody has been able to persuade [the Macy chain of newspapers] to change their viewpoint."[80] On the other hand, there is no evidence that the secretariat was in contact with the Westchester press between September 1962 and February 1963, when a letter was written to the editor. It was not until March 14, 1963, ten days after the final vote, that Harold Riegelman of the Citizens Budget Commission in New York City visited Edward J. Hughes, Editorial Director of Westchester County Publishers, Inc., as "amicus curiae" to explore the possibility of overcoming his objections to MRC. Riegelman found that Hughes's main fear centered about the possible development of an MRC with legal status into a level of "supra government which could impose regional solutions on regional communities whether they liked it or not." Lacking "tangible assurance" that this would be effectively resisted by MRC and its sponsors, he "felt obliged to oppose any first step, which might lead in that direction."[81]

As a result of this meeting, Riegelman suggested that a declaration affirming the voluntary character of MRC and the noncompulsive character of its decisions be drafted in negotiation with Hughes and his associates, and that the "mechanics of reconsideration" by Westchester be worked out, this time with Macy chain endorsement. In compliance with these suggestions, Riegelman proposed a draft of an amendment to the interlocal agree-

[78] E.g., Prager sent a batch of materials to Case for distribution on October 25, 1962; Lehman wrote a "Letter to the Editor," *Reporter Dispatch*, February 13, 1963, pointing out errors in a recent editorial; Prager sent copies of the interlocal agreement and other informational items about MRC to Supervisor John A. Lombardi of White Plains on February 21, 1963.

[79] "Foes of MRC Say Message Proves Point," *Reporter Dispatch*, February 26, 1963.

[80] Letter from Lehman to McKeon, February 14, 1963.

[81] Letter from Riegelman to Lehman, March 18, 1963.

ment as follows: "It is not the intent of this interlocal agreement nor shall it be construed to restrict or diminish, any powers heretofore or hereafter conferred by law, upon any political subdivision of the state or any governmental agency, interstate, state or local, including without limitation powers related to planning and zoning."[82] This amendment was never incorporated into the interlocal agreement because MRC abandoned the attempt to achieve legal status soon after and a new agreement was to be drawn.

Once more, MRC's efforts were insufficient and tardy. As in Suffolk, the Council misread the situation and failed to realize the extent of opposition that would develop. But the danger signals were there. As early as July 1960, the Macy chain of newspapers had found MRC's decision to seek legal status "regrettable." When Suffolk voted against participation in May 1962, the papers applauded the move as "sensible."[83] In September 1962, only two persons appeared to testify in MRC's favor at an open public hearing; in October, it was suggested that "things don't look too good"; and, by December, it was recognized that "Michaelian couldn't get it passed."[84] It was clear that the interlocal agreement was destined for trouble when the Board of Supervisors side-stepped the issue, first at the open public hearing and again at the budget meetings. Finally, it was unusual for the county executive to propose such a matter to his Board of Supervisors and let it dangle. Once MRC realized that the county executive had political troubles of his own, it might have attempted to form coalitions of support and neutralize the opposition.

Instead of engaging in a systematic political analysis of the Westchester situation, MRC continued to ignore the realities of

[82] *Ibid*. When Lehman sent Michaelian a copy of the suggested amendment to the interlocal agreement, the latter pointed out that it was identical in wording to an amendment which had been introduced by Westchester legislators and appended to the Tri-State Transportation Commission Bill (sec. 2, art. 6), at Macy chain suggestion.

[83] "Another Layer of Government," *Reporter Dispatch*, July 5, 1960, and *Herald Statesman* and *Reporter Dispatch*, May 16, 1962, respectively.

[84] Memorandum from Prager to Lehman, October 25, 1962, quoting comments of George Case, and records of William Cassella, December 11, 1962.

urban-suburban politics. One of the blunders at the time of the Westchester vote was the publication of the article in the *New York Times Magazine*, under Wagner's name, which lent weight to the fear that New York City would impose its will on the suburbs.[85] This created great uneasiness about the intent of MRC and was used as effective propaganda against it. This article made it even more important for MRC to engage in a program which would emphasize the broad areas of mutual interest shared by *all* of the communities in the region. If Westchester were to join, it had to understand that it had much to gain and little to fear.

Westchester's defeat of the interlocal agreement was a severe blow to the regional cooperative movement in the New York metropolitan area, a blow from which the Council has never recovered. Lacking basic understanding and support from local political officials, community groups, and the public at large, MRC provoked fears of bureaucratic supergovernment and loss of home rule which were disseminated by the local press and reiterated by the extremists. With little positive support from its own proponents, the MRC cause was used by political officials for their own ends, to advance their own interests. Neither Michaelian nor the MRC secretariat made a consistent effort to enlist friends, combat the opposition, or reassure those who were fearful. Perhaps much of the explanation for this seeming lack of attention can be found in the inadequacies of the MRC organization, whose lack of funds and staff hampered it from taking positive action whenever the need arose. These inadequacies will be discussed further in the next chapter.

[85] *New York Times Magazine*, October 7, 1962, p. 47.

VII

ORGANIZATIONAL WEAKNESSES

A Challenge to Leadership

It has now become clear that a voluntary council cannot measure the existing governmental arrangements against a set of predetermined principles, prescribe a formula for formalized cooperation, and then sit back and wait for results. In order to join the planning function with the practical realities of politics, councils of governments need strong and imaginative leadership to initiate and sustain programs, secure public recognition of their efforts, and cope with attacks from opponents. The diffusion of power interests in the New York metropolitan region means that a complex network of lines of influence must be created in order to mobilize support for a new undertaking. This requires time, dedication, and hard work.

A successful leader knows the relation between intelligence, knowledge, and skill, as well as the political compromises that have to be made. He must be alert to changing political situations and circumstances. Since any action may bring a counteraction, future developments must be anticipated, and responses must be made to current situations. Much depends upon how the leader relates to the community and its interest groups, upon his skill in communicating—in articulating goals and stimulating interest— and upon the strategies of his operation, in terms of meeting priorities, planning the work, setting time schedules, and informing the public.[1]

[1] For further discussion of political leadership in metropolitan areas, refer to Martin, *Metropolis in Transition*, pp. 35 and 131; Willbern, *Metro-*

MRC was hampered in all of these efforts by a lack of basic organizational necessities. The Council kept waiting for formalization of its voluntary status to provide it with full-time leadership, specific budget revenues, professional staffs, the right to contract for federal and state funds, and the authority to seek solutions for area-wide problems. In the meantime, it struggled along with an executive secretary who provided *part-time* leadership to MRC and served *full time* as First Deputy City Administrator of New York. His salary came to him as a result of his formal position in city government. He received no extra remuneration for his job with MRC.

Maxwell Lehman served as Secretary of the Council when it was founded in 1956. His title was changed to "Executive Secretary" in 1958 in order "to give proper recognition to the magnitude of his task."[2] The membership expressed approval of this move, and the *New York Journal American* commented: "Mr. Lehman is that rare combination of a scholar in government and a get-things-going man. He has won the respect of both Republican and Democratic officials and has succeeded in getting them to work in harmony on problems that none of them could ever solve alone."[3]

Many others have expressed admiration for Lehman and the work he performed for the Council over the years. Michaelian feels that he did a "very good job" with MRC and helped to pave the way for developments that might not have otherwise taken place. Specifically, Michaelian noted that Lehman acted as a "wonderful referee" in facilitating the acquisition of surplus watershed lands by Westchester County, for use as a recreational area, from New York City which owned the lands but no longer used them. (Michaelian felt that negotiations between the various agencies of the two governments might have ended in a "big

politan Issues, ed. Birkhead, p. 59; Smallwood, *Metro Toronto*, p. 37; and Advisory Commission, *Factors Affecting Voter Reactions*, pp. 28–31.

[2] Minutes of MRC membership meeting, February 5, 1958, pp. 43–44. The original motion was made by Karl Metzger, was enthusiastically seconded by A. Holly Patterson, and was "thirded" by Griffith Harris. (At this time Patterson also moved that the Conference render thanks and appreciation to Wagner for his "very generous leadership . . . and for [his] very warm friendship" [p. 45]).

[3] "Splendid Choice," *Journal American*, June 20, 1958, p. 29.

fiasco" had Lehman not been so helpful.)[4] At the joint congressional hearings held in New York City in June 1963, Representative Rosenthal was impressed with Lehman's "obvious experience and learning and know-how." Senator Muskie likewise felt that Lehman's responses indicated "wide experience in the field [of intergovernmental relations] , . . . a great deal of thought, . . . and certainly a great deal of dedication to [his] own responsibilities."[5]

But "experience and learning" and "dedication to responsibilities" are not sufficient to comply with the requirements of a post as demanding as that of executive officer of a voluntary regional council. A fragile new agency of government cannot be launched successfully in the New York metropolitan region with the expenditure of a few minutes each day. The MRC chairman could not be expected to devote much time and attention to MRC's needs. Because of the overwhelming nature of the responsibilities adhering to the office of Mayor of New York City, Wagner gave time to the Council and presided at meetings only when required. Otherwise he seems to have given his executive secretary free rein. The chairman was probably briefed on Council operations and lent his authorization when requested, but he did not assume a direct, policy-making role.[6]

The executive board as well seems to have played a relatively minor role in initiating policy. Because of its shifting membership and irregularly scheduled meetings, it frequently appears to have met in order to ratify decisions already made and action already taken.[7] The general lack of time and interest, and the primary job obligations of the officials whose communities were members, were such as to create a situation in which the success of the

[4] Interview with Michaelian, April 12, 1966.

[5] *Joint Hearings: Government in Metropolitan Areas* (1963), pp. 45 and 50.

[6] Interview with Keith, April 22, 1966, and with Slote, May 5, 1966. This was a different set of circumstances from the Metropolitan Washington Council of Governments where the chairman was very prominent in Council operations and the secretary assumed "indirect leadership. . . . He took the classical view of the technician's role in government and may fairly be said to exhibit a 'passion for anonymity' " (Hanson, *The Politics of Metropolitan Cooperation*, p. 10).

[7] MRC records, and interviews with Prager and Slote. The only instance in which the executive board overruled a suggestion of the executive secretary in Slote's memory concerned a proposed budget for the Council drawn up in 1960.

Council depended in large measure upon the vigor, personality, and personal attitudes of the executive secretary.

There is considerable agreement among people who were close to MRC in its formative years that the executive secretary's manner of operation often had the unfortunate effect of alienating the very officials and agencies whose friendship and assistance he needed. A sophisticated, urbane New Yorker, Lehman was regarded with suspicion by some important state officials and legislators. Because of his handling of the proposed MRC legislation in Albany, and his failure to furnish sufficient information about MRC's operations and objectives to the New York State legislature, mistrust of a possible new power center was fostered. The apparent reluctance on the part of the New York City Mayor and City Administrator to relinquish their posts with MRC is reported to have done nothing to dispel this fear.[8]

Moreover, the exclusion of a broad spectrum of regional interests from membership and/or participation in MRC was probably a deterrent in gaining legislative and state acceptance and may have alienated other groups as well. Despite recommendations against setting up a rival civic organization to gain public support for MRC, the executive secretary continued to support this idea, thereby offending RPA, which had already gone out of its way to stimulate and support MRC's efforts in the regional arena.[9] Lehman's unwillingness to cooperate with other groups manifested itself in the use of some of RPA's projections "often without credit to the source." The distribution of a press release crediting MRC with preparation of *The Race for Open Space* and failing to mention the essential contribution of RPA also rankled.[10]

---

[8] Interviews with Prager on a number of occasions between February 1962 and April 1966; with Zimmerman, February 16, 1966; with Keith, April 22, 1966; with Edward Kresky (then assistant to the chairman of the Metropolitan Commuter Transportation Authority), April 27, 1966; with Slote, May 5, 1966; and with Koppelman, January 23, 1968. Some of the state officers specifically mentioned were Barrett, Ronan, and top officials of the Interstate Sanitation Commission.

[9] Interview with Keith. For further confirmation, see memorandum from Cassella to Lehman, April 14, 1959, discussed in Chap. IV, p. 73.

[10] Letter from Keith to James Schrader, American Society of Planning Officials, December 31, 1962. RPA hoped MRC would be less hesitant about giving credit when it had its own staff and could carry on work on

Lehman's actions sometimes offended some of MRC's most devoted members. His release of statements to the press without prior consultation irritated Westchester County on a few occasions and provoked a letter from Michaelian to Wagner suggesting that the timing of the releases was such as to give the entire question of legal status "a political flavor, . . . the last thing that any of us affiliated in any way with MRC would desire."[11] The secretariat's choice of Grossingers, a resort in Liberty, New York, as a meeting place for Council members "horrified" Karl Metzger, who was "violently opposed to the idea" and asked Lehman to "please forget it." Metzger felt that Grossinger's was improperly situated, from the Council's point of view, because it was located outside of the MRC region. He also thought that its atmosphere was "unsuitable for conducting the region's business," and that "the public might get the wrong impression."[12] Despite this request, the meeting was held as scheduled.

Finally, the executive secretary's conception of the nonpartisan manner in which MRC was to function should be noted. Although Lehman was a product of New York City politics and had an insider's view of city problems, he looked upon his work with MRC as devoid of partisan politics. This view was not shared by state officials or by members of local legislative bodies, particularly those from Nassau, Suffolk, and Westchester counties.[13]

---

its own. For a discussion of *The Race for Open Space*, see Chap. VIII, p. 190.

[11] Michaelian stated that the publicity emanating from news releases concerning the future of MRC provoked an adverse reaction from his Board of Supervisors (August 31, 1961). As a result of what they read, the legislators regarded legal status for MRC as an "urgent crash program" to be foisted on them. Michaelian wished to see no further releases on the subject unless proper clearance was sought from the Committee on the Future, of which he was a member. An answer from Lehman to Michaelian, September 14, 1961, explained that both stories were solicited by the *New York Times* and that neither came from a press release.

[12] Letter from Metzger to Lehman, January 17, 1963.

[13] E.g., according to Michaelian, the "wrong guy" made contact with Governor Meyner in New Jersey when the enabling legislation was pending. This allegation is borne out by Koppelman as well. For more general comments about the need for political judgment in directing a council of governments, see Hanson, *Metropolitan Councils of Governments*, p. 32.

Full-Time Independent Leadership

The behavior and point of view of the executive secretary are significant insofar as they may have contributed to a less favorable climate of opinion for MRC, but they do not lessen the overwhelming need for full-time experienced people to give daily direction to a council of governments. In a voluntary and loosely knit association of officials, preoccupied with their own problems, energetic leadership is a necessary ingredient to identify problems, establish policies, and gain consensus among conflicting units. MRC functioned for ten years with an executive officer who devoted a small part of his time to its affairs, with an assistant who devoted nearly all of his time to MRC and to New York City's interlocal relations, and with temporary clerical personnel on leave from the Department of Welfare. This informal, part-time staffing from New York City's administrative hierarchy hindered MRC's programs and was a significant factor in the Council's failure to secure legal status.

MRC drew funds for stamps, office supplies, and equipment from the overall budget of the Office of the City Administrator. Its monthly *Bulletin* was financed through printing and reproduction funds which were also included in the total expenses for the City Administrator. The Council's semiannual meetings were largely self-supporting and were paid for by registration fees. The latter were MRC's sole incoming money. There were no funds to hire research staff of any kind, and MRC made use of experts from the government of New York City on an advisory or consultant basis when necessary. This was not always a satisfactory arrangement.[14] While Mayor Wagner's annual report

[14] E.g., in the course of an important MRC project, the preparation of a master map of water-pollution sources in the region, the Water Pollution Committee secured help from William T. Ingram, a sanitary engineer who acted as consultant to the New York City Health Department. As part of the program, Ingram personally paid for blueprints of a group of maps which he acquired from the Interstate Sanitation Commission. Lehman had to furnish a complete explanation to Abraham Beame, then Budget Director of New York City, concerning reimbursement of Ingram in the amount of $192.89 for the outlay he had made (letter from Lehman to Beame, July 10, 1958).

for 1962 indicated that he considered the provision of space, personnel, and equipment to the secretariat of MRC "a contribution by New York City toward more effective partnership between the City and its neighbors,"[15] other observers felt strongly that MRC should have an independent staff that was responsible to the regional organization itself.[16]

The importance of a permanent secretariat to give continuity to the operations of a voluntary agency is borne out by MRC's experience. As the attempt to achieve legal status consumed months and then years, and the various communities failed to ratify the interlocal agreement, MRC received less support from all of its members, including New York City. Arthur Prager, the Assistant Executive Secretary, became increasingly fretful with the unsatisfactory state of affairs, noting in October 1965 that the Council had been given "the lowest possible priority [in the City Administrator's office], the most inadequate and undesirable office space, and the most unacceptable equipment."[17] Clerical help was available only on a part-time basis, and MRC's addressograph machine was obsolete.

Prager's morale, which had started to deteriorate sharply after the Westchester defeat in 1963, sank to a new low. He found it impossible to schedule the customary semiannual membership meetings called for by the MRC charter since the meetings required considerable preparation and correspondence. His demands for office supplies were largely ignored. The MRC clipping file, which contained noteworthy news of member communities gleaned from seven suburban newspapers, was discontinued because of a lack of clerical help. Publication of the monthly MRC *Bulletin* was suspended in June 1965, because its

[15] *Ninth Annual Report of Mayor Robert F. Wagner to the City Council and to the People of New York City*, January–December 1962, p. 35.

[16] See George Deming, address to "Workshop on 'Voluntary Multi-Purpose Organizations,'" 1961; Robert F. Van Horn, address to AMA–NACO Workshop on Voluntary City-County Regional cooperation," 1965; and meeting of Technical Advisory Committee, MRC, 1964, described in Chap. I, p. 17.

[17] Memorandum to Robert H. Connery on "MRC Problems," October 15, 1965.

yearly contract with the printer had expired.[18] By the end of 1965, MRC was, in effect, out of business.

Early Recommendations for Secretariat

The organizational inadequacies which hampered the agency in its daily operations stemmed largely from the voluntary character of the organization. The Council planned to move quickly to set up a full-time secretariat and staff as soon as its legal status was secured. In 1960, the Committee on the Future of the MRC called on the executive secretary to prepare a plan for the organization of the secretariat, including a description of duties and responsibilities, staff requirements, and job specifications. The only difficulty in carrying out this assignment was that each person who worked on the project had a different view of the Council's regional mission. Therefore, different staff plans were presented.

A preliminary memorandum was drawn up by Frank Smallwood, then Assistant Professor of Government at Dartmouth College (on temporary assignment to MRC under the terms of an internship award from the Institute of Public Administration in New York City). Smallwood recommended that the secretariat be organized on a "generalist rather than a specialist basis." He saw little need to staff the organization with traffic, recreation, and water- and air-pollution experts, since technical personnel was already available in local communities and duplication of staff might create ill will. Instead, Smallwood recommended establishment of the positions of executive director; staff associate for special studies who would maintain personal liaison with all MRC study and survey committees; staff associate for community assistance who would maintain personal liaison with all member communities; and staff associate for regional relations who would maintain personal contact with the press and other metropolitan organizations.[19]

[18] The MRC *Bulletin* resumed publication on a bimonthly basis with the February–March issue in 1967 and has appeared at irregular intervals since.

[19] Memorandum from Smallwood to Lehman on the subject of the "Future of the MRC Secretariat," August 12, 1960.

Smallwood's plan was set aside in favor of a second, more complicated organizational arrangement, calling for staff positions of executive director, director of research and planning, and director of intergovernmental and community relations—with the latter two to have a staff assistant each. Positions of office manager, librarian, secretaries, and clerk-typist were also included. The total expenditure for staff services and other expenses under this second plan came to $110,500. This plan was likewise not used.[20]

The plan submitted by the executive secretary to the Committee on the Future was the most elaborate of all. It offered a detailed budget for MRC and included an organizational chart, staffing and salary schedules, duty statements, and job specifications. The proposed job titles and salary schedules are shown below. The amounts indicated represent an outlay of funds that Lehman considered necessary to maintain a permanent secretariat on an annual basis. It was also anticipated that funds would have to be provided for rent, office, equipment, car, chauffeur, and other miscellaneous items; these expenditures came to a total of approximately $70,000.

		Range	Annual Salary
1.	OFFICE OF THE EXECUTIVE DIRECTOR		
	A. Executive Director	$25,000 to 30,000	25,000
	B. Deputy Executive Director	15,000 to 17,500	15,000
	Office Manager (1)	6,400 to 8,200	6,400
	General Clerk (1)	4,550 to 5,990	4,550
	Librarian Clerk (1)	4,550 to 5,990	4,550
	Secretaries (4)	5,000 to 6,890	20,000
	Typists (4)	3,750 to 4,830	15,000
2.	COUNSEL	17,500 to 20,000	17,500
3.	INFORMATION AND EDUCATION		
	Director	15,000 to 17,500	15,000
	Illustrator-Writer	6,400 to 8,200	6,400
4.	ENGINEERING		
	Chief Engineer	17,500 to 20,000	17,500
	Jr. Engineer	7,100 to 8,900	7,100

[20] No one who was connected with MRC in 1960 remembers the author of this particular organizational plan. Lehman probably asked a staff member in the Office of the City Administrator to prepare it.

5. ECONOMICS

Economist	15,000 to 17,500	15,000
Research Assistant	6,400 to 8,200	6,400

6. TRANSPORTATION

Director	15,000 to 17,500	15,000
Research Assistant	6,400 to 8,200	6,400
Total Personal Services		196,800
Other than Personal Services (supplies, phone, etc.):		2,500
TOTAL		$199,300[21]

Many observers feel that the scale of operations that Lehman proposed was a fatal blow to MRC and its hopes for securing legal status. Both in terms of money and staff requirements, the proposal was considered unrealistic and inflated, and out of proportion to the present or contemplated role of the agency.[22] A letter enclosing the proposed budget and staff organization was sent by Karl Metzger to members of the Committee on the Future of the MRC warning them that their reaction to the enclosure "might be a little strong." The minutes indicate that committee members felt that the staff requests signified the "beginning of a new government."[23] The committee recommended that a new proposal for staff organization be drawn up at or around the figure of $100,000.

Further consideration of staff needs was postponed until the interlocal agreement was written. As approved by the membership at the February 1962 meeting, the agreement simply provided for a full-time director and staff "as may be necessary for the performance of the Council's functions." It is improbable that agreement could have been obtained with respect to more detailed specifications. The original report of the RPA committee, dealing with "The Future of the MRC," had called only

[21] A three-page memorandum on "Justification for Salaries of the Staff for the Permanent Secretariat of the MRC" accompanied the proposed schedule. It indicated that a salary range of $25,000–30,000 for the executive director was warranted because the person selected to represent the region should command a salary "that is at least on a par with the heads of the major agencies within the region."

[22] Interviews with Michaelian, Keith, Slote, and Prager.

[23] Remark made by Michaelian at meeting of the Committee on the Future, late 1960. No precise date is given.

for the employment of a "small, high-quality staff as secretariat." MRC members were reluctant to have the Council develop into a larger agency than was absolutely necessary and would probably have reacted to Lehman's proposal as negatively as the members of the Committee on the Future did.[24] Lehman, on the other hand, looked upon the Council as a major research organization, "staffed with experts in planning, transportation, water pollution, health, airports and other problem areas concerning the region."[25] Clearly, this was a different view of the Council's role. The uncertainty about MRC's objectives vexed the Council in dealing with its own members and confused the question of staff and budgetary requirements as well.

Overlapping Dues Payments

The determination of an equitable financial formula for MRC was another difficult question. With respect to "Finance," the pertinent parts of section 8 of the interlocal agreement had provided:

(a) The Council shall submit to the governing body of each contracting unit of government a budget of its estimated expenditures, revenues, and sources thereof in advance of each fiscal year. . . .

(b) Each of the Council's budgets shall contain specific recommendations of the amount or amounts to be appropriated to the Council by each of the contracting units of government. The total amount of such appropriations shall be apportioned among the contracting units of government on the basis of population, provided that the Council may make such by-laws with respect to appropriations by overlapping units of government as the Council shall deem equitable.

(c) . . . Except by three-fourths affirmative vote of the total votes on the Council, no budget of estimated expenditures shall be adopted if it contemplates appropriations of more than one cent per capita of population for each contracting unit of government.

[24] Refer to discussion in Chap. V, p. 89, concerning membership reaction to MRC's proposed role as a coordinator of regional authorities.

[25] New York Times, July 23, 1961, p. 58. This view of the Council's secretariat was at variance with that of RPA, which saw it as a "facilitative, agenda-drafting, coordinating headquarters," working in conjunction with RPA's own staff (letter from Keith to Schrader, December 31, 1962).

No contracting unit shall be responsible for any contribution to the budget unless such sum is appropriated by the contracting unit according to law.

In February 1962, when the interlocal agreement was adopted, a budget of about $160,000 was contemplated, based upon a population count of approximately sixteen million residents in the region. Some members opposed the one-cent-per-capita levy, pointing out that certain member municipalities would have to contribute to their counties' levy as well as their own or would, in effect, be subjected to double taxation. The *Record*, in Bergen County, New Jersey, pointed out that the city of Newark contained about one-half of the population of Essex County and paid about one-half the cost of county government. Under the MRC proposal, Newark would pay dues for each of its residents and, through county taxes, would pay about one-half the county's dues as well. The Director of the Essex Board of Freeholders, James McKenna, called this "double taxation," as did Steven Bercik, Mayor of Elizabeth, New Jersey, and Stanley W. Church, Mayor of New Rochelle, New York.[26]

This question of overlapping dues payments had been discussed on many occasions since 1959, and the Technical Advisory Committee, responsible for drafting the interlocal agreement, had spent many hours on numerous formulations. "We settled on a penny per head as the only justifiable approach because we felt that each unit of government involved had to have a financial stake, even though Newark and Essex might contribute on the basis of the same heads."[27] When the question was raised at the general membership meeting in February 1962, Lehman failed to support the formulation agreed to by the consultants, and returned the matter to the Technical Advisory Committee for further consideration. The proposal was amended to include a provision for by-laws to be written to ease this double appropriation (see [b] of section 8), but this did not serve to quiet the uneasiness which had developed.

Eight months later, the Council had not yet determined whether the assessment would be one cent a head or a ratio of the popu-

---

[26] *Record*, February 28, 1962.
[27] Letter from Keith to Joan Aron, December 22, 1967.

lation of the member unit to the population of the region as a whole. At a meeting of the Technical Advisory Committee in October 1962, the assistant executive secretary advised that "the members are reluctant to do anything about the inter-local agreement until they find out how much it will cost them." The issue of uncertain costs was used by opponents of MRC as one reason why they should not affiliate, and it proved to be one of the stumbling blocks in the path to ratification of the interlocal agreement.[28]

The technicalities of the assessment schedule were never clarified. In April 1963, when it became clear that the communities in the region would not accept the interlocal agreement in its (then) present form, Michaelian suggested that the secretariat draw up a budget for specific projects and that costs be divided among the members and included in their annual budgets. (He thought that this would be more palatable to MRC's members than a one-cent-per-capita tax to support MRC.) Some months later on, the executive secretary suggested that a revised agreement "ought to allow for some method of making the Council self-supporting," and the Committee on the Future recommended the imposition of "modest dues," based on a starting budget not in excess of $50,000.[29] In January 1964, a budget committee was created by the executive board to determine the amount of dues and the method of collection. The October 1964 issue of the MRC *Bulletin* mentioned that a system of payments was being considered based on a sliding scale similar to that used by the United States Conference of Mayors, but there was no further consideration of this question until 1966 when the articles of incorporation were written.

[28] E.g., see letter from Riegelman to Lehman, reporting that White Plains considered it a "double burden" to pay dues to MRC and also assume its part of the county's financial obligations to MRC (March 18, 1963). Also refer to minutes of the MRC executive board meeting, January 3, 1964.

[29] Michaelian's suggestion was made at a meeting of the Committee on the Future, April 11, 1963; for the suggestion of the executive secretary, see memorandum from Lehman to all members of MRC concerning the interlocal agreement, July 15, 1963; and for the recommendation of the Committee on the Future, see letter from Metzger, Chairman of the committee, to Lehman, October 30, 1963.

During all of the time when the proposed budget was being diminished from its 1960 peak, the secretariat continued to function with an executive secretary, an assistant, and a typist. Assistant Executive Secretary Prager estimated that New York City spent an average of approximately $50,000 per year on behalf of MRC, a figure which included salaries (one-half the salary of the executive secretary, the total salary of the assistant, and salaries for one full-time secretary, one half-time secretary, and a half-time multilith operator), postage, printing, office supplies, transportation, and telephone calls. (For a more realistic consideration, Prager suggested that funds for legal fees, office space, and equipment be included as well.) He felt this "stripped MRC down to the absolute minimum for existence and would just about keep it alive."[30] The Council maintained a fluctuating bank balance of about $50 to $1200 from 1962 to 1966, the years for which "Treasurer's Reports" are available.[31]

Current Financial Status

A recent survey of regional councils in the United States indicates that all suffer from financial problems to a greater or lesser extent. Most councils receive annual contributions from member governments through the use of an assessment schedule based primarily upon population, but the amount of financial support contributed by members varies widely. For the majority of the councils, federal grants are the largest single source of revenue and are vital to the implementation of programs and activities.[32]

Once incorporated as a legal entity, MRC also turned to the federal government for help in establishing itself. Under the ur-

[30] Letter from Prager to James Steed, Office of the County Executive, Westchester County, February 14, 1963.

[31] MRC had $48.04 in its bank account at the end of 1962, $673.15 in 1963, $710.27 in 1964, and $1,173.97 at the end of 1965, of which $680.74 was administered by the Law Enforcement Committee and $493.23 was in the MRC general fund. At the end of 1966, MRC had $534.89 in its law-enforcement fund and $671.23 in the general fund.

[32] Hanson, *Metropolitan Councils of Governments*, p. 9. See also Citizens Research Council of Michigan, "Research Brief on Financing of Eight Selected Councils of Governments." (1966), pp. 1 and 2.

ban planning grant for which it applied on May 31, 1967, the Council requested federal funds of $210,000, to be matched by a total nonfederal contribution of $105,000. This was to be budgeted roughly as follows:

SALARIES—planning agency personnel	$139,974
SERVICES—technical consultants	133,026
TRAVEL	5,000
REPRODUCTION AND PUBLICATION	11,982
OTHER:	
Books, periodicals, maps	4,500
Office supplies, postage, telephone	10,000
Rent	9,500
TOTAL	$313,982[33]

MRC planned to raise its share of one-third of the total amount by a contribution of $50,000 from the Old Dominion Foundation —to cover the cost of a joint project of waste management with RPA—and by contributions of $55,000 from local municipalities.

In the spring of 1968, MRC learned that it would receive $100,000 from the federal government. By this time, the joint RPA-MRC project specified in the grant application was already completed, and MRC was financing itself with dues from some of its members. The new by-laws, adopted March 3, 1967, provide for the annual payment of dues by members, with contributions ranging from a high of $40,000 for a community with over

[33] The staffing chart for the "planning agency personnel" as submitted in the application was as follows:

Title of Position	Annual Salary
Executive Director	$25,000
Director of Program and Planning	18,000
Director of Public Affairs	15,000
Research Associate	10,000
Planner	10,000
Engineer	10,000
Research assistant	8,000
Administrative assistant	8,000
Secretary	6,250
Secretary	5,250
Secretary	5,250
TOTAL	$120,750

Fringe benefits and other allowances were to be added to the total.

four million in population to a low of $500 for a community with a population of less than 50,000. The question of overlapping payments by counties and municipalities has been settled. Where a county, which is an MRC member, includes municipalities which are also members, the county's share of dues will be reduced by the amounts paid by the cities and towns within its confines.

If all of the communities which are presently considered to be MRC members were to pay their scheduled dues according to their 1960 population figures, a total of $113,728 would be forthcoming. By the time the federal grant came through in 1968, eight of MRC's members had paid dues according to the new population schedule as follows:

	Population (1960)	Dues
NEW YORK STATE		
Nassau County	1,300,200	$10,000
Orange County	183,700	1,500
Putnam County	31,700	500
Rockland County	136,800	1,500
White Plains	50,400	1,000
New York City	7,782,000	40,000
NEW JERSEY		
Linden	39,900	500
CONNECTICUT		
Westport	21,000	500
	TOTAL	$55,500

As a practical matter, no community has been excluded from participation in the Council's activities because of nonpayment of dues.

MRC hired an executive director in January 1968, and other employees have been added since. The Council plans to apply to the federal government for further financial assistance for the fiscal year 1969.

Organizational Framework for MRC

In addition to budgetary and staff deficiencies for the period under consideration (1956–1966), MRC lacked a framework for intergovernmental cooperation to which local communities could relate.[34] The proposed legislation for a tri-state metropolitan council drafted in June 1960 had outlined a structure for the new agency, authorized a method of financing, and set forth its proposed functions. This bill was later scrapped in favor of the interlocal agreement, approved in 1962. There were no by-laws; they were to be written and submitted to the membership as they became necessary after the interlocal agreement was ratified. Everything depended on legal status, and this became less and less certain with the passage of time.

Meanwhile, if regional cooperation was not to be left to the good intentions of a few, well-meaning local officials, there were many questions to be solved. One of the most taxing dealt with the question of membership. At one of the first MRC meetings, in July 1956, it was decided to include as members all counties in the metropolitan area (outside of New York City), all cities in the area, and representation from Fairfield County, Connecticut. There would be, in addition, two representatives at large for all noncity municipalities within each county. Under this proposal, seventy-eight units of government were contemplated as members, including fourteen county representatives, thirty-six city representatives, and twenty-eight representatives at large.

The question of individual membership within counties was reconsidered in September 1956, and MRC's steering committee recommended that the selection of governmental units within each county eligible for membership in MRC be determined by the county itself. It was also suggested that all communities, regardless of size, which had attended the original MRC meeting should retain membership and that all counties in the New York metropolitan area which had not been included at the original meeting should be invited to join. In Connecticut, where counties no longer existed, towns were to be the basic unit of membership. At the December 1956 general meeting, the Council adopted this plan. (At this time, it also decided that all conference members would have equal voting powers, that the top elected official in

---

[34] Hanson points out that there is no standard structure for a council of governments and that much depends upon governmental arrangements in the particular metropolitan area in which a council operates (*Metropolitan Councils of Governments*, p. 15).

each participating unit would represent his community, that the organization would be voluntary in composition, and that the full council would meet twice a year, in the spring and fall.)

The rules governing additional memberships were never finalized. In drafting legislation to establish a regional council in 1960, the Committee on the Future of the MRC reopened the question and found itself faced with such vexing problems as: population criteria for membership; New York City representation; the fate of smaller cities then in the Council (such as Linden and Hackensack, New Jersey); large unincorporated areas (such as Hempstead, New York); and representation from Connecticut. In an effort to use criteria that would avoid further fragmentation and representation of narrow interests in the region, Slote recommended that the county be used as the basic unit of membership and that membership be provided also for the major cities (such as Newark, Jersey City, and Yonkers).[35]

Meanwhile, varying practices had developed in different counties. In Passaic County, New Jersey, for example, the municipalities of Passaic and Paterson were members. Clifton, the second largest city in the county, had never joined. Bergen County, New Jersey, with a much larger population than Passaic County, had only one municipal member, Hackensack, which was smaller than other Bergen municipalities.[36] It was a confusing time for

[35] Memorandum from Slote to Lehman, May 20, 1959. Mayor Wagner suggested that "population figures" alone were unacceptable as a basis for membership on the Council because (1) some large communities had little control in actuality over metropolitan affairs since control resided in the counties, and (2) some small communities shared a great many problems in common with their neighbors (address to the United States Conference of Mayors in Los Angeles, California, July 14, 1959). The Special Committee on Metropolitan Governmental Affairs of RPA also debated this question of membership and found it most difficult to resolve. After much deliberation, this committee recommended that membership in MRC be provided for each county in the region, each municipality with a population of 50,000 or more, the town of Greenwich, Connecticut, and groups of municipalities; and that representatives from the states, national and regional governmental agencies, and nongovernmental groups be included as nonvoting members (January 5, 1959).

[36] See "The Council Wants to Be Official," *Passaic Herald News*, February 27, 1960. In the editor's opinion, this incomplete representation from counties and cities raised doubts about the Council's right to act as spokesman for the metropolitan area.

potential members as well. The applications of East Orange, New Jersey, and Rye, New York, were tabled pending review of the criteria for membership, and they never became members.

The Committee on the Future considered the various possibilities of requirements for membership and drafted legislation for consideration by MRC members in June 1960. Section 4 of the legislation establishing a tri-state council originally read as follows: "The council shall be composed of the elected chief executive officer of (a) each county in the metropolitan region; (b) each city in the metropolitan region with a population of 45,000 or more, . . . and (c) such additional governmental units within the metropolitan region with a population of less than 45,000 as the council by a majority vote of its executive board may admit to membership."[37] Between June 1960 and February 1961, section 4 was changed to provide that "each municipality in the metropolitan region with a population of 50,000 or more" might be a member of the Council. While this provision was acceptable to the general membership, the legislation itself was never passed by the state legislatures. Instead, the interlocal agreement was drawn up, establishing MRC pursuant to enabling legislation passed by the three states.

The interlocal agreement circumvented the specific question of population standards. It established an interlocal advisory board composed of "contracting units of government," the latter to "mean any local governmental unit party to this agreement but [not including] a public authority, a school district, an improvement district, or other special district." Since the interlocal agreement was never ratified by all of the communities which regarded themselves as members, a frame of reference for membership still did not exist. This lack caused considerable confusion. Union County, New Jersey, for example, requested the congressional subcommittees on intergovernmental relations in 1963 to strike "officially" its name from membership in MRC. However, since

[37] The use of the 45,000 figure as the minimum population for cities to be represented on the Council was a compromise. It furnished a means of retaining as members some of the small New Jersey municipalities which had joined previously, and the figure was "open-ended" since other smaller communities could join the Council by a majority vote of the executive board (notes of William Cassella, June 17, 1960).

the request was not made directly to MRC, the council continued to regard Union County as a "voluntary informal member."[38]

In 1964, the assistant executive secretary considered as a "member" any county or municipality which regularly participated in MRC activities and which had not officially informed MRC that it was withdrawing from membership (like Suffolk). On the other hand, he pointed out that some communities felt that a "member" was a community whose local legislative body had ratified the interlocal agreement calling for legal status for MRC. The interlocal agreement had provided for payment of an annual assessment as a condition of continued membership with voting rights and privileges. Since the annual assessments were never determined, MRC could not attract new members, or induce old ones to join "officially." Conversely, it could not assess local communities until the criteria for membership were definitely established. The need for a framework for cooperative action was obvious.

Current Membership Requirements

MRC was incorporated on November 2, 1966, pursuant to the Membership Corporations Law of New York State. The certificate of incorporation defines the region for MRC purposes (with the same boundaries as heretofore) and limits membership in the corporation to the elected chief executive officer of a "municipality" in the metropolitan region. The term "municipality" is broadly defined as "a county, city, town or village, except a county wholly contained within a city." The by-laws provide that any elected chief executive officer of a municipality in the metropolitan region may become a member simply by notifying the execu-

---

[38] Letter from Prager to Mrs. George W. Mann, December 2, 1963, in answer to a question about Union County's status in MRC. Prager wrote that the Union County Board of Freeholders had approved the interlocal agreement on August 16, 1962, but that about six months later, Union County had been informed that the resolution had been improperly passed since the New Jersey enabling legislation called for two public hearings on such a resolution and only one had been held. In July 1963, a letter had been sent to all MRC members asking them not to take action on the interlocal agreement because of the possibility it might be revised.

tive secretary of his desire to join and upon payment of his annual dues. After long years of deliberation over population criteria, the Council has now decided that all local communities, regardless of size, may be admitted as members. MRC members presently show an enormous variation in population, ranging from a high of 7,782,000 in New York City to a low of 17,700 in Morristown, New Jersey (based on 1960 population figures). If all of the "municipalities" in the region were to join, MRC would have close to 550 members.

The by-laws continue the tradition of one vote for each member, regardless of size. A nine-man board of directors—four from New York, three from New Jersey and two from Connecticut—is provided, to serve for one year. A chairman and vice-chairman may be elected from these nine members to serve as president and vice-president of the Council respectively. The by-laws provide for membership on MRC committees and participation in MRC activities by representatives from the three states and from interstate agencies, but do not confer on such representatives the right to vote.

Lack of Clear Sense of Purpose

Up until now, this chapter has been concerned with questions of leadership, staff, money, and organization, which were of great concern to the secretariat, MRC members, and outside advisors, and which consumed long periods of time and vast amounts of attention. A more important question still remains: What did MRC plan to do with the money, staff, and organization when these became available? Because MRC did not answer this question satisfactorily during most of its first ten years, it was inevitable that confusion about its role developed.

As far back as 1958, before the public hearings on the future of the Council were scheduled, MRC defined for itself four possible directions in which its activities might proceed: (1) to continue as a voluntary agency; (2) to become a supervisory agency to which existing bodies would be answerable; (3) to act on regional matters which were inadequately handled; (4) to become a regional government and deal with "regional" matters.[39] Examination of the Council's activities in subsequent years indicates that it seemed to pursue each of these alternatives in turn. When it was unable to venture too far in any one direction (such as developing into the kind of supergovernment that was decried in the Council's public statements), it backtracked into a relatively safe berth as a forum for study and exchange of information. This ambiguity about its own objectives made it difficult for MRC to sell itself and its services as a purely advisory agency with limited powers to the local communities which feared it.

It also made it difficult for the secretariat to define its own role. The secretariat was established at an early date to serve as a center for the exchange of information, "calling together committees, making arrangements for . . . meetings, issuing to all participating members information relating to the area, maintaining liaison with agencies engaged in metropolitan problems, and related duties." In 1959, these assignments were augmented by the establishment, which MRC announced in a press release, of a central office of information on governmental problems of the metropolitan region; this office was to conduct research into "various aspects of the metropolitan area." A few months later, the secretariat proposed to render a fairly large array of services to MRC members in line with its function as "the Council's central information and fact-finding office."[40]

In 1960, more assignments were added. The executive secretary announced the formation by MRC of a permanent regional statistical committee, in conjunction with other regional organizations including the Metropolitan Council of Planning Agencies, RPA, and the Port of New York Authority, to advise the federal

[39] Fact sheet on MRC, "Metropolitan Regional Council," October 20, 1958.

[40] Minutes of MRC steering committee meeting, July 18, 1956; press release, April 20, 1959; and report of executive secretary to MRC membership, June 16, 1959, respectively. "Services" to be furnished by the secretariat included information concerning the governmental machinery of every community in the region and sources of state and federal aid for specific purposes, data on special projects of interest to members, answers to questions about public administration, and the conducting of extensive research projects.

government of the region's statistical requirements. In 1962, plans were announced for the establishment of a regional statistical service for all of MRC's members, as well as for a study of population changes and shifts, to make advance projections on a continuing basis. This created some concern at RPA, which was then working on an economic report of the region, "the forerunner of a regional data center under RPA jurisdiction."[41] RPA's concern was groundless. No record of work on these projects by MRC can be found.

Equally ambitious projects were proposed for MRC committees. In October 1960, for example, the Committee on the Future of the MRC was made a standing committee of the Council with a broad scope and function, "possibly even to [plan] the future development of the region."[42] Karl Metzger, Chairman of the committee, felt that MRC might evaluate and analyze the nine-volume study made by Harvard University for RPA of the economic and demographic features of the New York metropolitan region and emerge with a recommendation for a revision of existing governmental policies. The Council's time and attention, however, were spent on its legal and organizational problems, and this monumental study was not scheduled.

Other interesting projects also lacked the means of implementation. A "Scope of Activities" for MRC, drawn up by the Technical Advisory Committee in June 1961 for use by the Committee on the Future in drafting the interlocal agreement, called for MRC to organize research efforts on regional matters, accept grants for research projects, and seek implementation of recommendations resulting from such efforts. These activities could not be undertaken. MRC files carry ample evidence over the years of "MRC resolutions not acted on, . . . future role of MRC, . . . future plans, . . . long-range objectives, . . . immediate-action programs . . . and forces needed."[43]

[41] Letter from Keith to Schrader, December 31, 1962.

[42] Report to MRC members from Karl Metzger, February 28, 1961. In November 1960, the Committee on the Future of the MRC was renamed by the executive board "Committee on the Future Development of the Region." Metzger retained the chairmanship.

[43] See memoranda from Slote to Lehman, August 17, 1960, and from

One of the few areas in which MRC was able to function effectively was in communicating with the public via the press, and it was vigorous in its issuance of press releases. On the other hand, there is no evidence that the press coverage aided the Council in any tangible fashion except to direct attention to its own inadequacies. In 1962, the assistant executive secretary answered a request for information about MRC with the admonition: "Remember that we are as yet nothing but a twice a year meeting and a few vague projects plus quite a few good plans for the future."[44]

Routine Work of the Secretariat

In addition to dreaming up plans for the future, the secretariat was faced with the task of keeping MRC operating. During the years when MRC was functioning with reasonable dispatch, this was a demanding job. The secretariat was responsible for all aspects of the semiannual meetings to which about 500 elected officials and staff people were invited.[45] It also prepared the agenda and did preliminary work for the meetings of the eight permanent committees dealing with traffic and transportation, air-pollution control, water-pollution control, housing and redevelopment, recreation and open land, water supply, future of the region, and law enforcement. In addition, the secretariat published a monthly newsletter, the *Bulletin*, which gave news of

---

Prager to Lehman (probably 1962); "fact sheet on MRC" prepared in 1961 and distributed in 1962; and an intra-departmental memorandum from Prager to Lehman, July 12, 1963. Some of the "future plans" enumerated by the Council in 1962 included: examination of local revenue-producing sources, including a study of inequities among localities and the fiscal relationships between local, state and federal governments; study of regional civil-defense operations; creation of a regional statistical service for members; and creation of a clearing house for coordinated planning.

[44] Letter from Prager to Nicholas Thomas, November 7, 1962. An example of one of MRC's "good plans" is found in the *New York Times*, June 16, 1964, p. 37, where it is reported that MRC was about to undertake a study of polluted beach waters in the city's suburbs in an attempt to identify sources of pollution in the region. Like other proposed studies, this one was never begun.

[45] The last meeting of this kind was held on March 19–20, 1963.

interest in the region, and wrote a booklet on *Home Rule vs. Super-Government* for popular consumption.[46]

Because of the new and experimental nature of regional co-operation, the secretariat had to answer a large number of requests for information from interested persons. As the drive for legal status mounted, the secretariat was kept busy refuting charges arising from malice, ignorance, and misinformation, and prepared a fact sheet on "Myths and Misconceptions" about MRC. It mailed out a large number of reports to its members covering a variety of matters ranging from the health aspects of metropolitan planning to the use of air space over and under interstate freeways in urban areas.[47] It made a study of population changes of counties and major municipalities in the metropolitan region from 1950–1958 and brought this up to date in 1960. It furnished "informal assistance" to members when it could.[48]

Public Relations

This left virtually no time for the secretariat to engage in other essential activities called for in the "Scope of Activities": "cooperative relationships" with other regional agencies; "technical and professional assistance" to members and other units of local government in the region; and "community relations" with public and private groups in order to foster public understanding of regional problems. MRC's inability to mount strong programs in each of these areas was a great handicap in its drive to win public acceptance. It is important for a voluntary agency to foster con-

[46] The first issue of the *Bulletin* appeared in September 1959. There were two more issues published in 1959, five issues in 1960, four issues in 1961, five issues in 1962, five issues in 1963, three in 1964, and seven issues in 1965 before funds for its continuance were disallowed. Lehman, Prager, and Smallwood collaborated on *Home Rule vs. Super-Government* for MRC in 1961.

[47] E.g., Hospital Review and Planning Council of Southern New York, "Hospital Planning for the People of Southern New York," 1963; U.S. Department of Commerce, "Instructional Memorandum on the Use of Air Space," 1962.

[48] E.g., letter from Lehman to George Deming, February 20, 1958, describing aid furnished by officials of New York City to the town of Greenwich, Connecticut, to resolve a space problem in Greenwich's town hall.

tinuous and close relationships with its members in an effort to determine the areas in which it can be most helpful. Continuing contacts with important civic organizations like the League of Women Voters, local chambers of commerce, and church groups, which are just beginning to show signs of regional consciousness, are likewise essential.[49]

MRC existed in comparative isolation from its members and from civic groups for extended periods of time. In moments of crisis, the executive secretary solicited business leaders, newspaper reporters and feature writers, public-spirited citizens, and consultants on urban affairs who might be useful in helping to solve an immediate problem. There is no evidence that these people were called upon to perform continuing services.[50] Similarly, the secretariat failed to stimulate vigorous contacts with member governments and to make full use of the information obtained from infrequent meetings. Visits to New Jersey communities in the summer of 1960 indicated that the latter would welcome MRC assistance in resolving specific problems. Some of the subjects recommended as appropriate for MRC working committees dealt with problems of industrial migration, garbage and trash disposal, the aged, water distribution, and mosquito control.[51] The recommendations which were easily handled by MRC were implemented. The others went unheeded.

A second round of visits to member communities was undertaken in 1962. Again, there seemed to be little concern with follow-up action on recommendations that were received. Free-

[49] E.g., a Tri-State Committee of the League of Women Voters of New York, New Jersey, and Connecticut was organized in March 1964 to explore problems of common concern in the tri-state metropolitan region. The committee hoped to increase League interest in metropolitan issues and to create a heightened awareness in the local communities of metropolitan needs.

[50] E.g., memorandum from James S. Ottenberg to Lehman, January 14, 1960, enclosing a list of suggested members for a proposed citizens committee for MRC; letter from Walter H. Jones, State Senator from Bergen County, to Lehman, May 10, 1961, suggesting names of newspaper reporters and feature writers whom MRC should contact to arouse New Jersey support and interest in regional programs.

[51] Memoranda from Smallwood to Lehman, August 12, 1960, and from Slote to Lehman, August 17, 1960.

holder John Jay Sullivan and Planning Director Harvey Mosko-
vitz of Passaic County, for example, both thought MRC needed
more publicity and that "a vigorous program ought to be undertaken to explain to . . . the people who must vote to accept or
reject the interlocal agreement . . . what it is and how Passaic
County will benefit." These officials felt, moreover, that MRC
ought to take advantage of the clause that gave the Council legal
status as soon as New York City and four other communities
ratified the agreement. With the dues appropriated by five communities, MRC could "start rolling . . . and the remaining members will follow suit in short order." County Executive Nickerson
of Nassau also felt that "full-scale projects by MRC" would stimulate interest among its members.[52] Once again, however, no
action was undertaken. Other MRC visits were scheduled for
March 1964, but no record of these was kept.

Gradual Deterioration

Because of ineffectual leadership and a lack of money and staff,
MRC was able to do little more than maintain itself in existence
in the 1960s. Research and study were needed to develop new
policies and recommendations, and MRC was not in a position
to provide these. Its main concern was with short-run problems
rather than with long-range planning to meet future regional
needs. The Council's preoccupation with legal status after 1961
was overwhelming and time-consuming, and militated against an
innovative role. Because of a changeover in political leadership in
the region that resulted in new membership on the executive
board, a change of personnel within the secretariat itself, and setbacks to its hopes for legality, the Council started a slow downward movement from which it has never recovered.[53]

Adequate records and reports of MRC appear for the formative
years only. They were no longer kept in coherent fashion there-

[52] Memorandum from Prager to Lehman, September 9, 1962. For further
discussion of ratification by New York City, refer to Chap. II, p. 40.

[53] Leslie Slote, who had helped direct MRC activities for many years,
left the Office of the City Administrator in early 1962 to join Mayor
Wagner's press staff. He is now working as Governor Rockefeller's press
secretary.

after. In 1963, the executive secretary considered MRC's public image "laughable" and deplored the lack of "mechanism" to carry out the "good ideas." Faced with a meeting of local officials on the problem of reducing jet-airplane noise in Nassau County, he needed staff to do basic research before anything else could be done. Despite the fact that all of the work of MRC originated in the City Administrator's office, there had been no budgetary appropriation for MRC since its establishment, and the City Administrator seemed reluctant to continue using funds that might be put to a more profitable purpose elsewhere.[54]

[54] Interview with Lehman, April 1963.

VIII

MRC PROGRAMS:

A STUDY OF GOOD INTENTIONS

MRC established its first working committees in 1956 to deal with problems of transportation and teen-age drinking. Over the years, more committees were added in the functional fields of water pollution, air pollution, water supply, housing and redevelopment, recreation and land use, future of the region, and law enforcement. These committees were headed by the elected officials; a technical official could participate and serve as a staff member only with the consent of the top elected officer of his community. Because of the high turnover of the region's elected officials, as well as the many pressures on their time and attention, the MRC secretariat had to provide basic continuity and staff work for the committees. The Council's continuing lack of staff and funds meant that it was frequently unable to furnish adequate support to the standing committees. Only in rare cases was a committee able to carry a project forward to a reasonably satisfactory determination. A brief review of the more important of MRC's functional programs will illustrate the different fields in which MRC operated and the difficulties it encountered in sustaining the work of the various committees.[1]

---

[1] A survey undertaken in 1966 of the major regional councils then in existence indicates that their programs were generally similar to those of MRC. All of the councils used standing committees to deal with functional fields such as open space, air pollution, transportation, water supply, sewage treatment, water pollution, physical land planning, and uniform codes. Most councils operated with larger staffs than MRC and still experienced

Traffic and Transportation

In 1959, the Special Committee on Metropolitan Governmental Affairs of RPA suggested that MRC assume a role of leadership in the regional transportation field that would serve as a prototype of the important role which the Council might perform "in all other present and emerging problems of the region."[2] Unfortunately, the Council was not able to take advantage of the leadership opportunities provided by regional transportation problems any more than it could do so in other functional fields. However, the attempt was made—and sustained—over a number of years.

The critical condition of the region's mass-transportation facilities was acknowledged by the membership shortly after MRC was organized, and a Traffic and Transportation Committee was created in July 1956. The committee's early programs and recommendations were most ambitious. They included: the coordination of existing communication facilities in the metropolitan area for traffic-control purposes; a study of the possibility of assuming operation of abandoned ferries between New York and New Jersey; a study of the region's heliport facilities; a recommendation to Congress that the 10 percent excise tax on railroad passenger fares be removed and that railroad commutation expenses to and from work be allowed as a proper income tax deduction to all workers; a recommendation to the public service commissions of the region to postpone all requests for curtailment of commuter service pending completion of the study of the Metropolitan Rapid Transit Commission; and the formation of a special commission to study a uniform traffic code for the region.

In 1957, this list was augmented by a proposal to examine the rolling stock of all commuter rail carriers in the area. In 1958, the committee expressed reservations about the structure of the governing body of the transit district proposed by the Metropolitan

---

difficulties in providing adequate staff support to their standing committees on a continuous basis. (Citizens Research Council of Michigan, "Research Brief on Staff Services and Programs of Councils of Governments" [1966], pp. 1–2.)

[2] *New York Times*, January 9, 1959, p. 16.

Rapid Transit Commission, recommended a reduction in the size of American-made automobiles, and proposed a thorough study of commuter services in the region. As the proposals became more numerous, the need for some kind of follow-up work to perform the studies and implement the recommendations became imperative. The secretariat, however, could only devote attention to the most urgent matters. It took steps to help defeat the proposed New York–New Jersey transit district, approved of the distribution to all members of a uniform vehicle code, moved that all jurisdictions notify the executive board whenever a change in parkway tolls was contemplated, and created a special committee to study commuter problems.[3]

In February 1959, the Traffic and Transportation Committee began to focus the greater part of its attention on the creation of a single regional agency to prevent the collapse of existing rail service for commuters. A subcommittee met with the governors of the three states in 1960 and explored the possibilities of creating a tri-state agency and securing tax relief and other financial aid to keep the New York, New Haven and Hartford Railroad in operation. MRC reiterated its proposal for the formation of a tri-state transportation agency in later years. When a Tri-State Transportation Committee was created in 1961, MRC urged that it be replaced by a tri-state agency "with power to determine the extent of the need, and to contract for, receive and coordinate the expenditure of public funds for regional passenger service in the public interest."[4]

MRC proposals received less attention as the Council suffered setbacks in its attempts to gain official recognition. MRC tried,

[3] See Chap. V, pp. 85–86, for a review of the action taken by MRC to defeat the creation of the proposed bi-state transit district.

[4] Report of the MRC Traffic and Transportation Committee, June 1962. During this same period, MRC also endorsed a program of federal assistance to the urban commuter problem, recommended a thorough investigation of the Port of New York Authority by New York and New Jersey, requested a thorough audit of the New Haven railroad by the New York State Public Service Commission and the Connecticut Public Utilities Commission, and recommended a study of airport facilities in the metropolitan region. Refer to Chap. V, pp. 99–101, for a discussion of MRC's further actions with respect to the formation of a Tri-State Transportation Committee in 1959 and 1960.

for example, to gain the support of the Tri-State Transportation Committee in 1962 in its effort to prevent the Erie Lackawanna Railroad from abandoning a seven-mile stretch of railroad line between Paterson and Mountain View, New Jersey. MRC felt that the segment of the railroad line in question should be preserved to meet the future needs of high-speed passenger train service between northwest New Jersey and core areas of New York City. William Ronan, then Tri-State Chairman, refused to intervene, stating that this was a "local" matter to be handled directly by New Jersey and the localities involved.[5] In 1967, Eugene Nickerson, the new Chairman of MRC's Traffic and Transportation Committee, lamented publicly: "Nobody takes us seriously that counts . . . not Ronan . . . not the Tri-State Transportation Commission. . . ." Nickerson felt that MRC would not be successful in handling transportation problems until it became independent and financially able, with a staff that could assist the committees in realizing "concrete accomplishments."[6]

It is difficult to evaluate the extent to which the Council was effective in influencing regional transportation policy. The record indicates that there was a great difference between what MRC intended to do and what it actually did. For one thing, it would have been impossible for the secretariat to attend to *all* of the recommendations emanating from the Traffic and Transportation Committee. In addition, outside New York City many of the region's local governments displayed little support for regional approaches to rail problems and feared proposals which might threaten local autonomy or generate new financial burdens.[7] With uncertain support from its members and a lack of cooperation from other regional agencies, MRC's role of leadership in the regional transportation field was tentative at best.

On the other hand, MRC's activities may have generated some unmeasurable benefit in the regional transportation arena. The Council did facilitate enactment by the states of the tax-abatement

[5] Correspondence between Lehman and Ronan, December 13 and 17, 1962.
[6] Report of the Traffic and Transportation Committee, June 1967.
[7] Danielson, *Federal-Metropolitan Politics*, pp. 22 and 184; and Doig, *Metropolitan Transportation Politics*, pp. 141–144 and 221–228.

program important to the continuation of commuter service by the New Haven Railroad insofar as prior consultation among Council members and state representatives familiarized the heads of local governments with each other and with the problem. MRC representatives testified frequently before the federal and state governments concerning this matter. MRC's efforts were likewise important and effective in urging the states to undertake a regional approach to the planning of transportation needs in the New York metropolitan area. Finally, the Council's constant prodding of the Port of New York Authority probably played a part in the Authority's assumption of responsibility for operation of the former Hudson–Manhattan rail line in 1961.[8]

Water Pollution

The Water Pollution Committee convened for the first time in the office of A. Holly Patterson, County Executive of Nassau, in November 1956 and agreed on the need for an "inventory of the water pollution problem" in the region that would include an assessment of the capacity of receiving waters to assimilate pollution and an investigation of present practices of handling industrial-waste discharges. In January 1958, the committee assumed the task of assembling on one comprehensive map all information regarding existing and proposed pollution-control projects in the region. The membership of the Council resolved to support the committee's efforts in compiling this information and to provide, "through the several municipal departments involved, material aid and assistance required in transferring information and data in the possession of each community to the regional sewage map." In 1959, the committee reported that the basic structure of the map was well under way.[9]

[8] For further discussion of MRC accomplishments in the transportation field, see Sayre, in *Metropolitan Problems*, p. 69; statement by Edwin G. Michaelian in *Joint Hearings: Government in Metropolitan Areas* (1963), p. 165; and RPA, outline of statement on "Commuter Transportation Problems in the New York Metropolitan Region," February 27, 1962.

[9] This account is derived from records and minutes of meetings of the Water Pollution Committee from 1956 to 1964. The name of the committee was changed in the late 1950s to the Water Pollution Control Com-

In 1960, the Water Pollution Committee decided to enlarge its membership so that more areas in the region would be represented. In this way it would gain increased staff support and more general participation. Chairman Patterson hoped that MRC member communities would follow Nassau's lead in supporting analysis and control of metropolitan water pollution, and would budget funds, as Nassau had, to defray the cost of preparation of the map. Some months later, the committee recommended that the sewerage map be completed with "the greatest dispatch possible," and that means required for its final preparation be obtained from MRC member communities "by direct appropriation." In 1961, it was suggested that all communities which would benefit from the map's completion undertake to pay for the necessary work, or else a foundation grant should be sought.[10] In February 1962, progress on the development of the comprehensive sewerage map was "brought to a standstill due to lack of funds for staff operation." Six months later, the Interstate Sanitation Commission denied MRC's request for funds on the grounds that the proposed map would probably duplicate those already published by the Commission.

MRC next turned to the federal Department of Health, Education and Welfare for funds leading to a comprehensive program of water-pollution control in the tri-state metropolitan area. In 1964 federal funds were approved and planning begun for a management study of water quality and water supply in the tri-state metropolitan region to be carried out by the United States Public Health Service. MRC's sole participation in the project

---

mittee. Henceforth both names appear in reports of meetings. For purposes of this study, and to avoid confusion, the name of the committee will remain as originally stated.

[10] Report of the Water Pollution Committee, June 28, 1961. Patterson, Chairman of the committee from 1956 to 1961, was reluctant to use private funds for the completion of the map since he considered this "primarily a government responsibility" (letter to Lehman, January 19, 1961). A "Draft of a Comprehensive Plan for Sewage in the Metropolitan Region of New York, New Jersey and Connecticut," submitted to the committee in May 1961 by William T. Ingram, engineering consultant, estimated that the project might be developed for about $100,000–300,000. The committee felt that this would involve a "relatively small" contribution by member municipalities and would make an MRC staff operation possible.

consisted of a briefing, co-sponsored by the Council and the Public Health Service, for officials of local governments and their staffs.

This account of the lengthy, unsuccessful attempt of the Water Pollution Committee to obtain funds illustrates some of the hazards of voluntary cooperation. Nassau County considered the project to be of the utmost importance and was one of the first communities in the region to supply the necessary technical information and to appropriate funds for its execution. Other communities which did not feel the need as keenly as Nassau were unwilling to spend money or contribute staff. By the time MRC realized that it was unable to sustain the project on its own, it could no longer represent itself in its dealings with federal agencies as the united voice of local governments in the New York metropolitan region.

The account also points up the financial inability of local governments to solve area-wide problems on their own without help from other levels of government. Recent federal legislation, such as the Federal Water Quality Act of 1965 and the Housing and Urban Development Act of 1965, Title VII, provide direct aid to local public bodies and agencies, among others, for programs of water-pollution control. In addition, New York State has recently mounted an extensive six-year program of water-pollution abatement in which financial and technical assistance is provided to localities in meeting sewerage requirements.

Water Supply

The Water Supply Committee of MRC also suffered from a lack of material aid and staff assistance. In early 1958, the MRC executive board recommended that an inventory of water resources and water needs in the metropolitan region be undertaken by the Water Supply Committee and the secretariat. Nothing was done about this until a permanent chairman for the committee was found, a process which took a year and a half. Mayor Kristen Kristenson of Yonkers was appointed to the post in August 1959, having been preceded by Mayor Edward J. O'Byrne of Paterson and Mayor Leo P. Carlin of Newark.

In January 1960, MRC issued a press release announcing that an inventory of the present and anticipated water-supply needs of the 550 communities in the tri-state metropolitan region would be undertaken shortly. Questionnaires were prepared and distributed to MRC members seeking information about their present sources of water supply, their estimated needs, and the sources available for future development. By February 1961, a total of thirty-four counties and municipalities had answered, and it was suggested that research be continued on a more detailed scale to present a more precise determination of the region's needs.

In 1962, the Water Supply Committee recommended that further study of the region's water resources should be made by a professional engineering consultant rather than by the MRC staff. An estimate of $20,000–25,000 was secured for a review of regional water needs and facilities. In March 1963, the executive secretary announced that the secretariat was attempting to find a source of funds for the study. Apparently none was found. A news release issued by MRC in December 1964 stated that MRC "will start action to find solutions for the annual water crises which threaten the tri-state metropolitan area . . . by the simple expedient of sitting down voluntarily around a conference table and . . . using the legal tools now at our disposal."

The experience of MRC's Water Supply Committee highlights the risk of using elected officials, subject to the vicissitudes of political fortune, as chairmen of functional committees. With three changes in personnel over a two-year period, the Water Supply Committee could not continue to operate unless all of the preliminary work, research, and routine business were performed by a professional staff. The MRC secretariat was unable to do this; nor could it make effective use of the information furnished by local communities in answer to the questionnaires distributed by the committee.

Air Pollution

In November 1956, a meeting of a newly created Air Pollution Control Subcommittee of MRC agreed that "something . . . [had] to be done about the increasing pollution" in the New York metropolitan area. Hope was expressed that MRC "might be an appropriate medium through which a warning system could be developed during periods of atmospheric inversion whereby the danger to health of high levels of pollution would be minimized." A permanent Committee on Air Pollution Control was created, and included many technical officials among its members. The committee started to work on a plan to establish an area warning system.

In 1957, the committee again agreed on the need for action at the local level, reiterated its belief that MRC "constitutes the most effective medium for an approach to the solution of the . . . [air-pollution] problem," and decided that meetings should be arranged with local mayors, other municipal officials, and appropriate state agencies "to provide the beginning of education and control measures." In early 1958, the MRC executive board requested the committee to "continue to work on the establishment of an areawide pollution warning system to prevent the creation of emergency conditions in this area."

There is no record of progress with regard to the development of the warning system in 1959 and 1960. In February 1961, a subcommittee was created to study the "practicality of a region-wide air pollution warning system," and the MRC membership directed the secretariat to take all necessary steps to provide for its full implementation. It was again recommended that conferences be held with public officials and that a technical committee, comprised of members of the New York–New Jersey Cooperative Committee on Interstate Air Pollution and MRC's Air Pollution Committee, be charged with formulating the mechanics of the system.

Once MRC showed an inclination to move, it received unprecedented offers of support and cooperation from state agencies dealing with the same problem.[11] The technical committee met several times during 1962 and drew up a "Proposal for a Regional Air

[11] E.g., the top officer of the New Jersey Department of Health, Dr. Roscoe P. Kandle, considered MRC "a very high-level, responsible agency . . ." (letter from Alexander Rihm, Jr., Executive Secretary, Air Pollution Control Board, New York State, to Slote, May 29, 1961). See also letter from Rihm to Lehman, September 9, 1961, offering assistance in developing a warning system.

Pollution Warning System," which was presented to the MRC membership at the March 1963 general meeting. The proposal set forth specific recommendations with respect to a system of alerts that would be activated when pollution of the air reached "dangerous proportions."

The proposal left unanswered certain questions concerning the establishment of appropriate standards for measuring pollutants, the location, financing, and operation of monitoring stations, possible action by the United States Weather Bureau relating to continuous upper-atmosphere temperature monitoring, and the appropriate organization to administer the system. The proposal was to be submitted to the appropriate public officials so that these points might be clarified. In December 1965, Wagner advised the New York Joint Legislative Committee on Metropolitan and Regional Area Studies that, while the tri-state alert system proposed by MRC was "finally in effect" it still had many "weaknesses"; suburban communities did not possess the proper equipment to carry on continuous monitoring, and the Interstate Sanitation Commission, which administered the system, lacked legal authority to enforce compliance with the system of alerts. Development of a unified program of air pollution control for the New York regional area is still pending.[12]

The many meetings of the Air Pollution Committee at which the need for a warning system was discussed illustrates the Council's propensity to *talk* about problems rather than act on them. The executive secretary recognized the intense public interest which surrounded the subject from 1957 on and deplored MRC's lack of authority to assure follow-up action. "At the beginning," he said, "great enthusiasm is generated. . . . This is dissipated as time goes on. . . . The Council can only make pleas—in the same

[12] Wagner's appearance before the New York Joint Legislative Committee was made on December 16, 1965. The federal Air Quality Control Act of 1967 provides for a two-year study of national air-quality standards and permits the states to set their own standards in the meantime. A Mid-Atlantic Air Pollution Control Compact, providing for the creation of a new interstate commission with power to set and enforce minimum air-quality standards, was approved by New York, New Jersey, and Connecticut in 1967. The compact becomes effective upon enactment of concurring legislation by Congress.

way as private organizations. . . ." On the other hand, the committee itself was inactive for relatively prolonged periods of time between 1956 and 1961. Moreover, once it established its own jurisdiction in handling the matter, it never made use of the public interest that had been expressed; the committee could have done so by calling together citizen advisory groups or holding public meetings.[13]

MRC's proposals for a regional warning system might have provided the Council with a definitive regional project by which to enhance its own prestige had the Council taken advantage of it. By 1963, however, MRC could no longer sustain the interest which had been engendered in both official bodies and local communities. Commissioner Arthur J. Benline, then head of the New York City Department of Air Pollution Control, described the Council publicly as an organization "evolved under the Mayor's prodding . . . which occasionally gets very active and very interested in the many problems which interest the entire area. . . . From time to time one or another of the . . . counties thinks their particular interest is being stepped on, and they lose this interest and activity."[14]

In 1966, the *New York Times* commented on the recommendations of Mayor Lindsay's Task Force on Air Pollution and suggested that New York City use the findings as an opportunity to "breathe new vigor into . . . MRC, which has already shown interest in the problem."[15] One year later, the newly invigorated Air Pollution Committee of MRC reported at the annual meeting that it would continue its support of air-quality standards for the

[13] Lehman's comments were made in a letter to Mayor Steven Bercik of Elizabeth, New Jersey, October 17, 1957, and in an interview, April 1963. In this connection, the Citizens Research Council of Michigan finds that all councils use "pragmatic ways and means of exerting regional and subregional influence with respect to policy considerations" ("Research Brief on Staff Services," p. 19). These include informal relationships with private and quasi-governmental agencies within the regional sphere of action, use of citizen advisory committees, sponsorship of citizen conferences, and a vigorous public relations program.

[14] Letter from Benline to Lehman, October 15, 1963, offering a copy of "News from the *Readers Digest*" concerning an air-pollution helicopter survey of the New York metropolitan area made by Senator Edmund S. Muskie, Chairman, Special Senate Subcommittee on Air and Water Pollution, and regional air-pollution officials.

[15] *New York Times*, May 10, 1966, p. 44.

region, inform local officials of alert procedures, and undertake a program of public information.

Housing and Redevelopment

MRC's Housing and Redevelopment Committee had a relatively short-lived existence. It assembled in February 1958 for the first time under the vigorous but temporary chairmanship of Hugh Pomeroy, then Planning Director of Westchester County, and recommended that the secretariat undertake a survey of housing conditions in the region and collate the information received in a form suitable for use by the committee. Some months later, Mr. Pomeroy prepared a questionnaire for distribution to each constituent jurisdiction covering such subjects as: the amount and condition of housing as indicated by the 1950 Census on Housing; additions made to the housing supply since 1950; housing and urban renewal projects completed, pending, or anticipated; and current housing needs of low-income families, lower middle-income families, and aging and minority groups.

In February 1959, the committee reported that the questionnaires which had been returned "fail in number to provide an adequate basis for definite conclusions." They did, however, indicate a need for an "accelerated program to cope with the problem of substandard dwellings and to provide additional housing for middle-income and low-income families." It was recommended that the Council encourage an expanded federal program to aid in reviewing and redeveloping the older sections of the region's cities.

Subsequently, the Housing Committee experienced great difficulty in gaining consensus among MRC members with respect to the approach to be taken vis-à-vis the federal government. It was first recommended that MRC members pass a resolution endorsing general Housing Bill S. 57, then under consideration by Congress, and urge the Senate-House joint conference committee to withstand "administration efforts . . . [to] water down" provisions of the bill. Some Republican Council members objected to the "attack on the administration," and Vice-Chairman Michaelian, officiating in Mayor Wagner's absence, suggested that the Housing Committee's recommendation be "filed" and ballots be sent to all Council members before a final recommendation was made.

Six months later, in February 1960, the Housing Committee recommended that MRC lend its support to recent resolutions of the United States Conference of Mayors and the American Municipal Association requesting the federal government to authorize capital grant funds of $600 million a year for urban renewal over a period of ten years. Again, objections were raised. A few Council members questioned the use of specific figures because of "insufficient study," one member questioned the relevance of the housing issue for regional consideration, and another member took exception to the inclusion of the words "population explosion" in the body of the resolution as being too "controversial." The final MRC recommendation carried no specific figures, and the words "projected population increases" were inserted to replace the offending ones. No further meetings of the MRC Housing Committee were held, and the Council restricted its discussions to less sensitive subjects.[16]

Planning

In 1957, RPA suggested that the Inter-County Planning Conference, a loosely structured organization of planning officials of New York City and counties in the New York metropolitan region, affiliate with MRC as the "Metropolitan Council of Planning Agencies" (MCPA).[17] This was done, and MRC and MCPA worked closely together with other regional agencies and officials of Middlesex and Somerset counties, New Jersey, in 1959 in preparing a statement of "Measures of Metropolitan

[16] Voluntary councils are not alone in their avoidance of controversial subjects. In studying the municipality of Metropolitan Toronto, Smallwood attributed much of its ability to achieve consensus among its member municipalities to the fact that "the basic problems that have represented its primary fields of concern have been relatively obvious in their priorities and relatively non-controversial in their implications" (*Metro Toronto*, p. 38). He anticipated little agreement on newly emerging issues of social reform.

[17] At the time, RPA hoped that the affiliation would "assure performance . . . [of the planning function] within the framework of policies determined by the top elected officials of . . . governments" (letter from Henry Fagin, then Planning Director of RPA, to Mayor Wagner, April 16, 1957).

Growth—the argument for maintaining the integrity of census statistics for the New York–Northeastern New Jersey metropolitan area."

In 1960, MCPA issued a report on the status of municipal, county, and regional planning within the New York metropolitan region and suggested that MRC give serious consideration to the need for coordinating actions of individual municipalities with respect to policies of land use. One year later, MCPA presented testimony on behalf of itself and MRC to a congressional subcommittee with respect to the desirability of initiating a mid-decade census of population and housing for the metropolitan region.[18] The proposal was well received and the two groups were asked to report further. Unfortunately, nothing more was done about this, nor about coordinating land-use planning in the metropolitan area.

Hampered by insufficient personnel and deeply immersed in its own organizational problems, the MRC secretariat was unable to pursue meaningful programs of metropolitan planning. Unlike some of the other regional councils then in existence,[19] it did not take advantage of the opportunities to work closely with MCPA, the planning group in its metropolitan area, and to seek federal grants for regional planning activities. Since then, the Tri-State Transportation Commission has emerged as the official planning agency for the New York metropolitan region.

Law Enforcement

The Law Enforcement Committee is the newest functional committee of MRC. Created in September 1963 to provide closer liaison among law-enforcement agencies in the tri-state area, it was called the "first attempt of its kind in the nation to coordinate police activities in a metropolitan region which crosses state and local boundaries."[20] Its first meeting was enthusiastically received

[18] Statement by MCPA at a public hearing in New York City of the Subcommittee on Census and Governmental Statistics of the House Post Office and Civil Service Committee, 87th Congress, November 29, 1961.

[19] E.g., councils located in San Francisco, Seattle, Washington, D.C., Southern California, Salem, Oregon, and Atlanta, Georgia (Citizens Research Council of Michigan, "Research Brief on Staff Services," p. 21).

[20] MRC press release, January 27, 1964.

by the police chiefs and sheriffs in attendance, and Commissioner Michael F. Murphy of the New York City Police Department voiced the "certainty . . . [that] the underworld will have cause to rue this day which might well be considered Apalachin in reverse."

Robert R. J. Gallati, then Planning Chief of the New York City Police Department, became the first permanent secretary of the committee. An advisory committee composed of representatives of sheriffs, police chiefs, and state police from each state was formed, along with functional subcommittees. Three more meetings were held in 1963 and 1964. An annual report issued by Secretary Gallati in September 1964 pointed up the rather remarkable fact that "this was the first time that a comprehensive listing of . . . the approximately five hundred local police jurisdictions . . . in the New York metropolitan area was ever compiled."

Gallati left the New York City Police Department in September 1964 and the new chief of the planning division succeeded him in his post as secretary of the Law Enforcement Committee. In 1966, another member of the planning division who had been active in the work of the committee, also left the City Police Department. Reflecting the changes in personnel, the committee was relatively inactive for a time. It has now started to hold meetings with greater regularity, but, as with other MRC committees, its program suffers from a lack of staff work. Neither the committee itself nor its thirteen subcommittees can function effectively unless some kind of vigorous follow-up activity is provided between the periodic meetings.[21]

Other MRC Projects

EMERGENCY AIRCRAFT PROCEDURE.—In September 1962, the station operations manager of Trans-Canada Airlines wrote to

[21] A pilot program in law-enforcement planning has recently been started by the federal Department of Housing and Urban Development, in cooperation with the Justice Department, whereby urban planning assistance will be made available to regional councils for the design of programs in law enforcement and criminal justice. Perhaps MRC can take advantage of federal aid to do a more effective job in this field.

Mayor Wagner asking for help in updating emergency procedures in the event of an accident to one of its flights in the New York City area. Because this seemed to be a "metropolitan" rather than a "city" problem, it was given to MRC to handle. Questionnaires seeking information on emergency procedures in case of airplane accidents in populated areas were sent to all MRC members. The Council hoped to consolidate the answers and publish them in a master manual of emergency procedures for distribution to all airlines servicing local airports. Approximately one year later, MRC mailed the questionnaires back to Trans-Canada, advising: "Unfortunately . . . MRC cannot put the information into a manual or other form because of the widely different answers received." Trans-Canada likewise advised that it was unable to "tabulate the data in such a manner as to be useful."

EMERGENCY CONTROL PLAN.—In late 1962, MRC proposed to member communities that a cooperative plan be developed "to improve interlocal communications and to coordinate resources within the region to meet emergency situations." A committee of local officials agreed on the need to organize for swifter and more effective handling of major accidents and natural disasters that crossed local boundary lines and recommended the creation of a communications network for the transmission of emergency weather information. A workshop jointly sponsored by the United States Weather Bureau and MRC on emergency weather reporting was offered to police, fire, and civil-defense officials of the region and was well received.[22]

Some months later, a memorandum was sent to all mayors in the metropolitan area suggesting the creation of a "Weather Intelligence Network" to bring advance warning of severe weather conditions directly from the offices of the United States Weather Bureau to the local officials. The nominal cost of $10 per month for each subscriber was to cover installation of three direct telephone lines from key points in the region (Newark, New Jersey; Mineola, New York; and Hawthorne, New York) and a small

[22] The Suffolk County Director of Civil Defense was especially grateful for the opportunity to work with MRC on the emergency weather communications system, calling the information "of vital concern" to his county (letter from Edward H. L. Smith to Lehman, January 3, 1963).

junction box in the Weather Bureau's headquarters. The project was eventually discontinued due to a lack of interest by MRC members. Stamford, Connecticut, was the only community willing to pay for the cost of the service.

JET AIR NOISE.—In March 1963, at the request of Palmer Farrington, then Presiding Supervisor of the town of Hempstead in Nassau County, New York, MRC adopted a resolution to call a conference of representatives of all areas in the United States affected by the jet-noise problem, to compile all available data with regard to jet noise, to develop appropriate criteria and standards of tolerance of jet noise, and to sponsor legislation in Congress to deal with the jet-noise problem. (This was an ambitious order for an understaffed organization, but the Council wished to win the confidence of local officials of Nassau County and saw this as a possible means.)

Invitations were sent to all interested parties, including representatives of the aircraft industry, the Air Transport Association, the Air Line Pilots Association, the Port of New York Authority, the Aviation Development Council, the Federal Aviation Agency, and the local newspapers, to attend a luncheon meeting featuring a panel discussion of "The Jet Noise Problem and Local Government's Role in Solving It." In further compliance with the membership resolution, MRC turned over a large volume of data on jet noise to the Nassau County–Village Aircraft Safety and Noise Abatement Committee, requested the president of United Acoustics Consultants, a private firm in Darien, Connecticut, to develop appropriate criteria for jet-noise tolerance, and advised Congressmen Rosenthal and Wydler from Nassau and Queens respectively that the MRC resolution supported bills which they had introduced in Congress dealing with jet-noise abatement. Thus, MRC fulfilled its obligations to Nassau County.

Recreation and Land Use

In contrast to many of the projects described previously in this chapter, which never reached fruition because of MRC's lack of a strong internal organization, the work of the Recreation and Land Use Committee was outstanding. In this particular field,

MRC was able to perform a real service to its members, to RPA, and to the development of the region at large. It warrants further consideration at this point.

In January 1958, Harold S. Osborne, then President of RPA, proposed to the MRC executive board that a recreation and open-space study be made. The purposes of the study were to estimate the region's future needs for open spaces for parks and recreation, to inventory the parks and natural areas in the region, to develop a plan for a regional system of recreational facilities, parks, and other open spaces, and to recommend action programs to meet these needs. To accomplish these purposes, RPA had received a grant of $60,000 from the Old Dominion Foundation. (This was later supplemented by smaller grants from the Taconic, Avalon, and Victoria foundations.) RPA proposed that the study be undertaken as a joint project of RPA and MRC with the cooperation of the Metropolitan Council of Planning Agencies, that MRC seek the active cooperation of state, county, and local park agencies of the region, and that RPA provide staff work with assistance from the staffs of the various governmental agencies concerned. The study group was to report its findings and recommendations in the spring of 1960.

The executive board accepted RPA's proposal and designated Griffith Harris, First Selectman of Greenwich, as Chairman of the Recreation and Land Use Committee. The agreement was unanimously approved by the MRC membership in February 1958, and letters were sent to all members asking them to designate their chief park or recreation aide to work with the RPA staff in assembling information on park facilities. A joint steering committee was appointed by RPA and MRC in June 1958 with Otto L. Nelson, then Vice-President of RPA, and Griffith Harris, MRC, as Co-Chairmen, and including as members representatives from the National Audubon Society, the National Recreation Association, the Metropolitan Council of Planning Agencies, and staff associates of RPA. RPA provided staff to the project under the direction of the joint steering committee. Inventory forms covering municipal properties, public school properties, and private recreation properties were sent out by MRC to its members for distribution to their designated representatives.

A progress report from the Recreation and Land Use Committee to MRC members in February 1959 indicated that a total of 380 municipalities out of 519 in the area covered by membership in MRC had completed at least one of the inventory forms and 287 municipalities had completed the first two forms. These 287 municipalities comprised 55 percent of all the municipalities in the area and represented 83 percent of the region's total population. "Steady progress" was reported by the committee in June 1959, and the work was completed on schedule with the publication of *The Law of Open Space*, *The Dynamics of Park Demand*, and *Nature in the Metropolis* in mid-1960. The fourth and final volume, *The Race for Open Space*, also published in 1960, contained the findings and recommendations of the project's staff. It emphasized the great need for additional open space to meet the recreation requirements of an expanding population, and called for the acquisition of several specific areas of unique regional significance.[23]

Public and private response to the Recreation and Land Use Committee project was "universally affirmative. . . . Unquestionably the efforts of MRC and RPA have greatly stimulated action throughout the region aimed at meeting mounting pressure for recreational facilities."[24] In the first two years following completion of the study, more than 32,000 acres of open land were acquired for parks and recreational areas by the region's counties and municipalities, using *The Race for Open Space* as a blueprint. Six years later, 80 square miles of public open space had been purchased for park use, a 30 percent increase over what had existed in 1959. Moreover, the reports were instrumental in stimulating state and federal programs. By 1966, all three states in the region had passed bond issues providing for the purchase and develop-

[23] The report also covered a series of related subjects such as the additional legal and financial tools necessary to meet open-space requirements, the importance of preventing encroachment on existing parks, and the need for better highway access to parks. *The Race for Open Space* concluded that the New York region had fallen far behind in providing parks for its existing population and considered it essential for the region to acquire additional land immediately before it was developed for housing and other purposes.

[24] Report of MRC Recreation and Land Use Committee, February 28, 1961.

ment of parklands, and the federal government had provided open-space grants of $2.8 million to governments of the New York metropolitan region.[25]

The need for a continuing regional survey of the acquisition of open-space lands was discussed at many MRC meetings after 1960. The secretariat announced itself ready to supply legal assistance to members wishing to take steps to implement technical recommendations made by *The Race for Open Space* and to issue questionnaires to all MRC members. No follow-up on this offer can be found. The Recreation and Land Use Committee was reactivated briefly in 1965 to discuss the possibility of drafting a memorandum of agreement among the local governments in the region with respect to the acquisition of open space. The agreement was not pursued after the passage in 1965 of the Housing and Urban Development Act which provided a flat 50 percent grant of aid for the acquisition of open space and for the development of recreational facilities. A new MRC Committee on Recreation and Land Use is now attempting to compile data to update its information and has distributed a questionnaire to all local governments in the region seeking details about land acquisitions for park and recreational purposes between 1960 and 1967.

The park, recreation, and open-space study has been described variously as "the most constructive action of the MRC to date," the "only real accomplishment" of MRC, and "the best example of teamwork by MRC and RPA."[26] Given financial and staff aid from RPA and a clear sense of direction and purpose, MRC was able to contribute the active participation of park, planning, and other technical officials in aid of a critically important regional effort. However, MRC's contribution went beyond merely serving as a vehicle through which information was collected. Because its membership included the top elected officials of the region who were intimately involved throughout the duration of the project in a program of material benefit to their individual

[25] RPA, "Results of Regional Plan's Park, Recreation and Open Space Project—1958–1966," Appendix II.
[26] Statement of Griffith Harris in the report of the Recreation and Land Use Committee to the MRC executive board, October 18, 1960; interview with Cassella, April 12, 1963; and letter from Keith to Schrader, December 31, 1962, respectively.

communities, the acquisition of open-space land became their effort as well as that of the two sponsoring groups.[27]

MRC members helped to sell the idea of acquiring open space lands before they disappeared into subdivisions and built-up areas. MRC support also provided RPA with a forum from which to discuss and proselytize, and made available to RPA documents and data which it might not have had otherwise. RPA's contribution must be underscored as well. Left to its own "resources" after 1960, MRC was unable to carry through with the necessary collection of data to implement the recommendations of *The Race for Open Space*.[28]

Balance Sheet of Accomplishments

On balance, the accomplishments of MRC seem to be more good intentions than anything else. The MRC secretariat tended to overstate its case and consistently promised more than it could deliver. A list of the "current studies underway by MRC" in 1958 included items such as an inventory of housing needs, a master map of water pollution, an air-pollution warning system, a study of railroad commuter lines, and the achievement of legal status. Many of these projects appeared on similar lists during the next five years until, one by one, they were eventually discontinued. In 1963, when most MRC activity had tapered off, Mayor Wagner addressed the Citizens Budget Commission and RPA and enumerated a list of projects in which MRC was then engaged. This included the creation of a coordinated emergency control system and a weather communications network, a study of ways to expand the region's industrial and commercial poten-

[27] E.g., Westchester County adopted the report's recommendations as its own goals and began to acquire additional parkland. By 1966, Westchester had acquired 3,500 acres of parkland to add to its 1960 base of 10,000 acres.

[28] RPA and MRC have recently collaborated on a study entitled *Waste Management: Generation and Disposal of Solid Liquid and Gaseous Wastes in the New York Region: A Report of the Second Regional Plan* (1968). MRC circulated questionnaires dealing with refuse disposal to its members to aid RPA map out a proposal of waste management looking to the year 2000.

tial, a study of means to assure the peaceful accommodation of new population groups, and ways to preserve the region's eroding shoreline. A "progress report for MRC" in 1965 showed more of the same empty plans.[29]

On the other hand, MRC's experience illustrates anew the difficulties inherent in attempts to "solve" substantive problems by voluntary action. A council's relative influence on other programs and agencies in its metropolitan area depends in many cases upon factors beyond its control, including money and staff, legal power, the nature of the particular problem, political considerations, and the consequences of lack of action. When a regional problem becomes sufficiently pronounced so that reorganization is necessary—as in the administration of an air-pollution warning system—simple cooperation is not enough. An agency with the requisite authority is needed.[30]

MRC first took note of its limitations in March 1964 when Mayor Wagner suggested that "an advisory or study group which limits itself to recommendations should not be challenged to produce its record of concrete achievements. . . . We are not an operating agency and . . . should not be judged in those terms."[31] It is ironic that, in detailing a long list of "specific accomplishments" and "future plans" every time MRC convened, the execu-

[29] See memorandum prepared by Lehman for George H. Deming on "Current studies now underway by the MRC," June 16, 1958; memorandum from Slote to Lehman concerning "MRC resolutions not acted on," August 17, 1960; MRC's answer, December 4, 1963, to a questionnaire distributed by the Metropolitan Washington Council of Governments with respect to MRC's progress during 1963 (for use by John C. Bollens in preparing a review of metropolitan-area developments in the annual edition of the *Municipal Year Book*, published by the International City Managers' Association). See also Wagner's address, February 4, 1963; and memorandum from Prager to Connery, October 15, 1965.

[30] The Citizens Research Council of Michigan finds few cases of complete sucess or failure as a result of action by a regional council. The implementing process is "gradual" rather than "spectacular," with partial success most common ("Research Brief on Staff Services," p. 17). For further discussion of the inability of voluntary councils to make enforceable decisions on important issues, refer to the Advisory Commission, *Alternative Approaches*, p. 36; and Hanson, *The Politics of Metropolitan Cooperation*, pp. 27 and 67.

[31] Address by Wagner to MRC membership, April 24, 1964.

tive secretary might have been the Council's harshest critic.[32]

Perhaps a balance sheet of MRC's record would look less blurred if its objectives had been spelled out more realistically. While the results of MRC's endeavors have never been as impressive as the secretariat has claimed, they are not insignificant either. The Council *did* play a role in support of proposals in the regional transportation arena, in the preservation of open space and recreational lands in the region, and in the proposal for an air-pollution warning system. Of equal importance, it provided the informal contact through which regional problems that required action by several governments could be negotiated and handled more expeditiously. The county executive of Westchester said about this: "If we want to get something, say, from the City of New York, . . . we can cut out the protocol and get right down to the meat of the problem."[33] Both New York City and Westchester County subsequently credited MRC with the satisfactory completion of negotiations for resolving a long-standing New York City sewerage problem and simultaneously furnishing the means for Westchester to acquire lands for recreational purposes.[34]

Moreover, the mere fact of MRC's existence in a complicated region of 1,500 governments merits important consideration. The

[32] E.g., a fact sheet on MRC prepared by the secretariat for general distribution in October 1962 listed twelve "accomplishments" in different functional fields, including the following:

> It has presented to the federal government the regional case for increased aid for public housing and urban renewal. . . .
> It began a nation-wide campaign for smaller automobiles. . . .
> It took the lead in developing a coordinated approach to the region's mass transportation problems, . . . which resulted in the creation of the Tri-State Transportation Committee. . . .

See also Lehman's report to MRC members, June 10, 1958, his address to the Women's City Club, December 2, 1958, and his address to the Home Builders' Association of Northern New Jersey, May 5, 1959, each of which outlined MRC's accomplishments for the recent past.

[33] Public hearing conducted by the Committee on the Future of the MRC, Stamford, Connecticut, November 18, 1958.

[34] News release, City of New York, Office of the Mayor, July 19, 1962, and *New York Times*, March 20, 1964, p. 35. To RPA, this was a "matter of some significance because previously lack of contact on just such sales had allowed important park sites to pass into the hands of private developers" (letter from Keith to Schrader, December 31, 1962).

Council's continuing stimulation of communication and cooperation between New York City and its neighbors opened up for
many suburban officials new ideas and new possibilities about the
New York metropolitan region. A planning official from Hartford found the "large gathering of officials of the many municipalities . . . heartening to us in Connecticut"; the chairman of the
Planning Committee in Orange County, New York, felt that participation in MRC "was of great value in assessing the County's
position in the region"; and the chairman of the Board of Freeholders of Middlesex County, New Jersey, found MRC to be
"the right agency for helping me to do a better job as a local
government official almost overwhelmed by problems plaguing
my particular responsibility, but which extended far beyond my
jurisdiction and reach."[35]

Thus MRC served over the years as a useful meeting ground
for the exchange of information and knowledge concerning certain common problems by elected and technical officials. Its past
ten years of regional experience provide a valuable blueprint of
conduct, procedures, and policies which can be studied and
evaluated by its new administration. The important question facing the Council now that it is a legal and independent body for
the first time in its existence is whether it can move beyond its
hitherto moderate activity to become an effective governmental
force, influencing decision-making in a region which is far different from that in which it was originally conceived.

[35] The officials in question were Horace H. Brown, Senior Planner,
State Development Commission, Hartford Connecticut (letter to Lehman,
March 3, 1960); R. Preston (report to the Orange County Board of Super-
visors, July 14, 1961); and Karl Metzger (statement in *Joint Hearings:
Government in Metropolitan Areas* [1963], p. 246), respectively.

IX

NO FINAL SOLUTIONS

The limited nature of MRC's accomplishments described in the previous chapter makes it clear that the Council did not develop into the "central general-purpose official leadership institution of the tri-state metropolitan region" envisioned in 1959 by Wallace Sayre, Luther Gulick, and other members of RPA's Special Committee on Metropolitan Governmental Affairs.[1] As Royce Hanson has pointed out, an organization which merely brings elected officials together periodically to discuss regional problems is far different from an institution of political leadership which identifies area-wide substantive problems and aids in their solution within a broad framework of total community welfare.[2]

When consideration is given to some of the difficulties attending the establishment of a metropolitan institution in a tri-state area, such as legal obstacles, city-suburban antagonisms, city-state hostility, political differences, lack of regional consciousness, and competing regional agencies, the question arises: Is there sufficient justification for MRC's struggle for survival in the past and for its revitalization, with federal help, at present? A second question, closely related to the foregoing, might also be asked: Are the drawbacks which have been associated with voluntary cooperative efforts—such as difficulties in reaching consensus, inadequate financial support, insufficient staff, turnover of membership—so limiting as to make them ineffectual undertakings?[3] Or can volun-

[1] *New York Times*, January 9, 1959, p. 16.
[2] Hanson, *The Politics of Metropolitan Cooperation*, p. 68.
[3] It has been suggested, in addition, that voluntary councils merely serve to delay solutions to metropolitan problems by neutralizing conflict

tary councils surmount these obstacles and provide a means through which local officials can learn to deal with common problems in a regional framework? Can these officials then participate affirmatively in the regional planning of their own communities?[4] While no positive answers can be furnished as yet, particularly in the rapidly changing New York region, guidelines by which to examine MRC's future role are presently emerging in other councils in other metropolitan areas.

The New Look of Federal-State-Local Relations

Wallace Sayre has pointed out that "the 1950's were marked by an effort to form metro-type government through local action. Now the effort is shifting to get metro government through federal and state action."[5] Since 1956, when MRC was originally conceived, it has become increasingly clear that many of the problems with which the Council dealt cannot be handled by local governments acting alone—or in concert. The very nature of the urban community makes it impossible for the Council to do more than provide weak, ineffective remedies for the community's problems. None of the local governments possesses the financial or legal resources or the jurisdictional authority to become involved in the massive future commitments required to deal successfully with urban problems spilling over jurisdictional lines. Interlocal cooperation is part of the answer. Local-state-federal cooperation is essential as well.

---

among local officials or by acting as a palliative to more drastic approaches to metropolitan reorganization. See, for example, Bollens (ed.), *Exploring the Metropolitan Community*, p. 94; Martin, *Metropolis in Transition*, pp. 49 and 143; Banfield, "The Political Implications of Metropolitan Growth," *Daedalus*, XC (Winter, 1961), 70; Herman, *New York State*, p. 27.

[4] See Victor Jones, "Associations of Local Governments," address to Conference on Government, 1961; Henry J. Schmandt, "The Area Council—Approach to Metropolitan Government," *Public Management*, XLII (February 1960), 30–32; Winston W. Crouch and Beatrice Dinerman, *Southern California Metropolis: A Study in Development of Government for a Metropolitan Area* (Berkeley: University of California Press, 1963), pp. 401–403. See also authors cited in nn. 6 and 14 to this chapter.

[5] Opinion Reporting Workshop of Columbia University, "Seminar on Effective Community Reporting," Pt. II, p. 9.

The history of local community action in the United States indicates that most of the motivation must come from the states or from the federal government, with a trend toward the latter in recent years. The federal government has been playing an increasingly important role in the metropolitan scene, including intervention in matters long thought to be "local." The federal emphasis on comprehensive urban planning as a prerequisite for funds will probably continue to be a positive factor influencing innovation in urban affairs. With financial pressures imposed by Washington, local officials have been forced to expand programs and to face problems they avoided in the past. Urban planning programs generated by the federal level are expected to continue to involve local political leaders in area-wide planning activities, in conjunction with the efforts of other regional planning officials.[6]

A greater number of states may play a more positive role in responding to the needs of an increasingly urban population, though there is less direct evidence of this. Roscoe Martin finds that the states have been "unwilling to assume their share of . . . responsibility, particularly during the last three decades," and sees little prospect for change.[7] With the reapportionment of state legislatures, however, other observers find reason to believe that the states will devote more attention to urban problems and make greater appropriations for metropolitan activities. Increased efforts on the part of the states to revise outmoded constitutions and to restructure themselves in order to act as middlemen in federal-local relations furnish encouraging evidence of a more meaningful state involvement in the assault on metropolitan problems.[8]

[6] Norman Beckman, "The Quiet Revolution," *National Civic Review*, LVII (January 1968), 14–20; Royce Hanson, "Federal Air Spurs Area Councils," *ibid.*, LV (July 1966), 401–403; Henry J. Schmandt, "The Emerging Strategy," *ibid.*, LV (June 1966), 325–330. For more general discussion, refer to Martin, *The Cities and the Federal System*, particularly Chap. VII, "The Expanded Partnership: Appraisal."

[7] Martin, *ibid.*, p. 47.

[8] Adrian, *Annals*, CCCLIX (May 1965), 42–43; Advisory Commission, *Ninth Annual Report* (Washington, 1968), p. 9; Scott, *Public Administration Review*, XXVI (December 1966), 336–337. See also discussions by John E. Bebout, "The State and Local Government," pp. 39–50, and Nor-

While federal and state governments are generating programs to be carried out at the local level, local communities must accept some measure of responsibility for shaping the programs which will guide their communities. In the same way that higher levels of government, which possess the financial ability to provide solutions to area-wide problems, should not proceed without due consideration of local preferences, local communities must reorganize themselves in such a way as to have their influence maximized. The federal government is asking for more than weak gestures of communication leading to cooperation; it would like to see the local governments help to plan the appropriate policies and achieve the necessary coordination.

Response by Local Governments

An increasing number of local governments have responded to the federal challenge by forming regional councils in their respective metropolitan areas. Many of these councils have undertaken regional planning on their own, and some have branched out into other fields as well. The Puget Sound Governmental Conference in the Seattle metropolitan area, for example, prepared a comprehensive transportation proposal, and the Supervisors Inter-County Committee in the Detroit metropolitan area, the oldest council of governments in the United States, merged with the Detroit Metropolitan Area Regional Planning Commission to become the Southeast Michigan Council of Governments and assume new responsibilities in regional and transportation planning.

The Association of Bay Area Governments (ABAG), the first voluntary council to move strongly into the field of comprehensive regional planning, became the official planning agency for the entire San Francisco metropolitan region in 1962, the only organization in the Bay Area eligible to receive and administer federal grants and funds related to comprehensive planning processes. In addition to performing studies in a wide range of

ton E. Long, "The Role of State Government in Regional Development," pp. 52–65, *The State's Biggest Business*, Policy Papers (1967).

functional fields, including transportation, conservation, and open space, it presently acts as the regional review agency for applications from local governments for federal grants-in-aid. In 1966, the general assembly of ABAG voted to request the California legislature to reconstitute it as a regional government for the Bay Area with initial authority in three fields: regional airports, parks and open space, and refuse disposal. Enactment of such legislation was considered a "likely possibility" in 1967; it now appears to be in doubt because of "internal dissension" and the alleged delinquency of ABAG's assistant director.[9]

The Metropolitan Washington Council of Governments (MWCOG), another active council, serves as the comprehensive regional planning agency for the Washington, D. C., metropolitan area and is involved in transportation planning and in studies of air pollution, water supply, waste disposal, and open space. In 1967, with federal financial assistance, MWCOG expanded its staff and programs to undertake regional planning in the fields of environmental health, public health and welfare, public safety, and data systems. MWCOG presently serves as the regional review agency and has embarked on new metropolitan activities in housing, uniform crime-statistics reporting, manpower development, and vocational rehabilitation planning programs.[10]

Councils as Policy-Making Bodies

As councils have become more active in comprehensive and regional planning, there has been a tendency for them to become

[9] Willis Hawley and Stanley Scott, "Bay Area Looks to Regional System," *National Civic Review*, LVI (November 1967), 595; and *Metropolitan Area Digest*, ed. Joseph F. Zimmerman, XI (Graduate School of Public Affairs, State University of New York, March–April 1968), 5, respectively. For further information about ABAG's recent proposal to convert itself into a limited multipurpose agency, refer to Robert G. Miller, "Regional Home Rule and Government of the San Francisco Bay Area," statement to the California State Assembly Committee on Municipal and County Government regarding Assembly Bill No. 50, February 22, 1967, mimeographed (Berkeley: ABAG, 1967).

[10] Metropolitan Washington Council of Governments, *Annual Reports, 1966, 1967*. Also see U.S. Department of Housing and Urban Development, *Cooperative Ventures in Urban America* (Washington, 1967), p. 70.

operational in character. Even without the new authorization it seeks, ABAG is presently considered to be a "quasi-governmental" agency which administers programs at a regional level.[11] Other councils which perform the regional review function exercise jurisdiction over a large number of regional programs and may soon become involved in the determination of priorities among competing programs and competing jurisdictions. In spite of their drawbacks, councils seem to be moving away from "mere social gatherings of local elected officials into rather elaborate intergovernmental organizations."[12]

Many questions are raised as a result of these new activities. Once a council takes on governmental functions and becomes the funnel for federal grants, can participation in its activities still be considered "voluntary," and would its recommendations remain "advisory" only? Martin points out that, in theory, no participating government of a voluntary council loses any of its decision-making power over matters which are purely local in scope. But the decision between what is "local" and what is "regional" is not always clear. Moreover, a participating community is not likely to agree with all of the decisions that its council may make.[13]

Proponents of voluntary councils welcome their growing involvement in the formulation and implementation of metropolitan plans and defend them as a practical means of linking planners and elected officials.[14] It is felt that there is no way to solve metropolitan problems without limiting the options available to local communities. Consensus does not necessarily involve agreement by all who participate, and the resulting range of choice "may still be greater than that which would result from a settlement

[11] Citizens Research Council of Michigan, "Research Brief on Staff Services," p. 31. See also Randy H. Hamilton, "ABAG—Five Years of Accomplishment," *Public Management*, XLVIII (May 1966), 142–146.

[12] Hanson, "Councils of Governments and the Demise of Service Regionalism," address to ASPA, March 29, 1968, p. 6.

[13] Martin, *Metropolis in Transition*, p. 36.

[14] E.g., Hanson, *National Civic Review*, LV (July 1966), 401; Schmandt, *ibid.*, LV (June 1966), 325; Hanson, *Metropolitan Councils of Governments*, pp. 33–35; Victor Jones, in *The State's Biggest Business*, Policy Papers (1967), pp. 81–95.

by a central authority."[15] If the regional viewpoint is necessary for the proper development of the region, some organization has to speak for the local governments involved. If the council does not do this, a special-purpose district or higher level of government might, and it would be less responsive to the people than their elected local officials.

Another important question deals with the representative nature of councils. The Supreme Court has extended its "one-man, one-vote" doctrine to local governments and has ruled that single-member election districts in local elected units with general legislative power over the community must be substantially equal in population. At the same time, the Court has left the door open to "the emergence of a new ideology and structure of public bodies, equipped with new capacities and motivations," and does not intend to set roadblocks in the paths of innovation and experimentation by local communities.[16]

While the decision suggests that the one-man, one-vote requirement may apply within local government more strictly than among local governments, the question of representation remains a thorny one. Reflecting the ferment of interest in this problem, ABAG has recently restructured its executive committee to reflect population differences among its members and has provided for state and federal representation as well. On the other hand, the mayor of Milwaukee has refused to join the council of governments in his metropolitan area on the basis that the city would be underrepresented and the power of the suburbs would be thereby increased.[17] In addition, it has been suggested that the political influence of minority groups, with established political bases in the central cities, would be submerged in the metropolitan planning bodies called for by current federal requirements.[18]

[15] Ostrom, Tiebout, and Warren, *American Political Science Review*, LV (December 1961), 842. See also discussions by Harold F. Wise, "More Than Planning," *National Civic Review*, LV (May 1966), 241–246; Hawley and Scott, *ibid.*, LVI (November 1967), 593; and Institute for Local Self-Government, *ABAG Appraised: A Quinquennial Review of Voluntary Regional Cooperative Action through the Association of Bay Area Governments* (Berkeley: 1965), p. 21.

[16] *Avery* v. *Midland County*, 390 U.S. 474 (1968).

[17] *New York Times*, April 28, 1968, p. 58.

[18] Frances Fox Piven and Richard A. Cloward, "Black Control of Cities:

The problem of providing all political groups in a regional area with equitable representation in a regional agency is complicated and will be difficult to resolve. Similarly, the problems facing area-wide planning bodies in metropolitan areas are expected to become more difficult and controversial. Federal programs are becoming increasingly oriented to problems of low-income and minority groups and the advancement of "physical" solutions in regional planning efforts is no longer looked upon as sufficient. If the councils evolve into decision-making bodies, therefore, their structures and scope of activities will have to be revised accordingly. Councils are still in a marked state of flux.

New York Metropolitan Region: The Current Scene

In contrast to the more advanced councils which have been assuming new tasks in the metropolitan areas of Detroit, San Francisco, Seattle, and Washington, D. C., MRC is just beginning to review and evaluate its own position in the most complicated metropolitan environment in the country. Until this is properly done, MRC will not be able to play a role in programming the development of the region or in helping to provide solutions to any of the critical issues facing the region.

The need for regional cooperation is greater than ever. A projection of the region's population to the year 1985 indicates that there will be about six million more people living in the New York metropolitan region than in 1960, and that this increase will spread far out from the central city and change all aspects of the region's physical structure. Because of this projected period of rapid growth, RPA has recently adopted a new regional study area, which includes a ring of nine additional counties and adds nearly 6,000 square miles to its original twenty-two-county, 6,900-square-mile region. According to the most recent RPA projections, the population of the New York metropolitan area is expected to increase by 58 percent to thirty million

Heading It Off by Metropolitan Government," and "Black Control of Cities: How the Negroes Will Lose," *The New Republic*, CLVII (September 30, 1967, and October 7, 1967), pp. 19–21 and 15–19, respectively.

persons by the year 2000, almost two times the population increase of the last thirty-five years. Tri-State also projects a vast
increase in people, income level, construction, and travel, with
many new demands for additional housing, jobs, education, and
other essential services.[19]

The projected population growth in the largest region in the
United States points up the need for better regional machinery
to coordinate the public policy decisions made by all the region's
governments. The growth cannot be accommodated in any kind
of rational manner as long as the 1,500 or so local governments
continue to function in their present unrelated fashion. The new
studies made by RPA and Tri-State provide basic research for a
wide variety of policy goals for the region, but there is little
expectation at present that official regional policy will be generated by the local governments.[20] Such an approach will have
to come from a superior governmental level, a process already
well underway.

Recent State Action: Takeover or Participation

To mention one obvious instance, regional centers of activity
are beginning to develop in the transportation field. In 1965, New
York State created a Metropolitan Commuter Transportation
Authority (MCTA) to deal with the development and improvement of commuter services within the twelve-county, New York
sector of the region. William Ronan, then Chairman of the Tri-
State Transportation Commission, became Chairman of the new
agency. In March 1967, the New York legislature authorized a
transportation capital facilities bond issue of $2.5 billion, "the

[19] RPA, *The Region's Growth* (1967); and Tri-State Transportation
Commission, *Regional Forecast 1985* (1967). See also RPA, *Spread City:
Projections of Development Trends and the Issues They Pose. The Tri-
State New York Metropolitan Region, 1960–1985*, Bulletin 100 (Septem-
ber 1962), and Arthur T. Row, *A Consultant's Report to the Tri-State
Transportation Committee on A Reconnaissance of the Tri-State Region*
(1965).

[20] For further discussion, refer to Doig and Danielson, "Politics and
Urban Development: The Case of the New York Region," *International
Journal of Comparative Sociology*, VII (March 1966), 76–95; Wood,
1400 Governments, particularly Chap. V, "The Political Economy of the
Future"; Chinitz, *Scientific American*, CCXIII (September 1965), 143.

largest state government bond issue in the nation's history,"[21] which, after submission to the voters in November 1967, was to be used for a variety of state and local purposes including highway construction, airport facilities, and mass-transportation facilities. A new transportation act, passed at the same time, created a Department of Transportation with responsibility for the development and coordination of a unified and balanced transportation system for the state.

Under provisions of the transportation act, MCTA became the Metropolitan Transportation Authority (MTA) in March 1968, with greatly expanded responsibilities in rapid transit, surface transit, bridge and rail commuter traffic. It already owned and operated the Long Island Railroad; it now exercises policy and planning control over most metropolitan-area transit, including the New York City Transit Authority, the Manhattan and Bronx Surface Transit Operating Agency and the Triborough Bridge and Tunnel Authority. Ronan has recently been appointed a Commissioner of the Port of New York Authority, a move which will further integrate transportation efforts in the region.

New Jersey is also adopting a new posture with respect to transportation. In 1966, it passed an act enabling the state to administer a comprehensive transportation program. In recognition of the need to plan highways in conjunction with other means of public transportation, a newly created Department of Transportation has taken over the existing functions of the state highway department and has established a commuter operating agency within the department to supervise operation of commuter service by the railroads. A large transportation bond issue has been proposed to modernize the state's transportation system and aid both highways and commuter lines.

Until now, regional action has been taking place within each state. Because of their mutuality of concerns in the transportation field, a regional approach may emerge. The proposed New Jersey bond issue, for example, is expected to complement MTA's program for New York, particularly in improving direct rail access to Manhattan. On the other side of the region, MTA and its counterpart in Connecticut, the Connecticut Transportation

[21] Advisory Commission, *Ninth Annual Report*, p. 7.

Authority (created in 1963), are presently undertaking joint action on behalf of their respective states to modernize suburban rail service on the New Haven Railroad, with the help of a large federal grant.[22]

Further instances of positive state action should be noted. New York State created an Urban Development Corporation in April 1968 with drastic powers to ignore city regulations, condemn property, and override building codes, if necessary, to carry out its program of rebuilding urban areas. While the plan calls for close cooperation with city governments, final decisions on urban renewal plans are left up to the corporation. New Jersey, too, has proposed creation of a Hackensack Meadowland Development Commission to oversee the development of a large tract of undeveloped land in Hudson and Bergen counties into an urban complex. Once more, local interests would be subject to veto by a majority of the commission's members.

Cumulatively, then, the state governments are beginning to act with power and initiative vis-à-vis the region. All of these programs raise the possibility of positive collaboration between state and local interests, but the extent of local participation that will be sought and permitted is far from clear. What *is* clear, however, is that the region will soon feel the effect of this increased use of state power; if local governments are excluded from participation, they will become progressively weaker and will have fewer and less important functions to perform in the future.[23]

Recent State Action: Institutional Arrangements

In addition to formulating new regional programs in specific functional fields, the states have been reexamining their relation-

[22] For further details, see the *New York Times*, March 12, 1968, p. 1, and April 9, 1968, p. 46.

[23] It is worthy of note that New York City's own plan for consolidating its transportation facilities was turned down by the 1966 state legislature. Arthur E. Palmer, Jr., Transportation Administrator of New York City, resigned when the MTA assumed supervision of mass-transportation facilities in the region because of his feeling that MTA would dominate the transportation field in the city (*New York Times*, December 1, 1967, p. 32).

ships with their own local communities. New York established an Office of Planning Coordination in July 1966 as an official planning agency within the executive department. Its purpose is to offer planning assistance to local communities and to coordinate the state's planning activities with those of local communities, other states, and the federal government. New Jersey established a Department of Community Affairs in March 1967 (headed by Paul N. Ylvisaker, a well-known specialist in community problems) to provide assistance to New Jersey municipalities and help them provide for local needs.

Connecticut has long promoted a regional approach to state and local programs through the formation of official regional planning agencies. In 1965, Connecticut created a legislative commission to study the "necessity and feasibility of metropolitan government" in regional districts within the state. With the assistance of prominent consultants in urban affairs, the commission rejected "metropolitan government" as a feasible solution and recommended, instead, a number of changes to help the state respond to its increased urban responsibilities.[24] Acting on the commission's recommendations, Connecticut established a new Department of Community Affairs in July 1967. Its purpose is to engage in planning activities and to provide funds and technical assistance to local communities to help them plan their own programs, particularly in economic and social affairs.

Tri-State Transportation Commission and the Review Function

In addition to the new planning agencies which have been created within each state, the region has its own official planning body, the Tri-State Transportation Commission. Created by interstate compact among the three states in 1965, its function is broader than its name implies. Not only does Tri-State perform its pri-

[24] *The State's Biggest Business—Local And Regional Problems,* Report of the Connecticut Commission to Study the Necessity and Feasibility of Metropolitan Government (January 1967). In addition to recommending the creation of a new state department of community and urban affairs, the commission also suggested the establishment of a new advisory commission and also a joint legislative committee on urban and regional affairs.

mary role of regional transportation and land-use planning, it also provides information to other regional agencies, administers mass-transportation demonstration programs, conducts special studies when requested, and acts as the clearing house for local proposals for federal programs in different functional fields. The only official regional instrumentality in existence at the time the Demonstration Cities Act was passed, Tri-State was designated by the regional office of HUD as the review agency for the New York metropolitan region, and was thus endowed with coordinating as well as planning functions.

Shortly after the HUD designation, the New Jersey members of Tri-State submitted a position paper which opposed giving Tri-State sole responsibility for the performance of the review function in the metropolitan area. Pointing out that Tri-State, because of the region it encompassed, was not an appropriate planning body for certain functional fields (such as water supply and open space), and that the Tri-State staff lacked expertise in many of the programs included for regional review (such as air and water pollution, sewer facilities, libraries, and hospitals), they suggested that a "Regional Review Coordinator" be designated for each state and for New York City to process applications and oversee the review function within his particular jurisdiction. Tri-State would then review only those applications with "regional or other intergovernmental implications."[25]

Responding to the suggestion, Tri-State adopted a resolution in July 1967, setting forth the procedure it would follow in reviewing requests for federal capital grants in the Tri-State region. Reaffirming its willingness to coordinate its planning programs with state, county, regional, and subregional planning programs, Tri-State stipulated that subregional planning agencies (that is, county planning agencies in New York and New Jersey, regional planning agencies in Connecticut) would review federally aided projects of "essentially local significance." Regional coordinators would be designated by the governor of each state to review proposed projects for consistency with state-wide planning programs and to determine, after application of certain specific cri-

[25] "Position of the New Jersey Members of the Tri-State Transportation Commission with Regard to Federal Regional Planning and Review Requirements," February 13, 1967.

teria and guidelines, whether a proposed project had "regional implications." In the latter instance, it would be reviewed by the Tri-State staff. If the appropriate level were found to be "subregional or state," comments would be sought from the state planning agency, the state functional agency, and the subregional planning agency in the area in which the project was to be located. In reviewing applications with regional significance, Tri-State planned to seek comments from these agencies as well. Tri-State hoped to restrict its review to regional projects for the most part, but recognized that it might become involved, as a practical matter, in subregional planning decisions which had "spillover" effects upon neighboring communities.[26]

Local Participation in Tri-State Reconsidered

In spite of the use of local planning agencies as an integral part of Tri-State's regional review procedure, the extent to which the procedure conforms with federal intent as set forth in Title II of the Demonstration Cities and Metropolitan Development Act of 1966 bears further scrutiny. It will be recalled that section 204(a) of the act provides for applications for federal grants to be submitted for review to any area-wide agency "which is to the greatest practicable extent, composed of or responsible to the elected officials of a unit of areawide government or of the units of general local government within whose jurisdiction such agency is authorized to engage in such planning." Tri-State meets the qualifications presently being used for designation as an "areawide agency,"[27] but its responsiveness to local elected officials has been questioned.

Concerned about the lack of local representation on Tri-State itself, as well as Tri-State's limited functional responsibilities, the

---

[26] Tri-State Transportation Commission, "Resolution #30: Regional Review of Federal Capital Grant Requests in the Tri-State Region," July 26, 1967, and interview with J. Douglas Carroll, Jr., Executive Director of Tri-State, October 17, 1967. In special circumstances, such as those involving New York City and Nassau and Suffolk counties, New York, the New York City Planning Commission and the bi-county Regional Planning Board, respectively, are used as "subregional agencies."

[27] See Chap. V, p. 108, for the definition of an "areawide agency" given in Bureau of the Budget Circular No. A–82 Revised, December 18, 1967.

New Jersey members suggested, in their position paper on the review procedure, that local officials be designated by the governors of the respective states to replace one of each state's five members "perhaps on the basis of a recommendation to the Governor by MRC," and that the base of state representation on Tri-State be broadened by enlarging its ex-officio membership. In partial accordance with this recommendation, Tri-State called for greater local representation in its membership, but this has not been implemented by all the states. Thus far, the mayor of New Haven, Connecticut, and the chairman of the New York City Planning Commission are the only local officials who serve on the Tri-State board.

The question then arises: Would appointment of one local official by the governor of each state make the agency sufficiently responsive to local elected officials, or should some kind of standard procedure be established to bind Tri-State, which is basically a state-oriented planning agency, more closely to MRC, the legal organization of local elected officials in the region? Robert Smith, a recent observer of the regional review procedure in the New York metropolitan region, suggests that the implications of the pertinent sections of the federal legislation are such that "cooperation between a highly-skilled planning agency and a council of elected officials not only is desirable but is requisite."[28] Because of the size and complexity of the region, Smith suggests that consideration be given to the establishment of subregional councils which might work closely with the subregional planning agencies presently in existence in the counties and regions of the three states. The subregional councils could furnish membership to MRC, and MRC, in turn, could nominate a certain number of members to Tri-State. (In order to achieve a further degree of regional coordination, Smith recommends that MRC appoint some of the members of the boards of special-purpose agencies in the region.)

Tri-State, on the other hand, feels that it provides a "unique example of creative federalism" insofar as its commissioners are

[28] Smith, "Implications of the Federal Requirements for Regional Review" (1967), pp. 50 ff. For further discussion of a closer relationship between MRC and Tri-State, see Victor Jones, in *The State's Biggest Business*, Policy Papers (1967), pp. 88–89.

"persons with . . . operational responsibilities" and because it com-
bines planning and coordinating functions.[29] It suggests that its
liaison with the region's top planners offers its recommendations
an enhanced opportunity for implementation. The Tri-State
technical advisory group meets on a regular basis, and all of the
region's planning and technical officials, including subregional
planning commissioners, are invited to attend. Reports on current
projects are given by Tri-State and other regional agencies, including RPA, Port of New York Authority, Hudson River
Valley Commission, and the new transportation agencies. Presumably the technical officials who are present report back to
their elected superiors any new regional developments. Tri-State
feels that it has had poor experience with the mechanism of local
cooperating committees. It claims that local governments are not
interested in "planning procedures" as such but would like to be
involved at the point at which decisions are made: "When the
local governments are affected, they are interested." The problem
then becomes one of involvement at the "appropriate time."[30]

There is little doubt that the federal government would like to
see both states and local governments represented on the regional
planning body. In the new federal context, planning must be
closely related to decision-making, and the federal government
seeks a close working relationship between planning and elected
officials at all governmental levels. HUD's new guidelines for the
conduct of metropolitan planning again stress the need for local
participation on the policy-making body of a planning agency as
well as increased emphasis on a state role.[31] Confronted originally
with the need to develop a realistic approach toward the many
political institutions in the New York metropolitan region (or
else be a party to the deprivation of funds to the region), HUD
has embarked on a program of making the existing structure as
workable as possible. Thus HUD is helping MRC to develop its
own capabilities so that it may eventually engage in joint planning and policy-making with Tri-State. At the same time, HUD

[29] Tri-State Transportation Commission, *Annual Report, 1967*, p. 3.
[30] Interviews with Carroll, October 17, 1967, and with Kresky, April
28, 1966.
[31] U.S. Department of Housing and Urban Development, MD 6011:1,
"Requirements for Metropolitan Planning Assistance," April 1968.

would like to see Tri-State broaden its interests and enlarge its base of membership, possibly to include persons proposed and approved by MRC. Tri-State's designation as the regional review agency will be reviewed by HUD at regularly designated intervals to see if its programs are functionally consistent with area-wide planning.[32]

Its review powers notwithstanding, Tri-State has taken no stands thus far on controversial programs, such as the creation of a fourth jetport for the region. Created originally as a research organization, it has conformed to each state's conception of the proper role of a planning agency and has been hemmed in by the political considerations of the three states. But the federal government is asking for a total regional planning process in which the planner must assume responsibility for the impact of his decisions. Tri-State must now be concerned with the social and economic aspects of the environment as well as the physical. For this, it requires an intense combination of all interested parties.

The major moves will have to be made by the states acting in concert. Tri-State's mandate is up for renewal in 1969 and this will give the states an opportunity to review its membership base and its limited functional responsibilities. If Tri-State's representation can be officially broadened to include local elected officials and representative citizens, along with state and federal officials, the advantages would be many: local governments would gain in knowledge and regional perceptions; Tri-State's programs might become more venturesome and meaningful; and Tri-State's recommendations would have an enhanced chance of implementation, having been subjected to the reactions and comments of a representative cross section of the metropolitan electorate.

MRC: Link with Tri-State

It is obvious that the particular form that a regional council will assume varies from one metropolitan area to another depending

[32] Interview with Morton Isler, Director of Planning, Program Coordination and Services Division, HUD, Region I, September 22, 1967, and address by Judah Gribetz, Regional Administrator of HUD, Region I, to the Tri-State Committee of the League of Women Voters, New York City, March 12, 1968.

upon local conditions and desires. MRC must adjust its thinking to face the region as it now exists, with its proliferation of state and federal agencies. There is no longer any question about close cooperation with state and federal officials; MRC can no longer survive in dignified isolation from other governmental levels. Nor can it be unwilling to share credit for its regional "accomplishments." As the states become more involved in local problems, they are not apt to permit local officials to make plans for which the states must pay the bills.

The limited involvement of local officials in the Tri-State operation offers a reconstituted MRC an opportunity to furnish liaison between Tri-State and the region's top elected officers. In addition to a regional planning agency such as Tri-State that makes technical studies of regional trends and presents alternative proposals,[33] the region also needs an agency which is widely representative of local governments to provide a forum for discussion and debate of proposals and to secure reactions of local communities. However, for this collaboration to be effective, Tri-State must make its proposals known, through MRC, to local officials while these proposals are still in the formulating stage. The core level has a right to know about the nature of decisions that are hanging over it. If Tri-State reviews applications for federal requests with "regional significance," local governments, which closely mirror the sentiments of the people, should be included in the planning process.

The actual coordinating arrangements between Tri-State and MRC should be structured in such a way as to provide more local representation on the Tri-State board at the time that programs are initiated; during the formulation of plans, so as to ensure conformity to local expectations; and at the final stage, when political leadership is needed to implement the plans. MRC can provide the linkage for all of these activities. Preferably, local representation on the Tri-State board should be secured by recommendation from the MRC executive committee, rather than by gubernatorial appointment. If the local cooperating com-

[33] E.g., Tri-State Transportation Commission, *Regional Development Alternates* (March 1967).

mittees are not revived, some other arrangement, under MRC auspices, should be devised.

In addition, MRC must define its own role vis-à-vis Tri-State so that it does not perform as another technical planning agency but provides supplementary help for a large variety of regional planning efforts. Whereas Tri-State may have preempted MRC's regional planning role as such, neither Tri-State nor MRC can deal with all of the issues that confront the region. MRC now has a planning officer on its staff who can bring together the Council's technical group, the Metropolitan Council of Planning Agencies, and coordinate the input of local planners. Since MRC's planner presently attends meetings of Tri-State's technical advisory group—in contrast to the municipal planners, who do not—he can keep them posted about regional studies which may affect their own efforts. MRC might also participate in joint planning efforts with Tri-State or provide components of plans in specific functional fields in which Tri-State is engaged. Joint financing of planning programs (such as MRC has undertaken with RPA) might be another means of effecting coordination.

MRC has indicated its willingness to coordinate its arrangements with Tri-State. The work plan outlined in the Council's grant application to the federal government in 1967 provided for federal, state, and interstate agencies, in addition to local planning officers, to be represented on all functional committees. These representatives were to advise of actual or potential conflicts in work programs. When the possibility of overlap arises, MRC expects to take the proper steps to avoid duplication.

Successful implementation of these arrangements with Tri-State and other regional agencies will hinge in great part on the extralegal personal and political relationships which develop. This, of course, depends ultimately upon the quality of leadership furnished by the Council and upon the willingness of local governments to cooperate in a regional undertaking. MRC's past experience indicates a membership which was unable to adjust to a political environment which was no longer "local." If the local governments continue to view the region with a parochial eye, and are unable to respond constructively to suggestions emanating from other regional agencies, a greater impetus will be given to direct intervention by state and federal levels. If they wish to adapt to changing regional circumstances, MRC offers them a means of successful participation.

MRC: Link with RPA

MRC must also establish more extensive relationships with the private groups which are concerned about the future development of the region. RPA furnishes an independent source of goals and ideals to mobilize community leadership. Pressure from RPA will probably mount in the future, and it has recently made, as part of its second regional plan, strong positive recommendations for private and governmental action to counteract the region's haphazard growth.[34]

Here again the planning process must be related to decision-making. RPA is presently seeking comments from a broad range of citizen advisory groups on many different important issues. If local officials are to respond to the long-range conceptions proposed by RPA, they need a common meeting ground in which to react. RPA cannot implement its plans without the help of local officials. As it did in the open-space acquisition program, MRC can bring about a confrontation between planners and policy-makers, help select alternatives for local governments, and prose-lytize locally to push projects that are useful. In leading the way to acceptance of regional programs at the local levels of government, MRC can be a force in securing implementation.

Cooperation between RPA and MRC on joint planning projects would be mutually beneficial. Local officials would profit from their association with the professional competence offered by regional thinkers, and RPA can use the technical information and financial assistance for its projects which MRC might provide. Close association with RPA, which has ties with varied civic groups, would have the additional effect of informing the public at large about the activities of MRC and might serve to develop

---

[34] Regional Plan Association, *The Lower Hudson* (1966), *The Region's Growth* (1967), *Public Participation in Regional Planning* (1967), *Waste Management* (1968), *Jamaica Center* (1968).

enhanced awareness of regional groups and projects. MRC requires wide public understanding and a broad sense of commitment—a mandate from the public that the problems are so myriad and complex that regional cooperation is needed. MRC also needs a counterforce to opposition in the form of public education and orientation, which must be a continuous operation and couched in broader, more significant terms than the sharply focused opposition. Public discussion, research, and reports can focus attention on some of the critical issues at stake and help to arouse public interest in community planning and the values it represents.

MRC: Pressure Group

The present fragmentation of decision-making among the region's governments makes it difficult for one municipality to find out what another proposes to do. The New York metropolitan region needs a forum where economic, social, and political problems can be discussed in broad terms. MRC has functioned in the past as a valid communicating device in helping municipal and county officials develop an understanding of their neighbors' problems and become accustomed to working together. If the Council establishes itself to the point where cooperation becomes customary and respectable, its strength can be used in a regional way to enable it to serve as the united voice of local governments in dealing with federal and state agencies. If a solid program of recommendations were to flow from MRC to Hartford, Albany, Trenton, and Washington, these governments would be compelled to listen.

MRC: Service Agency

MRC can also provide useful services to local officials by helping them to deal with problems that originate beyond their local boundaries. Intergovernmental cooperation can be useful in such functional fields as uniform traffic codes, taxicab rates, joint purchasing, police communications, fire protection, building codes, bus systems, and sewerage disposal. The Council must establish rapport with local communities and find out what they want so that its program meets clearly recognized needs. If a common denominator of frustration with a common problem emerges, the need for a cooperative mechanism will be made clear. Initially, it would be wise for the Council to engage in a relatively minor but useful cooperative effort, perhaps in the field of law enforcement, and achieve a measure of success before it becomes involved in ambitious functional undertakings. For MRC to gain the confidence of all the local communities, there must be tangible accomplishment, in response to political demands, as well as highly publicized press releases.

Ultimately, in a region of this size, some form of subregional political action will probably emerge. It would be useful for MRC to provide assistance in drawing up intergovernmental agreements, consistent with a larger regional plan, to which local communities would have to conform. It may be that the best hope for local governments to survive as decision-makers in the New York metropolitan region will hinge on their ability to develop subregional equivalents of MRC, along the lines of Robert Smith's suggestion.[35]

In order to perform as a service organization for local governments, as a pressure group vis-à-vis the state and federal governments, as an implementing mechanism for public and private regional agencies, and as a research and educational arm for the region at large, MRC needs a full-time, professional staff. Now divorced from the New York City administrative hierarchy for the first time in its life, it is up to the new executive director to establish working relationships with local communities and competing regional agencies. MRC's budget is relatively modest for the moment. The amount of federal aid that will be forthcoming will probably depend upon the support it can enlist from its own members and its ability to work with Tri-State in developing regional programs.

A Major Challenge for MRC

The real test for MRC will come in terms of disagreements among

[35] Smith, "Implications of the Federal Requirements for Regional Review" (1967). See also discussion by Crouch and Dinerman, *Southern California Metropolis*, p. 402.

its own members—in achieving consensus among the disparate groups which make up the metropolitan region. If the suburbs fail to show more interest in aiding the central cities than they have previously, MRC cannot survive. Study after study of public service requirements in the region's older cities indicates that the cities are burdened with special kinds of problems which they cannot handle on their own. Already saddled with high tax rates and fiscal difficulties, they may also suffer an increased outward migration of middle- and upper-income families and industry because of increased obsolescence, deteriorating urban facilities, and the continued concentration of low-income and minority groups.[36]

New York City is far more important to the region than any other municipality. A sensitive balance will have to be struck in terms of meshing its needs with those of the suburbs. On the one hand, the city would obviously be dominant in any arrangement approaching representation of political units in proportion to population. At the same time, it was not inappropriate for Mayor Lindsay, in his first address to MRC members, to emphasize the need for suburban users of city facilities to contribute to the support of central city services. If a council does not point up to the suburbs their interdependence with the central cities, it has lost a large part of its reason for existence. Similarly, if MRC cannot serve as the mayor's channel for communicating indispensable concepts to suburban communities, it will have failed in another one of its primary purposes.

The challenge to the leadership of the Council is very great. Given the lack of homogeneity of the governmental units surrounding New York City and the presence of three states, the problems become even more difficult. The new leadership is going to have to depend upon its wits, persuasive pressure, and political judgment to establish MRC and work out its procedures and rationale. Until now, there has been more talk about regional co-

[36] Regional Plan Association, *Public Services in Older Cities* (May 1968). See also *New York Times*, August 13, 1967, p. 1, concerning recent studies by the federal Economic Development Administration, which indicate that the migration of white and Negro poor from the rural areas in the country to New York and other cities will continue into the mid-1970s.

operation by the local governments than action. At the same time, the region has made considerable progress in the realistic development of new programs. Paradoxically, the new, large, functional authorities launched by the states may serve to alert local governments of the need to organize themselves against a common enemy.

A Useful Beginning

To return to the questions posed at the beginning of this chapter, a regional forum of local elected officials, recognized by other agencies—public and private—can be a great help in effective regional planning. A firmer organizational structure than the MRC approach may be desirable, but the formal Council is better than cooperation on an ad hoc basis and offers the possibility of greater service. Some councils of governments in other metropolitan areas are beginning to develop into organizations with considerable influence over regional decisions. Their experience is sufficiently promising to warrant the revival of MRC in New York and its encouragement by other levels of government. The New York region, perhaps more than most, must begin to see and understand itself as a region. This requires dialogue. Furthermore, leadership from within local communities is needed if the localities are to have a vision of self-destiny and if total abdication of direction and control to state authority is to be avoided. MRC's efforts, discussions—even its trials and infirmities—can generate a regional sense of identity and its recommendations can provide stimulation for future action.

No supergovernment is foreseen for the New York metropolitan region. Rather, there will be large, functional authorities to supply the most critical area-wide services, with increased pressure from above for regional coordination. The important objective is to achieve an effective mix of responsibility so that the interests of all levels of government and the private sector can be accommodated and can work together. The federal government is playing a catalytic role; the states are beginning to act in unison. The big question is whether the local establishment will be represented; that is, whether the state and federal agencies will deliberately use their money and guidance to strengthen local governments so that they too can participate in planning and governing the region.

The particular type of machinery is not the important matter. What is important is the presence of some type of organization to furnish representation to local interests of the metropolitan region. MRC, as originally conceived, was well ahead of its time. The recognition by New York City and a few others of the need for a cooperative and coordinating mechanism in the New York metropolitan area was a sophisticated notion in the 1950s; it is becoming an actual necessity in the 1960s. MRC's past experience, though disappointing, furnishes sufficient reason to attempt to rebuild it into a more durable instrument of political responsibility. Its membership of local elected officials from a variety of heterogeneous communities, while a trial to the ingenuity of the executive director and his staff, may actually prove to be of benefit to regional programs.

No high-handed recommendations can be furnished as yet for the New York metropolitan region. The important thing is to set up some kind of flexible arrangement which can work with the functional authorities already in existence. The situation is such that an organization will have to be modified to meet changing opportunities presented by fluctuating environmental factors. MRC must be alert to fortuitous developments as they occur, and a pragmatic approach can meet regional needs as they are identified. Circumstances such as a prolonged electricity failure, intense smog causing physical discomfort, or severe drought inducing a water shortage, may pave the way for an expansion of MRC's role in regional affairs.

The voluntary approach to metropolitan cooperation may be regarded as the first plateau to be reached. If more orderly solutions for effective metropolitan planning are to emerge, they will have to be based on the insights that the public, the politicians, the business community, the labor leaders, and the elected officials have developed from experiencing the benefits of the regional cooperative approach. MRC is not an ultimate solution. But it may provide the metropolitan community in New York with its first demonstration that local governments *can* play an effective part in shaping their own destinies.

INDEX